bert Owen

Robert Owen

ROBERT DAVIS
FRANK O'HAGAN

Bloomsbury Library of Educational Thought

Series Editor: Richard Bailey

B L O O M S B U R Y

LONDON · NEW DELHI · NEW YORK · SYDNEY

Bloomsbury Academic
An imprint of Bloomsbury Publishing Plc

50 Bedford Square   1385 Broadway
London   New York
WC1B 3DP   NY 10018
UK   USA

www.bloomsbury.com

First published 2010 by Continuum International Publishing Group
Paperback edition first published 2014 by Bloomsbury Academic

British Library Cataloguing-in-Publication Data
A catalogue record for this book is available from the British Library.

ISBN: PB: 978-1-4725-1893-4
ePUB: 978-1-4725-1894-1

Library of Congress Cataloguing-in-Publication Data
Davis, Robert.
Robert Owen/Robert Davis, Frank O'Hagan.
p. cm – (Continuum library of educational thought; 25)
ISBN 978-1-84706-104-1 (hardback)
1. Owen, Robert, 1771-1858- 2. Eucators—Scotland—Biography.
3. Education—Great Britain—History. 4. Education—Great Britain—
Philosophy. 5. Social reformers—Scotland—Biography.
I. O'Hagan, Frank. II. Title. III. Series.

LB675.O94252D38 2010
370.92-dc22 [B]

209037920

Typeset by BookEns, Royston, Herts.
Printed and bound in Great Britain by the MPG Books Group

Contents

For Malcolm MacKenzie

Series Editor's Preface

Education is sometimes presented as an essentially practical activity. It is, it seems, about teaching and learning, curriculum and what goes on in schools. It is about achieving certain ends, using certain methods, and these ends and methods are often prescribed for teachers, whose duty it is to deliver them with vigor and fidelity. With such a clear purpose, what is the value of theory?

Recent years have seen politicians and policy-makers in different countries explicitly denying *any* value or need for educational theory. A clue to why this might be is offered by a remarkable comment by a British Secretary of State for Education in the 1990s: 'having any ideas about how children learn, or develop, or feel, should be seen as subversive activity'. This pithy phrase captures the problem with theory: it subverts, challenges and undermines the very assumptions on which the practice of education is based.

Educational theorists, then, are trouble-makers in the realm of ideas. They pose a threat to the status quo and lead us to question the common-sense presumptions of educational practices. But this is precisely what they should do because the seemingly simple language of schools and schooling hides numerous contestable concepts that in their different usages reflect fundamental disagreements about the aims, values, and activities of education.

Implicit within the *Bloomsbury Library of Educational Thought* is an assertion that theories and theorizing are vitally important for education. By gathering together the ideas of some of the most influential, important, and interesting educational thinkers, from the Ancient Greeks to contemporary scholars, the series has the ambitious task of providing an accessible yet authoritative resource for a generation of students and practitioners. Volumes within the series are written by acknowledged leaders in the field, who were selected both for their scholarship and their ability to make often complex ideas accessible to a diverse audience.

It will always be possible to question the list of key thinkers that are represented in this series. Some may question the inclusion of certain thinkers; some may disagree with the exclusion of others. That is inevitably going to be the case. There is no suggestion that the list of thinkers represented within the *Bloomsbury Library of Educational Thought* is in any way definitive. What is incontestable is that these thinkers have fascinating ideas about education, and that taken together, the *Library* can act as a powerful source of information and inspiration for those committed to the study of education.

RICHARD BAILEY
Birmingham University

Foreword

Born almost 50 years before Karl Marx, Robert Owen (1771–1855) built a school for his workers' children at New Lanark, furnishing one of the very first models of universal education at the birth of the nineteenth century. On his sojourn to America to establish a new colony in Indiana called New Harmony, he issued 'The Declaration of Mental Independence' in 1826 to commemorate the Declaration of Independence and to indicate the next step in the liberation of humankind.[1] It was unfortunate that both Thomas Jefferson and John Adams died on 4 July 1826, on the fiftieth anniversary of the Declaration of Independence. Owen's 'manifesto' for a 'mental revolution', though far-sighted and written over 180 years before the development of the 'knowledge economy', was poorly received. He was accused of preaching atheism, among other things, and his debate with Alexander Campbell, the Christian millennialist, in 1829, sealed his 'defeat' in the American context.[2] In his manifesto he referred to a mental revolution 'as superior in benefit and importance to the first revolution' on the basis of the alleged fact that 'the mental powers of man exceed his physical powers.' To this end he declared war on the three obstacles and 'monstrous evils' that stood in the way of achieving mental liberation: the system of private property, 'absurd and irrational systems of religion' and marriage founded on the concept of private property and sanctified by religion. There are many points of comparison with Marx, not least the shared belief that the individual is a product of his or her environment. Owen reasoned that if this be

---

[1] See the full text at http://www.atheists.org/A_Declaration_of_Mental_Independence_by_Robert_Owen_.
[2] See the comparison between these two thinkers by Rick Cherok (1999) at http://www.bu.edu/mille/publications/winter2000/cherok.PDF.

the case then we must change the environment, and unlike Marx he focused on creating community, a kind of sociological practical experiment, rather than trying to transform the whole of society. His efforts have been regarded by some as the founding of the American Left contributing to a new socialist vision of society, redefining 'community' and proposing a new form of economic cooperation as the basis of material well-being. His belief in education as the means for the formation of character, the elimination of poverty, and perfectibility of human beings distinguished him as visionary thinker and practical reformer. In his *Life of Robert Owen* published in 1858 he says: 'These writings are intended to effect an entire revolution in the spirit, mind, manners, habits and conduct, of the human race – a rational, practical revolution to be introduced gradually, in peace, with wise hindsight ... '

In this new book on Robert Owen, two distinguished scholars from the University of Glasgow provide a fresh intellectual biography of Owen as both industrialist and reformer, and a critical exposition of his work, including an insightful understanding of the key principles underlying his educational thought and practice. Robert Davis and Frank O'Hagan, both known for their historical studies, especially in the Scottish context, have provided us with a clear, sober, and scholarly account of Robert Owen as an educational thinker. As they explain, even though Owen was not a philosopher, nor is there much originality in his educational thinking, he was a powerful and practical reformer. Davis and O'Hagan locate Owen within the contours of the emerging patterns of his own industrial culture to elucidate and explore the relevance of his educational thought for the contemporary landscape. They examine his idea of the 'new,' his millennial utopian thinking and its uncanny resemblance to framing issues and ideas that define the topography of today's post-industrial society, or 'knowledge economy.' Their careful scholarship brings Owen and his works alive again for the twenty-first century at a point when contemporary reformers are contemplating again the connections between education, work, and community, and looking to educate citizens for the 'just society.'

Robert Owen provides a penetrating and compelling account of the influence and relevance of Owen today, an 'ambivalent legacy' as Davis and O'Hagan argue, balanced between a new world utopianism and Scottish Enlightenment rationality. This is an excellent, thought-provoking and exciting introduction to the educational thought of Robert Owen, one of the most remarkable reformers of the industrial age and one of its most impassioned educational thinkers.

Michael A. Peters
University of Illinois at Urbana-Champaign
November 2009

Acknowledgments

A work of this kind is indebted to a gifted generation of Robert Owen experts including Ian Donnachie, Gregory Claeys, George Hewitt, David McLaren, and Tom Markus. Behind them lies an older scholarship on which we have also drawn, including Lloyd Jones, Frank Podmore, Harold Silver, J. F. C. Harrison, and John Butt.

We wish to acknowledge the support of a number of people who have given us assistance in the writing of this book, in particular Jim Arnold, Director of New Lanark Trust since 1974, Lorna Davidson, Deputy Director of New Lanark Trust, and Aynsley Gough, Education Officer at New Lanark. We wish to place on record our gratitude to the staff of Glasgow University Library, especially Honor Hania. We are grateful also to numerous individuals who have been valuable sources of information and insight through conversations and interviews including the delegates at the 'Robert Owen and his Legacy' conference held in August 2008 at the Gregynog Conference Centre, in Powys, Wales. These include Pat Chandler, Malcolm Chase, Joe England, Margaret Escott, Alex Lawrey, Jose Ramon Layna, Ben Maw, Theresa Moriarty, Dewi Rowland Hughes, Geoff Powell, Bryn Purdy, Meg Purdy, Alan Spence, Noel Thompson, Chris Williams, and Stephen Yeo. Hatton Davidson, honorary curator of the Robert Owen Memorial Museum in Newtown, was also very generous to us in conversation and correspondence.

The book would not have been possible without the support and encouragement of our colleagues in the Faculty of Education of the University of Glasgow, especially the dean, Professor Jim Conroy and the deputy dean, Professor Ian Menter, the head of curriculum studies, Harry Blee, and the head of religious education, Stephen McKinney. Within curriculum studies, thanks are due to Alan Britton, Grant Stewart, and Maureen Farrell. The support of Raymond McCluskey has been invaluable. Within religious education thanks are due to Roisin Coll, Leon Robinson, Leonard Franchi, Karen Wenell, Catherine O'Hare, Mary Lappin, Alison Phipps, Victoria Harrison, Sr Andrea MacEachen, Fr John Bollan, Liz Brown, Denise Porada, and Sharon Cumming. Our friend and colleague in religious education, Fr Gordian Marshall, OP, died suddenly as this work was commencing. We remember him in its completion. Gratitude is also owed to Peter Gronn, now of the University of Cambridge, for many stimulating conversations at the outset of our research. Richard Bailey, the series editor, and Alison Clark at Continuum also merit our sincerest thanks.

Our two families have been constant sources of encouragement throughout the project. From the Davis family, this includes Ann, Christopher, Mark, and Gareth, Robert Davis Snr and Kathleen Davis. From the O'Hagan family, Helen, Pauline, Aileen, Siobhan, and Shaun. We would also like to thank Greg Murphy, OP, Raymond and Mary Taylor, Joe and Clare Fodey, David Carr, Tom Steele and Terence, Gerald, and Kevin O'Hagan.

Introduction

Robert Owen is in some respects an unusual figure to place in a library of educational thought. Owen was neither a philosopher of education nor a systematic theorist of learning and teaching. As we shall see, while he often claimed to have formed his educational ideas from first-principle reasoning about the nature of humanity and from careful observation of the times in which he was living, most of the concepts upon which he spent a lifetime reflecting were widely known and debated in the surrounding culture long before Owen took them up. There is little genuine originality in Owen's educational thought, though there is often a striking freshness in the style in which he communicated with his audiences and a passion in the confidence with which he sought to turn the principles he had borrowed or absorbed from Enlightenment sources into meaningful social action.

Robert Owen was first and foremost a man of business, even if his entrepreneurial instincts were from his earliest days tinged with a strong social conscience and an impatient desire to address the often formidable problems confronting his society. As such, he preferred action to words, movement to stillness, and change to continuity. From an early age, Owen intuited that he was living through a revolutionary epoch, where the old certainties of the past were being swept away by the forces of unprecedented economic, technological, and social transformation. Always an optimist, and alert to the huge potential for wealth creation in the historic shifts taking place around him, Owen devoted much of his creative energy – as well as considerable proportions of his growing personal fortune – to the implementation of an ambitious program of social and educational reform designed to harness the energies of industry and commerce to the improvement of the living conditions of the masses. These goals aligned Owen with a class of entrepreneurs in early nineteenth-century

Britain admired for their philanthropy and for their commitment to the amelioration of the frequently dreadful conditions in which the working classes found themselves. But Owen was distinctive even within this group for the dedication with which he pursued his objectives and for the status he accorded the reform of popular education within them. From his base in the Scottish industrial village of New Lanark, founded by his father-in-law, David Dale, on the banks of the River Clyde, Owen set out more assiduously than almost any other philanthropist of the time to put his theories into practice. He sought to demonstrate to the commercial and political elites around him that an entirely alternative approach to the planning and organization of production, labor relations, education, and community was possible − one which would preserve the tremendous creative dynamism of industrialization while ensuring that its fruits were more equally distributed between owners, producers, and consumers. As his schemes developed, and his reputation soared internationally, Owen went still further, suggesting that a reorganized society with cradle-to-grave education for all at its heart could inaugurate a new age of egalitarian prosperity and happiness for the whole human race, the ultimate potential of which was beyond calculation.

It is the purpose of this book to investigate and assess these elements of Robert Owen's thought and to explore their relevance to the educational preoccupations of the present day. More than most previous studies, this examination tries to place Owen's educational thought, and some of the paradoxes that surround it, in the context of the underlying patterns of his culture. Owen recognized that the new industrial civilization that was emerging all around him would require new institutions, new values and attitudes if it were to flourish in the interests of all of its members. The idea of the 'new' came to obsess Owen in everything from place names for his utopian communities to the remodeling of religious belief for the coming age of reason. It helped propel him to a position of leadership in what was for a brief period a genuine mass movement for social and educational reform in Britain and, to a lesser degree, the United States. While the measures Owen proposed and implemented at New Lanark undoubtedly reflect the limitations as well as the aspirations of the period in which he lived and worked, we who operate in what is often called the era of 'late industrial' or 'post-industrial' capitalism continue to face often remarkably similar challenges and find ourselves deliberating difficult philosophical and policy issues with powerful echoes of the themes close to the centre of Owen's many educational endeavors. In the unfinished quest for the provision of high quality education for all regardless of class or origin, the example of Robert Owen from the threshold of the Industrial Revolution, and the continuing inspiration of his New Lanark project, may have much still to teach us, even as that same unpredictable Revolution seems to be entering into another, global phase in its turbulent history.

Part 1

Intellectual Biography

Chapter 1

Robert Owen: Industrialist and Reformer

A Welsh childhood

It was Robert Owen himself who insisted that the life of the mind and the content of the individual character were shaped decisively by experience and environment. The emphasis in much of his educational thought on the crucial importance of *early* experience in the molding of personality suggests than any proper understanding of Owen and his ideas should pay due attention to the influences at work in his own childhood. One obstacle, however, to this otherwise promising approach – widely recognized by his biographers – is that the materials for reconstructing Owen's childhood and adolescence are incomplete and sometimes unreliable. Our principal source, an autobiography entitled *The Life of Robert Owen Written by Himself*, of 1857, is the partially dictated memoir of an old man with a failing memory and an understandable tendency to embellish self-servingly the recollections of his earlier years (Owen 1993e). While not without merit as a record of forces that shaped his values and outlook, the *Life* always requires to be treated with caution and there is little supplementary evidence with which to enrich its account of his childhood and its background. Nevertheless, and despite these limitations, the broad patterns of the elderly Owen's memories of his origins do provide a consistent enough foundation for pointing to several of the key factors in his family heritage that were to prove of lasting significance to his later development. Some of these factors were deeply personal and domestic; others part of the social and cultural fabric of the dramatic epoch into which he was born. Still more can be traced to the complex interplay between these two zones, where individual biography meets the processes of historical change. We shall see all three dimensions setting the terms of reference for our understanding of the man and his ideas throughout Robert Owen's long and remarkable career.

Robert Owen was born in 1771 in Newtown, Wales. He was the second youngest of seven children in a family of farmers who, in keeping with employment patterns of the time and region, moved in and out of other occupations such as innkeeping and saddlemaking as economic conditions in a sometimes unpredictable agrarian environment dictated. While never in penury, the family's fortunes were sometimes uncertain and they appear to have sustained themselves on a combination of strong, extended kinship ties and a domestic resourcefulness from which Robert was eventually to acquire almost inexhaustible reserves of self-reliance. Newtown itself was in many senses a classic Welsh borderland market town of the period, its appearance of rural stability signifying subtle and longstanding patterns of agricultural life evolved over several centuries, while at the same time conveying unmistakably an openness to commerce, trade, and the currents of new products and ideas emanating from the much larger population and economic centers of England. It is certainly possible to see that there were many features of the Newtown environment of his childhood that Owen expended much of his later philanthropic energy endeavoring to recapture in the many community-building projects with which he became associated: the self-contained sense of belonging; the low-key but pervasive practices of neighborly cooperation; the ready access to pleasant and uplifting natural surroundings with their attendant beneficial effects on individual well-being. It is also reasonable to conclude from Owen's own memories that something of the gradual but ultimately far-reaching economic changes beginning to affect the region of Montgomeryshire in which late eighteenth-century Newtown was situated played an important part in the formation of the young Owen's emerging self-awareness, highlighting for him both the tensions and the potential in settlements of people where the contrasting experiences of continuity and social change existed in such close proximity to one another.

Within his own family, Owen appears to have formed a strong initial bond with his mother, Anne, while the exertions of his father, Robert Snr, in seeking to provide for his wife and five surviving children seem to have rendered him an inevitably more distant figure. Certainly, in later years, Owen took pains to emphasize the distinction of his mother's lineage and her resultant interest in learning. Household resources were sufficient to enable the family to send Robert unusually early to school (perhaps as young as 4 years) where the intelligence he himself regarded as an inheritance from his mother's branch of the family swiftly established him as an able and imaginative pupil. Although the education available at Newtown Hall was by all accounts basic, its influence on the young Owen proved vital in two respects. First, it convinced him of the value of children attending school at a time when the education of the young was still in many quarters viewed skeptically. Secondly, it introduced him first-hand to the then increasingly fashionable model of learning and teaching subsequently known as the monitorial system, the key feature of which was the employment of older, talented pupils to teach younger children in return for fee exemptions. Developed in the following decades by Andrew Bell and Joseph Lancaster into a fully-fledged pedagogical method, the monitorial principle was essentially an application of the Factory System to education, whereby the more able and more senior pupils passed on their learning by rote to their juniors, often in very large classrooms. Owen encountered an early version of the monitorial system directly under the tutelage of his teacher, William Thickens, who, despite his obvious limitations as a provincial educator, recognized the academic potential in Owen and made him an 'usher' or monitor from age 8. We can in fact see in his acceptance of this early role Owen's first formal involvement in the instruction of others, a task to which he took enthusiastically and which in several respects formed a blueprint for many of his later approaches to education (Podmore 1906, pp. 4–12; Donnachie 2005a, pp. 6–8).

Like many a capable young person of the period, denied access to the benefits of the elite education reserved for only the wealthiest sectors of British society, Owen had to supplement his basic schooling in literacy and numeracy with much home education and self-teaching. Owen recollected that as a child he read widely in the literature customarily prized in Protestant artisan households of the period. Two books stood out for him, however, and can reasonably be said to have etched themselves onto his imagination as a child (Owen 1993e, 4.53; Donnachie 2005a, pp. 8–9). Daniel Defoe's famous and popular novel of 1713, *Robinson Crusoe*, described the adventures of a castaway on a desert island struggling to survive and prosper in a difficult and uncivilized environment, and then succeeding in forging a successful master-servant relationship with a Carib 'savage' also left abandoned on the same island. The appeal of *Robinson Crusoe* to the young (to boys especially) lay primarily in its sense of adventure and of survival against the odds. It was also, however, an emblematic text in the emergence of a particular set of eighteenth-century attitudes associated with the rise of a new class of self-made entrepreneurs, advancing and flourishing on the basis of individual effort and ingenuity rather than simply birthright. Similarly, *Robinson Crusoe*'s portrayal of exotic island locations and mysterious, 'uncivilized' races patronized by the innately superior European mind appealed to those elements of the same rising classes who attached themselves firmly to the expanding empire-building ambitions of the British maritime state, which, at the time of Owen's birth, had succeeded in subordinating or colonizing considerable stretches of overseas territory across the globe. The most celebrated of these British imperial possessions at the time of Owen's birth was, of course, the American colonies, only to be lost to British rule in a momentous revolutionary war when Owen was 5 years old.

A second text to which the young Owen was devoted was John Bunyan's spiritual masterpiece of 1678, *Pilgrim's Progress*. This was a staple book of pious Protestant households of the eighteenth century, a companion volume to the Bible prized for its edifying allegory of the Christian pilgrim's lifetime journey through the traps of temptation and sin towards the final goal of salvation in Christ. Bunyan's simple, unaffected prose style commended his book to children, and was pressed on them for its encouragement of individual zeal in the cultivation of moral righteousness. It seems evident that the elements of *Pilgrim's Progress* strongly critical of the luxury of worldly pursuits made an enduring impression on the young Owen, who absorbed Bunyan's promotion of plain living and the perils of material excess pursued for its own sake. There is in Bunyan's presentation of the Christian Gospel a powerfully egalitarian message, skeptical of worldly riches, privilege, and aristocratic hypocrisy. The roots of these ideas of course run deep into the New Testament, but they acquired fresh impetus when adopted by radical Protestant sects of the sixteenth and seventeenth centuries, of the type to which Bunyan himself belonged and which saw him persecuted for his beliefs by the authorities of his time.

It is impossible to understand the appeal of a book such as *Pilgrim's Progress* to young people such as the youthful Owen without also appreciating that the most superficially obvious sign of permanence and continuity in the community into which Owen was born was the pervasive presence of Christianity. The Christian faith in many respects sustained the fabric of life in late eighteenth-century rural Wales, subject as it often was to abrupt shifts in economic fortune. Owen's family appears to have been religiously observant without being unduly devout, with prayer and Church attendance part of the rhythm of domestic and community existence through the pattern of the agricultural year. The Established Church in Wales (i.e. the national Protestant Church equivalent to the Church of England and officially recognized by Crown and Parliament) operated through a network of rural parishes manned by local parsons mostly appointed by local squires, nominally (though rarely actually) in consultation with the bishops of the Welsh Church. Through their preaching and teaching, these parsons performed an important role in the pastoral support of the population and in the promotion of a distinctive tradition of Christian values that afforded shape and meaning to the often harsh and unpredictable lives of the majority of worshippers. In its more elite forms, the Welsh Christianity of Owen's time could be remote and authoritarian, encouraging uncomplaining submission to the will of an inscrutable God. At its most successful and popular, however, local clergy identified closely with the struggles of the indigenous people and preached a Protestant Gospel of hard work, social solidarity, and the equality of all before God (Williams *et al.* 2007, pp. 134–165).

In Owen's childhood, the relatively settled patterns of Welsh Christianity were shaken and revitalized by the arrival of missionaries acting on behalf of sects and reform groups with a strong resemblance to the congregations to which John Bunyan had belonged a hundred years before. Broadly speaking, these groups were commonly referred to as 'dissenters' because, though Protestant, they 'dissented' from the authority of the Established Protestant Church in key areas of Christian doctrine and Church governance. Some of these groups tried to stay within the Established Church and encourage reform internally. Others were more fully separatist, with a longstanding history of 'nonconformity' with the Established Church and highly critical of its alleged worldliness and complacency. Indeed, part of the motivation for the waves of evangelical renewal that swept Wales from the 1740s onwards was a growing perception that the Church was failing in its mission to the new classes of workers and townspeople emerging out of the processes of economic change steadily overtaking Welsh society. In the expression of these sentiments, the dissenters and nonconformists gathering strength in the Wales of Owen's childhood retained something of the revolutionary energy of earlier centuries, when puritan piety had reverberated with political grievance and helped fuel the series of tumultuous civil wars of the 1640s that had culminated in the execution of King Charles I and the creation for a short time in England and Wales of a republican Protestant Commonwealth. By the 1770s, much of this insurrectionist feeling had dimmed, but memories remained of the power of concerted resistance to authority when galvanized by shared religious conviction. In Owen's late teens, a rekindling of these forces was to take place in response to the still more convulsive revolutionary events unfolding in the France of 1789–1793.

The most immediately successful of the new Christian groups in the Newtown area of Owen's childhood and youth was the Methodists, who preached a strict Calvinist gospel of personal salvation, suspicious of many of the forms and rituals of the mainstream Church. The Methodists accompanied this austerity with a strongly motivated program of individual and social renovation, focused on the alleviation of poverty and the removal of the blight of vices such as alcohol and promiscuity from the lives of the poor. The young Robert Owen came into contact with a group of Methodist women in Newtown when he was about 8 years old. The women shared Methodist tracts and pamphlets with him, which he digested enthusiastically. In his autobiography, Owen was later somewhat smugly to suggest that the main consequence of this encounter with Methodism was to convince him of the pointlessness and inherent sectarianism of all religious attachment. It seems much more likely, however, that the rudimentary social gospel of Methodism, with its stress on spiritual renewal accompanying material improvement in the lives of the poor, played its part in the longer-term formation of the charitable dimensions of his thought while also contributing to the intense burst of personal piety he experienced at around the time of his meeting with the Methodist revival (Owen 1993e, 4:54; Williams *et al.* 2007, pp. 165–223).

In the decades after Owen's departure from Wales, movements such as the Methodists and then the Baptists were to make serious inroads into the territory of the Established Church in the principality, eventually eclipsing it in numerical strength. In Owen's childhood, this was still a relatively distant prospect, but the challenge of evangelical sects did provoke some sort of response from some of the vicars of the Established Church alert to many of the day-to-day challenges facing their flocks and troubled by the likely appeal of rival groups. In the person of charismatic Rev. Samuel Drake of the parish of Llanllwchaiarn, Owen appears to have encountered one such vicar, someone who became for a time his mentor and who helped encourage his interest in the moral and pastoral aspects of religious faith. While Drake remained firmly attached to the Established Church, Owen portrayed him as strongly committed to the welfare of his congregation and ready to imitate some of the moralism of the evangelicals in, for example, publicly reproaching the shortcomings of the local squire. Under Drake's guidance, Owen took to a sustained period of religious reading and reflection, stretching, he tells us, to the composition of sermons for which he earned the ironic local soubriquet 'the Little Parson' (Owen 1993e, 4.54; Donnachie 2005a, pp. 9–10). We know nothing of the content of these sermons except indirectly, because Owen claimed to have destroyed them after discovering their close coincidental resemblance to some of the sermons of the famous novelist and clergyman, Laurence Sterne. Recently, Geoff Powell has ingeniously suggested that a survey of the Sterne sermons to which Owen was referring reveals something important about the impact of Christianity on the development of Owen's thought (Powell 2008). The common theme of the sermons in question is the failure of vision that prevents one class or category of human being from identifying with the experience and the suffering of another. Sterne's preaching highlights the radical insistence of the Jesus of the Gospels on the urgent need for abandonment of the egocentrism handicapping human solidarity and evident most damagingly in the otherwise unbridgeable gulf separating the realms of the rich and the poor. It is possible that Powell takes a too literalist view of Owen's self-narration, here, and particularly his portrayal of himself as an emerging, enlightened Christian ethicist, free of the baggage of traditional metaphysical dogma. Certainly, it seems clear that Owen's estrangement from orthodox Christian belief took place over a much more protracted period than his autobiographical reflections suggest. Nevertheless, attention to episodes such as this, from Owen's earliest stages of development, correctly underscores the extent to which the pedigree of his later social and educational thought had roots in moral and theological questions of considerable longevity in British culture.

From Newtown to Manchester

It might have been anticipated from this portrait of his earliest years that a boy of Owen's obvious intellectual abilities could reasonably have expected to pursue his formal education beyond the provincial confines of rural Wales. Educational opportunity was for Owen and his class, however, severely restricted. While belonging to the Established Church removed any formal religious impediment to possible entry into one or other of the two English universities (Oxford and Cambridge) or the Inns of Court in London where the legal profession was trained, economic and social realities of the late eighteenth century made a move of this kind inconceivable for a youth of Owen's relatively humble origins. Instead, we find that from his earliest years, and despite his undoubted talent for learning, education was for Owen constantly accompanied by the experience of work. There was nothing unusual in this. In the absence of all but the most primitive forms of subsistence support for the destitute from local parish relief, families such as Owen's required that every member be economically productive in contributing to the family's earnings and sustaining often parlous living standards. With five children to look after, Robert Snr appears to have encouraged this in all of his offspring, combining their basic instruction with varieties of labor from which either money could be earned or services provided related to the various occupations in which he himself was active.

Robert Jnr's work experience seems to have begun locally, assisting his father directly and occasionally working casually for neighboring farmers and tradesmen. The rapid expansion of shops in the late eighteenth century was one of the most obvious signs of economic change taking place across provincial Britain and it is easy to see why a boy of Owen's noticeably precocious social skills and capabilities in reading, writing, and arithmetic proved apt to the growing retail sector. In a previous generation, this settled pattern of education and employment would probably have set the parameters for much of Owen's later life in rural Wales, with the ratio of one to the other tilting markedly in favor of employment as he matured. Hence he might in an earlier time have disappeared from history as one of the unremarked masses of shopkeeper artisans of the kind his own father typified. A new and complicating factor had entered into this long-established life schedule, however, in response to the wider economic changes of which the proliferation of shops was only one important signifier. Increasing numbers of people in the towns and villages of the Welsh countryside were staking their relatively meager resources on migration. They were drawn to the expanding economic opportunities available beyond the provinces and made newly accessible to them by the improvements to transport resulting from the growth of the canal system, the arrival of improved turnpike roads, and the spread of the coach network across large parts of the British Isles. The young Owen watched several of his siblings embark on this route out of Wales, seeking advancement in the new realms of employment and opportunity available in the major cities of England and with the full encouragement of their ambitious parents.

The backdrop to these changes in the detailed patterns of domestic and working life – reaching, it is clear, even into the backwaters of rural Wales – was the massive historical transition we call the Industrial Revolution. It is doubtful whether members of the Owen family or the community of Newtown more broadly were particularly conscious in the 1770s and 80s of the magnitude of the forces beginning to reshape the lives of the population of which they were a part. However, as we shall see, there is abundant evidence that as his career blossomed, Robert Owen, in common with many of the self-taught but practical innovators of his generation, did indeed acquire a sophisticated understanding of the processes of social and economic change overtaking the British Isles in the course of his lifetime. In their earliest stages, however, these developments impinged on Owen, as they did on many others, primarily as an implicit sense of widened horizons altering the previously fixed contours of life and work as these had been determined seemingly from time immemorial. This judgment is in keeping with contemporary scholarly perceptions of the complexities of the Industrial Revolution. Social and economic historians, indeed, now distance themselves from some of the sense of suddenness and upheaval associated with the word 'revolution,' preferring instead to dwell on much more gradual and long-term developments affecting the organization of labor and production, and the harnessing of new forms of energy, around industrial and manufacturing activities from the late seventeenth century onwards (Daunton 1995, pp. 125–173). This is not to minimize the scale of the changes overtaking Britain, nor to diminish their eventually colossal impact on the conditions of existence for rich and poor alike. It serves, however, to underscore continuity as well as innovation; incremental adjustment as well as rapid realignment; the strength of tradition as well as the appeal of the modern. The basic Newtown shops in which the young Robert Owen was employed stood at the end of complicated supply chains that drew upon extended networks of international trade, technologically-enhanced manufacture, banking credit and investment, and highly competitive national markets. At the same time, they were for the most part family units – cottage industries intimately bound up with traditional divisions of domestic labor and a continuing dependence on the land and its husbandry. There were many paradoxes associated with this transitional stage, now commonly labeled by commentators as 'proto-industrialization,' and they play an important part in setting the context – and the boundaries – for the subsequent conduct of Robert Owen as an industrialist and as an educational reformer (Quataert 1988; de Vries 2008, pp. 40–73).

It is not surprising that a boy of Owen's flair chose to follow his elder brother into England in pursuit of enhanced employment opportunities. Following a brief, successful stay in London working alongside his brother, William, Robert, still only aged 10, was offered in 1781 his first major opening in the form of a retail apprenticeship with James McGuffog, a prosperous linen and woolen drapers in Stamford, Lincolnshire, serving a diverse clientele including some of the wealthier elements of the Lincolnshire gentry. This move was decisive for Owen's future in several respects. It was his first proper introduction to the operations of the textile trade, then representative of the leading edges of the Industrial Revolution. It was also his first encounter with a much more elite and intensive form of retail management than anything to be found in Newtown, requiring the exercise of the skills of speculation, risk assessment, marketing, customer relations, the oversight of staff, and detailed financial calculation. At each of these activities Owen was quickly to prove himself adept. At the same time, McGuffog's small business was modest enough in scale to preserve much of the character of the older forms of household enterprise alluded to above. Owen was in consequence as much a foster-son as an apprentice in the concern. As his fledgling career began to flourish, he found himself integrated more fully into the McGuffog family routines, sharing something of their prosperity and gaining access to many of their elevated social connections and cultural pursuits. Despite his later protestations, he also appears at this stage to have retained at least the outward forms of orthodox religious observance (McGuffog, a Scot, was a devout Presbyterian) and to have enriched these with extended reading in translations from the Latin classics accessed through the McGuffogs' well-stocked library.

Upon the successful completion of his apprenticeship, Owen returned to London in 1785, joining the much larger but less select haberdashery firm of Flint and Palmer at the heart of the city. This was an altogether more sophisticated (if, Owen felt, somewhat chaotic and impersonal) business operation, which made correspondingly greater physical and mental demands on a boy of 14 in the form of frequently exhausting shift patterns running from early morning until late at night. From his time with Flint and Palmer, Owen gained his first direct acquaintance with the practices of wholesale buying and his first rudimentary understanding of the supply and distribution ends of the textile trade, which was beginning to burgeon across Britain. While his talents appear to have been both recognized and rewarded by his new employer, the young Owen clearly felt frustrated by the endless physical exertions of the job and its general humdrum lack of opportunity. He therefore seized readily the chance to take up a seemingly much more promising and financially rewarding situation with a well-known firm of silk mercers and linen drapers in the city of Manchester – John Satterfield and Company – for which he duly departed in 1788, aged 17.

It is no exaggeration to describe Owen's subsequent rise through Manchester commerce and society as meteoric. In keeping with the later Owenite philosophy, this astonishing transformation was as much about the place as the person. It may at first sight have appeared a retrograde step for a young man of promise to move from the metropolis to what was still widely regarded as a provincial Lancashire town. By 1788 Manchester was, however, becoming one of the hubs of the Industrial Revolution in Britain – a major center of trade, banking, engineering, and textile manufacture. The city's fortunes were in large part attributable to the activities of a class of wealthy merchant-industrialists who over the previous 50 years had stimulated far-reaching structural change in the production of cotton, shifting it from an essentially dispersed household occupation of the rural peasantry to a much more centralized and coordinated industrial system, which had in turn seen Manchester's population rise from 30,000 to over 50,000 in the 15 years prior to Owen's arrival. While the presence of large 'manufactures' was still comparatively rare, intermediate workshop arrangements were multiplying, augmented by a remarkable burst of technological innovation that overtook the cotton production process between 1760 and 1780. James Hargreaves' spinning jenny of 1764 was a multi-spool spinning wheel, the advent of which reduced dramatically the amount of individual work required to produce high-quality yarn, the raw material of cotton goods. In 1771, the industrialist Richard Arkwright installed the first water-driven spinning frame, or 'water frame,' providing for the cotton spinning process levels of energy far beyond that which could be supplied by human labor alone and consolidating the link between cotton production and towns and cities situated near fast-flowing rivers. As a consequence, Arkwright could legitimately lay claim to the creation in Cromford, Derbyshire, of one of the first proper 'factories,' established not simply to aggregate human labor at a single site but to link large numbers of workers to the operation of machinery. The practice was soon widely imitated across the North of England and Scotland, especially in expanding towns such as Manchester and Glasgow. The invention by Richard Crompton in 1779 of the spinning mule brought together the concepts of the jenny and the frame in a much more complex and efficient water-driven installation through which the production of a new quality of yarn that was both stronger, yet thinner and more adaptable, became possible. The speed and volume of technological change, and the enthusiasm with which it was embraced in Manchester, won the town the title 'Cottonopolis' and saw its wealth and its population grow with remarkable rapidity (Lloyd-Jones and Lewis 1988; Evans 2001, pp. 141–154).

Robert Owen stepped into this environment with all of the right qualifications, experiences, and attitudes to exploit the vast range of opportunities with which it almost immediately presented him (Podmore 1906, pp. 24–42; Donnachie 2005a, pp. 37–54). His career at Satterfield and Co. was marked by the singular dynamism and brio he had perfected in the service of his previous employers, even if Satterfield, it transpired, was the least successful businessman of the three. The restlessness that had eventually propelled Owen out of employment with Flint and Palmer proved a permanent asset in Manchester, where industrial developments moved at such an unprecedented pace that young men of enterprise were repeatedly in receipt of fresh offers of employment and partnership geared to the climate of opportunity with which the city was so clearly identified. Contemporary with Owen's arrival, cotton production had begun to enter into a third major era of mass production across Britain, with the steady incorporation of a number of variants of James Watt's new steam technology into the manufacturing process. The coming of steam in the 1780s effectively ended the older systems of cottage and workshop employment in cotton production, launching the first significant phase of the classical factory system and increasing almost immeasurably the money to be made from textiles. Watt and his partners strove to retain control of the cascade of vital developments in steam technology, such as the double-acting engine and the centrifugal governor, but spin-off companies, spare-parts providers and varieties of imitators and improvers mushroomed in cities such as Manchester, eager to capitalize on the many openings and niche markets available for exploitation.

It was not long before Owen was lured into this highly competitive world, drawn away from the retail end of the cotton sector into its industrial infrastructure. In collaboration with a young technician named John Jones, he embarked upon his first industrial partnership for the manufacture of what appears to have been a bespoke version of Crompton's spinning mule. This was a bold departure from his previous employment, both in terms of risk and expertise. Owen consistently pleaded in his autobiography his own comparative ignorance of the engineering aspects of cotton production, preferring to highlight as his contribution to the partnership his experience of resource management and personnel. It is unlikely that this division of expertise was ever as straightforward as Owen self-deprecatingly suggested, for the efficiencies he soon brought to what was in many of its key characteristics an early engineering production line involved advanced conceptual understanding of the operations of the technology alongside the confident leadership of a frequently untrained workforce. We can, in fact, discern in the youthful Owen's early career as an independent entrepreneur in Manchester the first glimmerings of the technocratic outlook that brought both of these skill sets together and that would come to inform much of his later success, including his larger vision of society and how it could be made more just and more efficient by the application of insights gained from industrial production.

It appears, indeed, to have been this highly profitable synthesis of scientific insight and leadership skill that drew the attention of one of Manchester's leading cotton magnates, Peter Drinkwater, to the rising fortunes of the youthful Owen. Perhaps in an effort to neutralize unexpected competition, Drinkwater succeeded in 1792 in recruiting Owen – still only 21 – into his own business, hiring him at some considerable salary cost as superintendent of his new, state-of-the-art mule factory and cotton mill, into which many of the latest steam technologies had been incorporated by Drinkwater and his planners. Owen's appointment to this position at such a young age was a minor sensation around Manchester, almost certainly responsible for bringing him his first taste of celebrity, albeit confined to regional social circles. The diligence and inventiveness brought by Owen to the venture soon vindicated Drinkwater's choice and silenced his critics. Owen introduced major quality control enhancements into almost every aspect of the production process – from the sourcing internationally of diversified strains of raw cotton, through the improvement of shop-floor working conditions, to the continued upgrading of the spinning machinery by the adoption of Watt and Boulton's latest instrumentation. By 1793, Drinkwater's faith in his new manager had reached the point where he laid before Owen the offer of a significantly increased salary and the promise of a full partnership within two years in order to retain his services indefinitely. In anticipation of such elevation, Owen's responsibilities were widened to include within his remit management of another local plant that Drinkwater was seeking to renovate. Owen responded by bringing to the enlarged enterprise still further breakthrough improvements in the successful exploitation of strains of American raw cotton previously regarded as of little commercial value, alongside the refinement of the resultant yarns produced by Drinkwater's factories to the point where the business looked set to assume dominance in the Manchester trade (Podmore 1906, pp. 30–35; Donnachie 2005a, pp. 40–50).

The proposed partnership did not in fact materialize, however, because of unforeseen changes to the overall ownership of Drinkwater's business from which Owen concluded that he would not ultimately gain. Resigning in 1795, he opted instead to capitalize on the enviable local reputation he had earned as a spinner of fine cotton and decided to pursue partnerships with other well-capitalized entrepreneurs then seeking to expand cotton production to the Chorlton suburbs of Manchester in a network of new purpose-built factories and mills. The eventual result of a series of complex negotiations and several ambitious but ultimately unviable speculations was the creation in 1796 of the Chorlton Twist Company, Owen's largest and most financially complex undertaking to date, at the heart of which he triumphantly installed a mill fuelled by the latest steam engine designed by Watt and Boulton. With his obvious strategic expertise, Owen was immediately appointed managing partner of the company, charged with establishing the enterprise on a sound economic footing and made responsible for its operational development and ongoing profitability. This was to be no straightforward task. Despite the seemingly insatiable appetite for all kinds of cotton clothing, from fustian to the new specialist muslin fabrics that Owen had himself helped popularize, Britain had entered a period of great economic turbulence brought on by political and dynastic upheavals on the European mainland and following swiftly on the traumatic loss of the American colonies in the War of Independence. These pressures were set to last through most of the 1790s and on into the first decade of the nineteenth century, drawing Britain into a series of damaging conflicts and eventually a spectacular international war from which it would finally emerge in 1815 as a victorious but radically altered nation. The economic fluctuations in the period caused immense disturbance to industrial production and the mass consumption on which it depended. Owen's success in launching and sustaining the Chorlton Twist Company at a time when many other cotton ventures were contracting or merging in a climate of economic uncertainty was one of the main factors in winning him the high levels of respect as a businessman and economic planner that would eventually propel him from provincial to national prominence.

The narrative of Owen's Manchester years is undoubtedly marked by an almost heroic sense of self-belief and inspired individual judgment. It was also, however, a key phase in the formation of his ideas, both economic and social. The background to these ideas lies in the wider historical forces impacting on British thought and culture of the time, as well as the peculiarly regional setting in which they were mediated to Owen as he rose through the ranks of Manchester society. The entrepreneurial class upon which the expansion of cotton manufacturing was centered spanned a mix of former gentry and landowners with deep roots in Lancashire society. They possessed a strong sense of regional identity, including proud traditions of education and learning drawn from their religious heritage in nonconformist Christianity. For the most part barred by creed and station from the universities, they cherished vibrant intellectual traditions of their own with a distinguished pedigree in the radical opinion of the previous century. At the onset of the Industrial Revolution, as these magnates expended the wealth and leisure time that accompanied the acquisition of their frequently huge financial surpluses, their impressive domestic libraries and municipal gathering places proved uniquely accommodating to study, scholarship, and the currents of radical thought associated with the growth of the European Enlightenment (Stobart 2008). Hospitality to scientific learning went almost inevitably with their professional and industrial interests, but this was richly supplemented by the circulation of books, magazines, and pamphlets in which the most controversial questions in contemporary philosophy, theology, politics, and economics were disseminated and vigorously discussed. At the same time, the obvious interests of the new industrial classes of northern England in the good governance of the towns and cities in which their fortunes were invested lent a markedly civic inflection to their intellectual pursuits. The intense academic discussion of rival views of politics and economics, for example, possessed an urgent and direct relevance to powerful men observing great social change occurring all around them. The ethical traditions out of which their dedication to work and their interest in material prosperity derived spoke eloquently of the responsibilities attendant upon the accumulation of wealth and placed a duty upon them to take an active involvement in the deliberation of wider social and political issues of the day at local and national levels.

With his solid educational foundations and extrovert sociality, Robert Owen entered this sphere of intellectual activism quite effortlessly. As the pattern of his working life in the city began to settle, he found himself invited to gatherings sponsored by the leading industrialists of Manchester responding to the controversies of the time. The most potent impetus to the wider intellectual life of the city in the 1790s was the unfolding spectacle across the English Channel of the French Revolution, embroiling Britain's most feared imperial rival in a political maelstrom of frightful proportions. At first welcomed by the reform-minded industrial classes of northern England as a justifiable protest against the monarchical despotism of the old continental order, the Revolution in France rapidly alienated many of its British supporters by its perceived indiscriminate attack on all political and religious institutions, including that of property itself. The Manchester elites were well aware of the potential appeal of the revolutionary ideals of liberty, equality, and fraternity to the most alienated and impoverished casualties of British industrialization, including sections of their own workforce. Initial support for the moderate parties in Paris, struggling to obtain necessary constitutional reform of the systems of representation and taxation in France, yielded to resolute opposition as the Revolution reportedly became more violent and more extreme in its political objectives. Responses to the guillotining of Louis XVI and the declaration of the French Republic served to reveal deep fissures in British society and threatened to expose dangerous patterns of discontent equal in severity to those that had prompted the insurrection in France (MacLeod 2007). Opinion in Britain rapidly polarized as the Revolution gave way to the show trials and executions of the Terror and factional violence threatened completely to engulf the French state. France declared war on Britain in 1793, opening a period of more than 20 years of hostilities and linking permanently the cause of domestic political reform in Britain to the deeply divided reactions of public opinion to the Revolution in France and its aftermath. In December 1792, Owen joined other concerned businessmen from the mixed community of Protestant dissenters in Manchester and Salford in signing a public declaration endorsing the British Constitution and affirming its existing capacity to deal with any justifiable social grievances of the sort that had wracked France. This was an important document. It was in large measure a response to the official alarm occasioned by the historic association of English dissenting communities with revolutionary sympathies, representing a public recommitment of mainstream nonconformity to the quest for gradualist political reform and designed to reassure an increasingly frightened and repressive government in London. His readiness to be associated with the declaration can be seen as Owen's first assumption of that sense of civic service that many in his rising class saw as a natural correlative of their growing affluence. Signing the petition appears also to have opened Owen to one the most significant educational opportunities of his adult life: membership of the Manchester Literary and Philosophical Society.

The Manchester Literary and Philosophical Society in many respects typified the kind of loose, informal, semi-academic association through which Enlightenment ideas and practices had been spread throughout Britain from the early eighteenth century onwards. All across Europe, as the tumult of the wars of religion of the previous century subsided, a new spirit of freethinking intellectual enquiry had begun to germinate, linked in part with the ancient universities (especially in Protestant countries), but dependent also upon the networks of unattached scholars, writers, and patrons motivated by a reawakened interest in the possibilities of philosophical reflection conducted independent of the perceived constraints of theology and the regulation of the Churches. Of particular appeal in Britain to the classes to which Owen belonged, this 'popular Enlightenment' developed as a grassroots movement based in the larger towns and cities and supported by the wealth and patronage of the newly prosperous elites. The Manchester Society appears to have begun essentially as a reading group, but it was soon attracting to its debating chamber in the house of the physician Thomas Percival interest in a wide range of scholarly activities, including scientific experimentation, exploration, the discussion of disease control and population growth, and wider speculation upon the future development of trade, economics, and industry (Silver 1965, pp. 75–86; Brnardi 2009).

The records of the Manchester Society shine a valuable light on this phase in the development of Owen's thought, even if they do not by any means compensate for the gaps in our direct understanding of what he was reading and absorbing from among the texts of classic Enlightenment literature at this time. Owen is surprisingly reticent in his autobiography about his own reading at this stage of his life, almost anticipating the paradoxical suspicion of books and book-learning that would be a hallmark of his mature educational philosophy (Donnachie 2005a, pp. 59–63). The operation of the Manchester Society depended upon the willingness of members to deliver papers for reading and discussion. This was sometimes supplemented by talks and lectures by visiting scholars drawn to the growing reputation of Manchester for industrial innovation and patronage of the arts and sciences. The range of papers presented to the Society, and the luminaries often responsible for their delivery, reveal the strength in depth of

Manchester's intellectual life in the 1790s and clearly reinforce the impression of the institution as a vital element in the municipal fabric of the town, central to the maintenance of its international standing in a period of tremendous intellectual ferment. Members included John Dalton, one of the founders of modern atomic theory, and Thomas Barnes, a Unitarian minister and first principal of Manchester College. James Ferriar, president of the Society when Owen joined in 1793, was a doctor trained at Edinburgh University and a pioneer of public health. Thomas Percival, the Society's principal patron, was himself a man of wide literary and cultural sophistication, drawing to the meetings of the Society many visitors from across Britain and abroad, including the famous poet and savant Samuel Taylor Coleridge, with whom Owen reported in his memoirs a prolonged and frank exchange on religion and morality.

Owen's involvement in the Manchester Society was expressed in several fields that were to become central to his later concerns. Commencing modestly enough with presentations to his peers on aspects of cotton production, Owen, despite his youth and comparatively limited formal qualifications, was soon extending himself into the delivery of papers on the importance of education, the cultivation of virtue in civic society, and the relationship between universal happiness and practical mechanics. None of the texts of these presentations has survived and it is hard therefore to determine their relationship to his subsequent thought. Beyond dispute, however, is the clear conclusion that his involvement in the Manchester Society initiated Owen into systematic study of many of the great issues of his times, teaching him the importance of acquaintance with a wide spectrum of opinion on controversial questions, and providing him with a platform upon which to perfect his communication with an audience. It seems equally obvious that the overall academic tenor of the Manchester Society, with its Enlightenment promotion of rational deliberation and its generally skeptical attitude to received authority, convinced Owen that educated debate had entered a new era of freethinking exploration, in which many of the seemingly incontestable truths of the past would be cast into doubt by the rigorous application of reason. In this regard, certainly, his experience in Manchester appears to have sealed Owen's final withdrawal from personal adherence to religious faith, carrying him into a state of polite but increasingly militant agnosticism that would intensify as he grew older.

Alongside this inner journey of self-fashioning, however, went another much more publicly engaged impulse consistent with the broad commitment of the Manchester Society to a kind of ethic of public service. Perhaps at Percival's prompting, Owen joined the Manchester Board of Health in 1796, just as it was beginning to coordinate the first wave of data collection from across Britain designed to assist in the lobbying of Parliament for legislation to address the worst excesses of the early factory system. Members of the Manchester Society had expressed concerns about factory conditions at many of their evening meetings. Ian Donnachie speculates that it was as a result of David Dale's detailed and conscientious response to the Manchester survey from his distant mill village on the banks of the River Clyde in Scotland that Owen first became acquainted with the existence of New Lanark and the interesting welfare experiments in which Dale was even then engaged (Donnachie 2005a, p. 63). This is difficult to verify from Owen's own memoirs, but it aligns persuasively with the wider currents of his thought as these had been channeled by his Manchester experience. Large-scale movements in European philosophical thought, cataclysmic political rebellion against revered and sacred authority, and technological advance of a wholly unprecedented character, had all found a point of focus in the city of Manchester and its cultural preoccupations in ways which made the international seem meaningfully local, the impersonal and anonymous profoundly immediate and practical. Owen's handling of these unpredictable forces reflected the optimism and pragmatism that had drawn him to Manchester in the first place: an almost unflagging belief that the unprecedented energies unleashed by the epoch through which he was living could be contained and directed by collective human action to produce for others the kind of advantage from which he had himself already enormously benefited. Owen's response to the classic forms of Enlightenment thought to which he was exposed by his omnivorous, if undisciplined, reading and his interactions with the learned minds of the Manchester intelligentsia assumed a shape close to that of his earlier absorption in radical Christianity. It took on, once again, a constitutively *ethical* character, where armchair philosophizing required to be targeted into bringing that same enlightenment, and that same imperative to reform the conditions in which men and women lived, into the darkest recesses of the restless society in which the youthful Owen had already found himself emerging as a figure of note.

Owen and New Lanark

Whether or not his curiosity about New Lanark was first stirred by the Manchester Society's national audit of factory conditions, Robert Owen most certainly did begin to learn of the mill town on the River Clyde as part of his professional responsibilities as chief manager of the Chorlton Twist Company. He records this fact conscientiously, if confusingly, in his autobiography (Owen 1993e, 4.94–96). His almost instinctive sense of the ebbs and flows in the cotton industry attracted to his factory intelligence about developments in matters such as new supplies of raw materials and various enhancements to the production processes that were beginning to appear across many areas of the British Isles. Manchester may well have retained for some considerable time its uncontested position in the fiercely competitive textile market, but the steady spread of the technologies of mass production in the 1780s and 90s, alongside the reawakening of guild traditions of clothing production and tailoring in a number of population centers across Britain, soon generated levels of textile manufacturing activity in several regions of England and Scotland that were quickly to match that of Manchester and its environs.

Perhaps prompted by the possible loss of custom to rival producers from the Clyde Valley, Owen in 1797 (or 1798: his chronology is muddled on this topic) embarked on his first commercial trip to Scotland, ostensibly to 'enlarge our business connections' (Owen 1993e, 4.94) in the Glasgow area (though quite possibly also to deal more effectively with the erosion of his customer base by the lure of local competition). Entering with his characteristic alacrity into the trading networks of a Scottish town that was beginning to mushroom in size and in industry very much in the pattern followed by

Manchester a decade previously, Owen soon found himself frequenting cotton manufacturing circles in Glasgow that were dominated by the name and the reputation of one man – David Dale. With his by now customary good fortune, Owen, while promenading one morning around Glasgow Cross, was introduced by a mutual acquaintance to David Dale's daughter, Caroline, who was also out walking, the Cross being only a short distance from the opulent Dale family home. This brief, casual encounter was destined to be one of the most significant meetings of Owen's life. In response to a polite invitation issued that morning by Caroline Dale, Owen embarked on his first journey from Glasgow to New Lanark to review a cotton producing enterprise in the possession of Dale and his partners that by the time of Owen's first ' visit was, he was soon to discover, well on its way to equaling, or even surpassing, anything operating in Lancashire.

Several leading commentators have noted that a singular feature of the autobiographical recollections set down by Owen in relation to his initial impressions of, and dealings with, New Lanark is the generally misleading portrait of what he in fact found there (McLaren 1999, pp. 22–24; Donnachie 2005a: 77). In some respects, this seemingly surprising bias on Owen's part may be rooted in a sense of mild professional envy associated with the impact of New Lanark on an industry over which the young Owen had formed an understandably proprietorial view. More profoundly, his sometimes subtly condescending representation of the state of New Lanark at or before his arrival, and, indeed, his occasionally patronizing descriptions of David Dale, may be seen as part of a larger trend towards self-hagiography in Owen's writings, in which exaggerated emphasis on the inadequacy of past conditions is repeatedly employed to magnify the achievements wrought by the subsequent interventions of Owen and his allies. We find this pattern of self-promotion recurring in his memoirs and letters, from his description of Drinkwater onwards. It is also reasonable to suppose that it would have taken Owen much longer than the *Life* and other writings suggest to form a reliable impression of New Lanark, its recent history and its complex business regime as these had been forged by Dale. It now seems clear that Owen in fact encountered a much more accomplished and sophisticated undertaking at New Lanark when he first came there than any of his memoirs would have us believe.

Born in 1739, David Dale had emerged into the Scottish mercantile class very much as one of the self-made men of the 1770s. From humble journeyman origins in Ayrshire, he had secured a position for himself in the clothing trade, which swiftly opened to him opportunities for profitable business partnerships and short-term acquisitions through which he expanded his interests in the growing textile manufacturing base of Southern and West Central Scotland. The major step up in his fortunes came with his highly advantageous marriage in 1777 into the wealthy Campbell family, then at the heart of the burgeoning banking syndicates of Glasgow and Edinburgh and close to the centers of political power in the capital. Dale was subsequently appointed a joint agent of the newly formed Royal Bank in 1783, exercising widespread discretionary authority over the bank's investment policies and assuming a founding position in the creation of the Glasgow Chamber of Commerce (Donnachie 2005a, pp. 69–70).

It was in this role that Dale played lead host to an important visit to Scotland in 1784 of the renowned English cotton baron Richard Arkwright, then deep in patent litigation in the English courts over various technological improvements he had introduced into the cotton production process and urgently seeking fresh scope for expansion of his textile interests north of the border (and in a separate legal jurisdiction). With Arkwright already committed to one important manufacturing venture in Stanley, Ayrshire, not far from Dale's birthplace, Dale took him on what was then popularly regarded as a Scottish leg of the fashionable Grand Tour: a visit to the picturesque Falls of Clyde near the historic county town of Lanark. As this trip suggests, long before it became even a potential centre for industrial development, the Falls of Clyde had occupied a prominent position in the imagination of visitors to Scotland as a place of outstanding natural beauty and elemental appeal. Attitudes to the spectacle afforded by the Falls were highly colored by then prevalent sentiments associated with the late eighteenth-century enthusiasm for the sublime: the raw, cleansing encounter of the individual sensibility with the unbounded vistas of nature at their least tamed and most romantic (Donnachie 2005b; Grenier 2005, pp. 15–49). Dale and Arkwright followed, in consequence, in the footsteps of poets, artists, and composers captivated by the beauty of the scene, where the Clyde appeared at its most turbulent and the landscape seemed far removed from the influence of human agency. In a response perhaps characteristic of the confluence of forces at work in the age, however, where artists saw only elemental force Dale and Arkwright saw with their entrepreneurial gaze massive kinetic energy at work. Arkwright as a result quickly recognized in the situation of the Falls the potential for the kind of industrial development that might take full advantage of his latest water-powered technological innovations for the manufacture of textiles. Whether Dale's choice of the Falls as a sightseeing destination included such commercial calculation is difficult to determine. Regardless of the range of possible motives, within less than a year, and as a result of their visit to the Clyde, Dale, in partnership with Arkwright, had embarked upon the building of what was then possibly the largest cotton mill complex in the world. Within less than one further year, by the spring of 1786, high-volume cotton production at New Lanark had commenced (McLaren 1999, pp. 17–22).

Dale's formal partnership with Arkwright did not endure, but the spur it gave Dale to invest in and develop the New Lanark site was momentous. Within five years of its inception, the village had grown considerably in size and immensely in productive capacity, establishing an enviable reputation with the cotton producing elites of the British Isles for the boldness of its industrial design and the drive with which its capacity was exploited. Later, Owen was to stress that New Lanark was only one of Dale's many business interests, implying that the distraction of other commercial projects and banking activities diverted his attention at key junctures from the village and its industry, leading sometimes to extensive delegation of decision-making and at other times even to a kind of benign neglect. This impression of Dale, while containing some truth, seems unduly partial and underplays the extent to which New Lanark was Dale's vision and its development for several years a defining fixture in his broader, evolving conception of industrial living. Like many of the early industrial leaders of his era, Dale was aware that the new patterns of production and consumption associated with the increasingly automated systems of manufacturing were altering the fabric of society in novel and unforeseen ways, with consequences that were sometimes dangerously unpredictable for the lives and fortunes of owners and workers alike. Shifts in the character of late eighteenth-century Scotland of the kind that had marked his own career pathway, underlined for Dale the movement of peoples, the disruption of agrarian communities, and the often grievous polarization of wealth and poverty in the newly-emerging social order.

Even before the founding of New Lanark, Dale possessed a wide reputation for philanthropy, patronizing charitable initiatives for the relief of indigence and the improvement of health and civic welfare in his chosen home of Glasgow, a town that was becoming one of the crucibles of the industrial revolution in Britain (McLaren 1999, pp. 77–89; Donnachie 2005a, p. 77). He also appears to have had some involvement in efforts to provide basic schooling in the poorest parts of the rapidly growing town, including the creation of Sunday Schools for elementary instruction in religion and morality. In certain respects, Dale's activities in these areas were typical of the philanthropic impulse that marked many of the great industrial plutocrats of the period. The precipitate accumulation of wealth accompanied by the frequently grim spectacle of displacement, squalor, disease, and illiteracy prompted many in the economic elites to devise schemes both local and national for the amelioration of the worst excesses of early capitalism in the workplace and beyond, especially as these afflicted the expanding laboring classes and their dependents (Wilson 2008). Undoubtedly, the fear of social unrest and the example of revolutionary violence across the English Channel provided incentives for these kinds of intervention in the operations of the unfettered market. The motives, however, were also frequently more complex and reflected wider ethical, and indeed spiritual, preoccupations of sections of the owning classes.

Dale's detailed, conscientious response to the Manchester survey underlines the depth of his interest in welfare questions and demonstrates that the transference of his philanthropic energies to the community of New Lanark may have been stirred by more than simply ameliorative motivations. The relationship of *place* to *work*, and the locus of *education* within that relationship, has an obscure ancestry within Dale's personal intellectual and spiritual formation that seems to have had a powerful impact on the early shaping of New Lanark and on the legacy Dale later bequeathed to Owen when ownership of the village passed to him. Throughout Dale's career as an industrialist the pursuit of prosperity was interwoven with the promotion of his religious and theological allegiances. Dale, indeed, developed an individual evangelical faith and a network of ecclesiastical connections not far removed from the Welsh Christian nonconformity to which Owen had been exposed as a boy. We have already highlighted the scale of theological ferment in the mid eighteenth century, as interest in the older traditions of radical Christian piety was reawakened in response to social and economic dislocation. Dale stood at the center of some of these developments, particularly as they affected the complex presbyterian politics of the Church of Scotland in the Glasgow area. Around the time of Dale's birth, a series of damaging splits had affected the national Church, largely in response to the issue of state and gentry control of the appointment of local Church ministers. Abstruse theological differences soon exacerbated these divisions, leading to the splintering from the Church of small but increasingly uncompromising Calvinist sects unhappy with the condition of doctrine and governance in the national institution. As a young man in the 1760s, Dale joined one such group of Glasgow secessionists angry at the interference of the town council in ministerial appointments. The group soon merged with other like-minded congregations to form the 'Old Scots Independents,' organizing Church communities in several towns and cities across Scotland, including eventually New Lanark itself (McLaren 1999, pp. 91–100; Donnachie 2005a, pp. 92–93).

Thomas Markus has recently drawn attention to the broader pietistic networks into which Dale's religious sentiments drew him (Markus 1993, pp. 286–288). Secessionist groups often sought out theologically congenial confederates in other Protestant jurisdictions experiencing similar tensions around the regulation of belief and practice. Dale's congregation, Markus suggests, possessed a natural affinity with one of the most powerful of the European secessionist bodies, the Moravians, or Church of the United Brethren. The Moravians were an early Reformation Church originating in Bohemia and Moravia that had experienced a surge in popularity and missionary activity in the 1730s. Successful Moravian missions to England and Scotland had resulted in the establishment of a number of congregations across the country, including at Fulneck in Yorkshire and in parts of Ayrshire, undoubtedly interacting with the rise of Wesleyan Methodism across the British Isles (Mason 2001, pp. 59–90). Dale's general sympathy with Moravian principles is vouchsafed by the design of one of his earlier business ventures, the 1786 mill village of Catrine in Ayrshire, which employed a Moravian model in the layout of the streets and main buildings of the community. Moravian belief specifically – and much eighteenth-century dissenting theology more generally – resonated with older Christian idealist impulses in radical Protestant thought of the Reformation period, which over a period of some two centuries had witnessed repeated efforts of breakaway sects and fringe Churches to found utopian communities erected in accordance with perceived New Testament principles and organized to live out the presumed values of the Kingdom of God. Many of these minorities were eschatological in outlook, meaning that they lived in expectation of the imminent arrival of the last days and the Second Coming of Christ as predicted by their millenarian interpretations of the Scriptures. Others were more quietist and interior in character, offering themselves as examples for the social and spiritual reform of a corrupt world. A shared theme of much of their life was the intertwined ideas of 'apartness' – physically detaching themselves from surrounding society – and an aspiration quite literally to build a new kind of community in which the design of the built environment would actively promote the formation of virtuous, godly citizens (Podmore 1998, pp. 97–120).

We are accustomed to thinking of this determinist understanding of the influence of the environment over the making of personality as a classic Enlightenment and secular formulation. Indeed, we shall see later in this book that in its standard Enlightenment construction it was to be of vital importance to the educational thought of Robert Owen. The experience of David Dale, however, and his various attempts actually to establish new kinds of industrial settlement, underlines the extent to which this set of beliefs was also rooted in older, theological, perceptions of the relationship of the individual to society. It is not misleading to suggest that what Owen encountered when he first came to New Lanark was a further stage in the ongoing experiment of Reformation Christian utopianism, of a kind to be found in an archipelago of such communities across Europe and America in the eighteenth century. These often otherwise theologically diverse places shared a deeply held belief in the need for *renewal* of society – hence the frequent invocation of the word 'new' in their place names and charters – that would begin from the base up, in the redesign of spaces and the fabric of living and working. Structure, pattern, and planning of the built environment commonly assumed an almost visionary or prophetic status in their programs, with the zoning of domestic and productive space shaped by sometimes arcane biblical principles, but nonetheless simultaneously rooted in the practical requirements of efficient wealth creation, self-sufficiency, and production. The architecture of authority and governance also shaped the organization of the community, representing the distribution of power within it and the active superintendence of almost every aspect of social life.

When Owen made his first excursion to New Lanark, he stepped into the midst of Dale's commercial and social experiment. While it is evident from the outset that he formed a very mixed opinion of the village and its activities, it is equally clear that he swiftly internalized some of the defining features of Dale's model and went on to replicate and adapt them as his own ideas developed. In Owen's mature thought, his sometimes obsessive preoccupation with the geometry of imagined, utopian social and industrial spaces is the most obvious demonstration of this. Plans and designs for perfect villages and towns – the majority fated to remain drawings and diagrams – were to become a hallmark of the Owenite movement in Britain and America, as well as a focus of much skepticism on the part of its critics. The template for these schemes throughout Owen's long career remained New Lanark, the only one of the sites to bear the stamp of an idealized conception of community from its foundation onwards. Owen without doubt sought firmly to distance himself from the religious pedigree of Dale's project, secularizing the underlying values and largely privatizing the place of faith in the life of the community, particularly as his own worldview grew increasingly nonreligious. It remains nevertheless significant (and ironic) that in several of his later ventures in utopian living, Owen found himself dealing with radical religious movements that possessed a strong family resemblance to Dale's sect.

Owen echoed the response of other visitors to New Lanark in immediately recognizing the distinctively benevolent regime under which Dale controlled his apprentices, including the care taken to provide for their education – an aspect of life at New Lanark that Dale had gone to great lengths to highlight in his feedback to the Manchester survey. The divergence of Dale's reforms in this area from standard early industrial practice can be exaggerated and their overlap with arrangements in other areas of the textile trade needs always to be recognized (Fitton and Wadsworth 1958. pp. 224–253). Moreover, some of Dale's much-commended approaches to education were dictated by the special circumstances of an immigrant and diverse workforce recruited from a wide geographical area and demanding more active efforts at community-building than the norm of locally sourced labor might ordinarily have required. Some of the limitations of Dale's provision were obvious to visitors other than Owen, and the subsequent changes introduced by Owen when he assumed ownership of the village represented undoubted improvements on what had gone before. That said, the record shows convincingly that Dale sought conscientiously to prioritize the education of children in the pattern of the working day at his mills. This included the teaching of literacy, numeracy, and religious instruction, the employment of a significant number of qualified teachers and the organization of a formal timetable of classes, including some scope for recreational activities such as music and dance. In addition, the commitment to the schooling of the young was embedded in wider attempts by Dale to provide the community with basic welfare services and moral direction. The results of all of this effort were curiously uneven – reflective, perhaps, of the inevitable, irreconcilable tensions within the early industrial system. While infant mortality rates and health care standards seem to have been better than average in Dale's New Lanark, delinquency and criminality caused concern to the surround-ing county. While some residents remembered Dale with considerable affection, the turnover of labor at his mills was no better than elsewhere in the volatile industry (Donnachie 2005a, pp. 78, 108–109).

Owen's captivation by what he saw at New Lanark – both in its actuality and in what he perceived increasingly as its industrial and social potential – was pursued on two fronts. Perhaps apprised even before his first journey to Glasgow of the ailing Dale's interest in selling the whole operation, Owen began tentatively to explore the possibility of its acquisition by the Chorlton Twist Company or one of its offshoots. At the same time, learning through intermediaries of Caroline Dale's rejection of a number of eligible local suitors, Owen embarked upon a courtship of Caroline that appears to have been prosecuted with his customary zeal and directness. Overcoming her father's initial opposition to both ambitions was achieved with the practical demonstration of intent for which Owen had won the respect of a succession of older businessmen and father-figures with whom he had collaborated profitably in the years of his adolescence. While Caroline's affections were fostered through a regular correspondence and the clever cultivation of support among David Dale's friends, Owen worked hard to secure the commitment and resources of his commercial partners to the purchase of New Lanark as a going concern. The two initiatives converged in 1799 when Dale, finally persuaded of Owen's sincerity and ability (if not his dubious religious credentials), assented to the marriage of Robert and Caroline and, almost as part of the same contract, agreed to singularly generous terms for the sale of New Lanark to Owen and his associates. Owen's Manchester partners were immediately aware of the advantage of the transaction Owen had sealed on their behalf in acquiring one of the most modern mill complexes in the world and in instantaneously neutralizing a major competitor. In the same spirit, it was quickly accepted that the most sensible arrangement for oversight of the new acquisition lay in the permanent relocation of Owen with his new wife to Scotland, where he could once again assume the role of managing partner that he had so successfully discharged in the Manchester venture. In January 1800, as Owen himself later solemnly put it, he as a consequence 'entered into the government of New Lanark,' where 'the groundwork on which to try an experiment long wished for' could at last commence (Owen 1993e, 4.109).

The Reform of New Lanark

It should be clear from this review of the first phases of his career that Robert Owen was essentially a man of practical action rather than a systematic philosophical or social theorist. Later in this book we shall examine key writings of Owen in which his vision of educational and social reform is set forth at length, largely as part of a prolonged propaganda effort on his own behalf to win political and economic support for the changes he believed were urgently needed to the social and educational structures of early industrial Britain. It remains nevertheless vital to recognize that the often discursive and sometimes derivative essays and pamphlets in which Owen laid out his main ideas are inseparable from his pragmatic sense of educational renewal undertaken in the communities over which he exercised leadership. These texts are not in design or execution abstract educational treatises. The crucible of almost all of Owen's most striking innovations was New Lanark, and it is in the functional development of the New Lanark system that we can see most clearly the objectives Owen had set himself and appreciate the emergent understanding of human nature and human society on which these objectives rested. New Lanark is, in a key sense, the central text of *all* of Owen's educational apologetics. In this same pragmatist vein, comprehending the roots of Owen's thought cannot be separated from his relations with several of the leading thinkers of his time, with whom he interacted personally in the examination of some of the most pressing social and political problems to occupy his generation.

For Owen's Manchester partners, New Lanark remained first and foremost a commercial enterprise and it comes as no surprise that Owen's first set of reforms when he took over related to the management and organization of cotton manufacture in the village. Owen had from the outset regarded Dale's workforce as inefficient and he introduced a new ethos of discipline and performance management into the mills, sacking two of Dale's managers and implementing a new structure of delegated superintendence copied from the Manchester owners and involving careful recording of each worker's efforts and output in an individual 'book of character.' To this Owen added an instrument which perhaps signaled his incipient awareness of the educational fashions of the day, while reflecting the increasing convergence of his perception of the control of production with the control of human beings. This was the device known as the 'silent monitor,' a four-sided piece of wood set above each workstation in the mills and color-coded in order to score each worker's daily performance. The origin of the device most probably lay in Owen's unacknowledged acquaintance with the ideas of the famous educationalist Joseph Lancaster, in whose *Improvements in Education* of 1803 the use of a similar object for the encouragement of pupils in classrooms was assiduously promoted. The silent monitor may strike modern minds as oppressive in its intrusive scrutiny of individual effort, but in its time it was seen as progressive, breaking with the far more coercive forms of oversight of classrooms and factory floors that still dominated the emergent industrial system (Donnachie 2005a, pp. 80–82).

The same comparative perspective needs to be brought to bear on the other changes initially introduced by Owen into community life at New Lanark. His decision to abandon the apprentice system favored by Dale, because of its reliance on pauper children imported from the major towns and then left mostly to fend for themselves when their apprenticeships were completed, undoubtedly reduced maintenance costs, but it also represented one of his first major efforts to galvanize the population of the mill village around some sort of sense of shared belonging. In an echo perhaps of the older forms of cottage enterprise from which he had himself originated, Owen proposed that the core of the workforce would no longer be orphans but families, attracted to live and work in the village by higher wages, increased automation, and superior living conditions. The corollary of increased rigor in the enforcement of production targets was the steady extension to this new, more coherent workforce of enhanced welfare standards in the form of better housing, health care, security, and even the availability of retail goods and services (Podmore 1906, pp. 160–170). Under Owen's management, several features closely associated with the more concerted regulation of production were also introduced explicitly into the governance of the social life of the community, resulting in a much firmer emphasis on civic virtues such as law and order, cleanliness, and temperance. It soon became clear that in Owen's evolving conception of community, social improvement would not be presented as fortuitous luxury dependent upon the generation of an economic surplus, but would be seen as absolutely integral to the attainment of it.

Nowhere was this relationship more publicly evident than in the provision of education at New Lanark. If Owen's quite exceptional performance as a cotton entrepreneur soon began to attract international business interest to his plant on the banks of the Clyde, it was the overhaul of education that over the course of time drew steadily increasing levels of philanthropic enquiry to his work. This was by no means immediate. Despite the reservations he clearly harbored about the scale and quality of his father-in-law's approach to the education of the populous, Owen began modestly enough by building on the enlightened practices inherited from the period of Dale's tenure. He extended the hours juveniles spent in school and made some limited changes to the curriculum and its resources. His decision to bring to an end the employment of the under-10s and to consolidate the working community around extended kinship units increased the numbers of school-aged children requiring education, with implications for their teaching accommodation. The scope for more far-reaching and immediate change was, however, at first very limited by several seemingly formidable obstacles. As Dale's health continued to decline, Owen was compelled to assume greater responsibility for his complex financial affairs and spent considerable periods of time overseeing and then offloading many of his less profitable assets, including less efficient mills and factories.

Vitiated by the upheaval of the Napoleonic Wars, the first decade of the nineteenth century was a period of dramatic political turbulence internationally, with damaging consequences for all forms of British overseas trade, especially that in textiles. Skilful management of the New Lanark enterprise helped Owen's company navigate the economic fluctuations intact when many other businesses succumbed to bankruptcy. His success at this won him increased levels of respect from his employees, especially at those points when only his charity stood between them and the loss of all of their household earnings in the wake of adverse trading conditions. Despite such approval from his workers, and the growing esteem of his peers, Owen was conscious that in times of severe economic strain the additional expense of ostentatious and sustained investments in philanthropy might place an unpalatable financial burden on the Manchester partnership in which ownership of the mills was retained. He was therefore forced to proceed at a pace quite at variance with his natural, impulsive style, constantly assuaging the suspicions of his partners and building alliances with other possible supporters in the political and commercial classes.

The result of these constraints was that while welfare conditions at New Lanark improved markedly in the first decade of Owen's leadership, more expensive changes to the organization of education appear to have progressed much more slowly, moving forward only incrementally as hard-won consensus and tight resources permitted. Owen's memoirs for the period are evasive on this point and in the material record of New Lanark it is actually surprisingly difficult to find evidence of significant educational advance of the kind Owen would subsequently pronounce essential to the flourishing of his ideal communities. By the end of a deeply challenging decade, in spite of his canny gradualism, Owen's daring plans for New Lanark had finally exhausted the patience of partners long skeptical of the financial benefits of his benevolence, while Owen himself had grown tired of procrastination. Seeing the opportunity begin to slip from his grasp, Owen determined in 1810 at last to press ahead with a far-reaching proposal 'to clear the foundation for the infant and other schools, to form the new character of the rising population' (Owen 1993e, 4.137). The boldness of his schemes, however, induced a crisis of confidence in the partnership, which had to be quickly restructured to avoid a complete collapse of the business. The revised partnership was to prove equally unconvinced in the face of his continuing ambitions and by 1812 Owen had been peremptorily sacked and a motion mooted by his former associates to sell New Lanark.

With his by now unrivalled skill as a broker and negotiator, Owen set out expeditiously to forge his third and final New Lanark partnership, opting ingeniously to produce a public prospectus for purchase of the mills that quite deliberately canvassed the advantages of combining at the village the potential for 'abundant profits' and 'a national benevolent institution' (Owen 1993a: 1.16). This intrepid maneuver outflanked his erstwhile partners and succeeded in soliciting the interest of a number of leading English philanthropists, including a group of prosperous Quaker businessmen centered on the wealthy factory owner and Fellow of the Royal Society, William Allen, and the radical utilitarian philosopher Jeremy Bentham. Around these men,

Owen believed he could at last establish the kind of ownership agreement that would allow him to pursue his transformation of New Lanark while maintaining the high profit margins of the mills. The clever and protracted campaign to free himself decisively from the limitations of previous contractual arrangements, which took him all over the country, also served sharply to raise Owen's public profile as a national champion of enlightened reform. This may well have figured in his strategy all along, because the composition of the prospectus, involving as it did the overt and unexpected promotion of those welfare aspects of the enterprise that had long troubled his Manchester partners, was accompanied by the writing of the first of his *Essays on the Formation of Character*, which would eventually become part of the major manifesto of his ideas, *A New View of Society* (Owen 1993f). The crisis of 1812–1813, from which Owen eventually emerged triumphant, formed the perfect backdrop to the launch of the next phase of his career as an industrialist and a reformer (Donnachie 2005a, pp. 104–108).

Owen had quite openly promoted the education of children as the flagship of his long-cherished innovations, despite the fact that some members of the first partnership had gone so far as to suggest that even the New Lanark school inherited from Dale should be closed to reduce costs. Owen's commitment to education seems to have been first aroused in the Manchester years, where it formed the content of at least one of his presentations to the Literary and Philosophical Society. From the Manchester period onwards, Owen would have been aware that the advent of industrialization and its shocking exposure of the immense scale of ignorance and illiteracy among the working classes had awakened interest in the possibilities of popular education for many concerned reformers. Before Owen, a number of enlightened employers associated with socially engaged religious movements such as the Quakers and the Hutchensonians had supported efforts to provide rudimentary education to working children as part of their employment packages. The notion of mass education remained an outlandish aspiration, but in the radical Christian movements to which, as we have seen, foundations such as New Lanark were obscurely related, schemes for the provision of large-scale schooling had been persuasively articulated and even in some cases actively realized in the late seventeenth and early eighteenth centuries. Indeed, possibly the greatest of all early modern educational theorists, the Czech John Amos Comenius (1592–1670), was a bishop of the same persecuted Moravian Church by which Dale had been heavily influenced in his early planning of Catrine and New Lanark. Comenius' *Didactica Magna* of 1657 was widely hailed as the first and most morally compelling call for the introduction of universal education across Europe. In Britain, from the time of thinkers such as John Bellers (1654–1725) to the initiatives of a former associate of Dale's, Patrick Colquhoun, at the Free School in Westminster, assorted proposals had been tabled and tested, some quite successfully, for funding and administering the basic education of the poor (Jennings 1928). The Scotland into which Owen had stepped in the 1790s also preserved, as we shall see, a long tradition of parish schools providing to a proportion of the Scottish peasantry significantly larger than the European norm a quite surprisingly varied curriculum. Core instruction in reading and writing had in consequence raised Scottish literacy rates to among the highest in the world. It has nevertheless been strongly suggested that the coming of industrialization to many parts of Scotland in the second half of the eighteenth century overwhelmed a national educational infrastructure predicated on the needs of an essentially agrarian society, further incentivizing novel interventions such as that offered by New Lanark (Houston 1982).

The detail of Owen's educational policies at New Lanark will be discussed in the next chapter of this book, alongside the important account of their implementation recorded by his son and amanuensis, Robert Dale Owen. Some of the key public statements made by Owen in defense of his innovations and their likely implications for society at large will also be considered. A revealing foretaste of his plans was offered by Owen when he welcomed the Quaker educationalist, Joseph Lancaster, to Scotland in 1812, as Lancaster was conducting a tour intended to promote the enlightened measures he had introduced into a number of schools in England as part of his trademark 'monitorial' teaching method. Owen's tribute to Lancaster once again implies something of the reading and reflecting on educational questions to which he must have been applying himself in the period leading up to the final coup by which he gained control of the New Lanark enterprise, but which were only very sketchily recorded in his memoirs. Lancastrian principles were destined to take deep roots in the village as Owen implemented his reforms, even if they were later subject to some significant amendment as his thinking became more cosmopolitan. In 1812, it was clear to Owen that progressive approaches to learning and teaching of the type championed by Lancaster went to the heart of the broader social transformation of which improved education would be the vital catalyst. Offered a more rational education, he insisted in his toast to Lancaster, 'all those in the lower walks of life, and the character of the whole community, will rise by many degrees [...] and [...] all be essentially benefited.' Moreover, in a telling gesture towards the potential for education within close-knit communities to effect wider social advance, Owen stated that schools which 'contain the younger children in the day time, will likewise serve for evening and Sunday schools, at which times those who may be past the proper age for the first [...] may be instructed' (Donnachie 2005a, p. 110). This last remark highlighted an objective of Owen's that he subsequently succeeded in incorporating, albeit vaguely, into one of the articles of the new partnership through which he secured his control of the business and which referred directly to the establishment of a school in a building in the village dedicated solely to that purpose. All along, it seems, Owen wished to utilize this article for the creation of something more than a school and involving, if necessary, the restructuring of premises at New Lanark inherited from Dale's original model. The aim of the building notionally identified as a possible school would be to locate education within a wider conception of civic belonging which, while resolutely focused upon the care of children, would not be confined to them. Instead, the education of the young would be highlighted merely as the first, if crucially important, stage in the development of rounded individuals situated in a healthy, flourishing community of contented citizens. This was the germ in Owen's thought for the concept that would later be realized as the Institute for the Formation of Character, the emblematic building finally opened in 1816 and which came in key respects to symbolize for the outside world the marvel of industry and enlightenment that was New Lanark.

The flurry of campaigning that preceded the forging of Owen's third New Lanark partnership took him, in the same year as his Joseph Lancaster speech, to London. The extent to which Owen's perambulations were deliberately intended to project a new public profile for himself and his ideas, as opposed simply to assist him in the finding of new business partners, is ultimately hard to determine – probably because Owen was himself unsure. It is clear that his impatience with the resistance of his second partnership to his plans for New Lanark energized Owen into setting down in writing the philosophical principles underlying his goals, possibly because he feared that they were about to be irremediably frustrated. If New Lanark was to be wrested from him and its development aborted, then his ideas at least would find their way into the vibrant public and political forums for which the metropolis was uniquely famous. Through his family and business contacts in London, Owen quickly connected himself to networks of dissenters and coffee-house radicals then urgently absorbed in the fevered political debates associated with the shifting fortunes of the Napoleonic Wars, the rising levels of protest against a corrupt and oppressive government, and the often dangerous lobbying for parliamentary and social reform. The legacy of the French Revolution still colored and divided these groups and the climate of opinion into which Owen plunged was heavily factionalized between those favoring a wholesale realignment of political and economic power – to be won by force if necessary – and those chastened by the violence of the revolutionary Terror and the expansionist Bonaparte dictatorship into accepting a more gradualist adjustment to the national institutions of government and representation. Owen gravitated to the second of these groups and soon secured important introductions to some of its leading figures, chief among whom was the bookseller and novelist William Godwin (White 2006, pp. 87–119).

When Owen met William Godwin in early 1813, the high tide of the older man's popularity as a social philosopher appeared to have passed. The combination of government intimidation, profound disappointment with the course of events in France, and often grinding poverty had diminished Godwin's former optimism and his militancy in equal measure, reducing his public following to a relatively small coterie. Godwin remained, nevertheless, the author of one of the

most important and controversial works of political philosophy of the
age, his *Political Justice* of 1793, which continued to command much
respect in radical circles 20 years after its first publication. The scale of
Owen's intellectual debt to *Political Justice*, and of the wider influence
of Godwin on his thought, has remained very hard for the biographers
of both men to resolve (Podmore 1906, pp. 119–121). It seems clear
that Owen had read *Political Justice* – though he makes no direct
acknowledgement of this – because many of its key concepts, and some
of its actual phrasing, recur in his writings. The depth of his
understanding of the book remains more ambiguous. Godwin's
foremost biographer, Peter Marshall, has pointed to the importance
of the lengthy series of meetings between the two men in the first five
months of 1813, as Owen visited Godwin's London home to discuss
their shared and unswerving adherence to the possibility of human
progress despite the seemingly bleak prospects for immediate reform
(Marshall 1984, pp. 220–222). Both men agreed on the preservation of
one of the central Enlightenment tenets articulated in *Political Justice*:
that the characters of people are not innate but determined by their
circumstances, and that rational intervention in those circumstances on
behalf of truth, justice, and reason held the potential to facilitate the
highest levels of human happiness. Both also rejected the alternative,
supposedly equally progressive, utilitarian analysis offered by the
philosopher Jeremy Bentham (ironically, destined to become a member
of the third partnership), which argued that the reorganization of
society could be achieved through the implementation of a system of
carefully calibrated rewards and punishments geared to the pursuit of
agreed rational outcomes. Owen echoed Godwin's hostility to this
instrumentalist view of the appetites, arguing instead in favor of the
intensive education from infancy onwards of all of the human faculties
as the most efficient means of implanting a shared moral desire for
attainment of common social outcomes. Marshall has also pointed out
that the essays in Owen's *A New View of Society*, in the process of being
drafted and refined during his stay in London, pay homage in large
measure to Godwin's understanding of the social and economic
structures most likely to guarantee the adoption by a better educated
working population of the principles of universal reason. These more
equitable structures would be secured, Godwin had suggested, not

through violent insurrection but by a process of consensual fiscal reform leading to the essentially voluntary redistribution of wealth and the dispersal of power to small self-governing cooperatives functioning in a decentralized pastoral-industrial economy. On simply a passing preliminary acquaintance with *Political Justice* in the late 1790s, the apparent foreshadowing of New Lanark in this semi-Arcadian model of social change must have resonated with Owen even as he first contemplated the potential of the Dale inheritance – its relevance deepening as his ambitions for the development of the village became more detailed (St Clair 1990, pp. 349–351).

The meetings with Godwin in London undeniably assisted Owen in perfecting the lines of argument that would go into the series of essays that made up *A New View of Society*, particularly the earliest one, 'On the Formation of Character.' Through Godwin, Owen was also introduced to one of the most revered radicals of Regency London, Francis Place, a figure from the same generation as Owen who had committed himself much more directly – and at some considerable personal risk – to the campaign for parliamentary reform and the extension of the franchise. Ian Donnachie has suggested that Place, together with his friend James Mill, with whom Owen had also become acquainted at this time, helped edit *A New View of Society*, lending it a lucidity of thought often absent from Owen's later publications (Donnachie 2005a, pp. 116–117). Place was obviously intrigued by Owen, perhaps seeing in him and his affluence an access route to power otherwise closed to the radical cause. He seems also, however, to have regarded Owen as a somewhat limited, even arrogant, thinker, gently chastising him for ignoring editorial advice and for failing to recognize that his theories of environmental determinism were in fact by 1813 a critical commonplace of Enlightenment social commentary. In his dealings with Place, we can begin to see much more obviously Owen's sharp divergence from the style of radical popular agitation that would come to dominate the politics of the ensuing 15 years in Britain, as the struggle for democratic change intensified and positions on the issue of electoral and economic emancipation polarized. Owen for the most part resiled from direct action of the kind increasingly advocated by Place and his circle, preferring to pursue his projects as successful pragmatic realizations, or models, of a better society by the example of which the decision-makers in the landed elites would be instructed rather than overthrown. In some respects, this made Owen at this specific juncture in his career, even as he returned to New Lanark as its inspirational leader and chief publicist, an eccentric, possibly even contradictory, figure: a radical conservative, perhaps, committed to the wholesale reshaping of society and its members from the base upwards, but unwilling to see this objective entailing any serious questioning of the differentials of wealth, privilege, and power as these were currently laid down in industrial society. His subsequent experience in actually implementing and then disseminating his long-cherished reforms would certainly alter some of Owen's perceptions of the forces both aiding and obstructing him, but his unswerving belief in his own righteousness and insight would maintain a marked separation between him and the other parties agitating for reform in nineteenth-century Britain, eventually inducing the birth of a quite distinct form of social and economic mass movement to which he enthusiastically lent his name: Owenism.

Owen at home and abroad

In terms of his intellectual formation, the period commencing in 1814 with his return in triumph to New Lanark in important ways marks a watershed in Owen's biography. The dealings with radical opinion in London confirmed the merit of his reforming initiatives and underlined their consonance with powerful currents of Enlightenment thought reaching back into the heart of the eighteenth century. The assessments and criticisms offered by figures such as Godwin and Place had perhaps highlighted a distinct lack of originality in the articulation of his main principles, but this was in no serious respect a repudiation of his objectives and it simply served to heighten his sense of mission and his growing conviction that any originality he did in fact possess lay in practice and not theory, in persuasion rather than description. He returned to New Lanark determined to complete the transformation of the community and establish it as an international showcase for the reforming values to which he was wedded. He would continue to explore, absorb and customize the ideas of others, but always in a spirit of practical advantage, seeking out ways in which the fresh perspectives on the human potential for self-realization and social improvement with which the early nineteenth century teemed might be harnessed and tested in the context of living and working industrial communities.

Owen had originally intended that his innovations in education at New Lanark would be the principal source of interest in him and his ideas for the world at large. The attraction specifically of his educational changes was at first overshadowed, however, by his association with factory reform, which gathered momentum in the period from 1815 to 1819 and which saw him propelled almost unwittingly to the forefront of a campaign for legislation to deal with some of the worst abuses of the manufacturing system (Podmore 1906, pp. 184–196). The general inefficiencies of the corrupt parliamentary process, together with its cynical manipulation by his peers in the commercial sector, reinforced Owen's overall skepticism towards electoral politics as a vehicle for genuine change. It also afforded him, however, further vital if sometimes bruising experience of conducting public debate with vociferous opponents in London and elsewhere and of lobbying to influence often very hostile public opinion in order to promote his desired objectives. In the case of factory reform, the results were ultimately a disappointment, with the parliamentary committee commissioned to respond to the progressive grouping he had helped to spearhead settling in 1817 for legislation much weakened by the pressure brought to bear on government by the rump of resistant factory owners. Owen's idealism was certainly dented by this outcome, but he had succeeded in bringing to the attention of leading politicians and landed magnates not only the injustices of the factory system but also his own idiosyncratic proposals for remedying a whole host of social ills, particularly those afflicting children and especially those that he believed could be cured by a national strategy for popular education. The educational elements of his petition were discarded in the discouraging response of the parliamentary committee just as assuredly as were his shop-floor proposals. He had succeeded, nevertheless, in once again publicizing his own intellectual ideals and in highlighting to a wider audience his efforts to embody them in the life of New Lanark. In consequence, far from abandoning the public platform in favor of his own private experiment on the banks of the Clyde, Owen came to see the two dimensions of his career as inextricably linked and used the largely fruitless experience of 1817 to press ahead still more vigorously with a nationwide campaign to replicate in a network of similar settlements across Britain not simply the educational philosophy of New Lanark, but its whole system of production and governance. This came to be known as Owen's 'Village Scheme' and was to remain from this point onwards a rallying point for him and his supporters. It secured him quite possibly his first burst of national public celebrity and resulted in a succession of open-air rallies, newspaper editorials (both for and against), and elite speaking engagements all over the country. The name of Robert Owen now excited comment from across the social and political spectrum in Britain, resulting in the close inspection of his initiatives by some of the leading writers and thinkers of the era. As we shall see, by no means all of the resultant responses to Owenism were favorable, but the publicity was priceless (Donnachie 2005a, pp. 122–131).

Returning to New Lanark in order further to pursue the development of the village as the proof of his concepts, Owen found communicated to him the first significant misgivings of some of his partners about the direction of his activism. The sensationalism of the factory campaign alarmed some of his quietist Quaker associates and highlighted for William Allen in particular – the partnership's chief financial backer – the disturbingly secular cast of Owen's rationalism. There was at this stage no question of any retreat from the project, but Allen's worries about the place of religious faith in the education of the youth of New Lanark, and in the life of the village more generally, were conveyed clearly to Owen, perhaps sowing the first seeds of mistrust between the two men. Allen was himself no provincial, but a gifted and generally open-minded intellectual with a distinguished track record in scientific research and philanthropy, as well as a network of European contacts that was to prove invaluable to Owen. He was also, however, President of the British and Foreign Schools Society, founded to promote the ideas of Joseph Lancaster and, like Lancaster, convinced of the centrality of religious instruction to the moral development of the young.

Typically, Owen responded to Allen's reservations by redoubling his efforts to establish the village as a focus of international attention, fostering a diverse coalition of patrons in Britain and abroad before the sheer stature of which any remaining doubts of his partners would be, he believed, entirely assuaged. This clever tactic succeeded for a long time, assisted by the reopening of the great highways of the European Grand Tour that came with the ending of the Napoleonic Wars in 1815. Prestigious visitors from across Europe and the British Isles flooded into New Lanark, eager to evaluate the experiments in education and welfare first hand, and keen to establish links with parallel initiatives in other European countries emerging from the shadow of war. In response to one such delegation, fascinated by the New Lanark approaches to schooling, Owen was once again persuaded to leave the village and undertake a European excursion organized by a highly placed and influential Swiss physician, Marc-Auguste Pictet-Turretini. The resultant trip through France, Italy, and Switzerland was another spectacular success for Owen, with Pictet skillfully combining appointments with some of the continent's foremost politicians with opportunities for Owen to visit a series of exciting educational ventures led by some of the leading progressives of the period. Owen hence gained direct working familiarity with many of the new approaches to schooling taken up in a number of European locations by figures such as Father Girard and Emmanuel Von Fellenberg, most of them in response to the legacy of the educational thought of Jean-Jacques Rousseau (Donnachie 2005a, pp. 146–150).

Owen's encounters with thinkers such as Girard and Von Fellenberg once again illustrate his characteristic style of intellectual development. Often impatient of abstract theories elaborated for their own sake, and increasingly skeptical of the merits of book learning, Owen could quickly form an intense absorption in ideas when he saw them operating in practical contexts, even when the conclusions he then often drew might leave him only partially persuaded of the principles being enacted. In the case of Von Fellenberg, and his celebrated school at Hofwyl, Owen responded very favorably to the vocational elements of the curriculum that Von Fellenberg had developed, with its close association with agricultural trades, its hospitality to children commonly excluded from orthodox schooling and its efforts at pupil self-governance. Indeed, so impressed was he with the methods at Hofwyl that he subsequently enrolled two of his own sons at the school to complete their education. Owen was less convinced, however, by Von Fellenberg's impassivity before the issues of social justice and his reluctance to link the purposes of the school to wider social change and cooperation. In these areas he felt New Lanark, for all its relative novelty, remained significantly ahead of Hofwyl.

By far the most elevated figure with whom Owen had direct contact in his European journey of 1818 was the great Johann Pestalozzi, by then an aged and venerated educational progressive whose philosophy of education had won acclaim and disciples throughout Europe and America, leading to the creation of schools bearing his name in many major towns and cities. Owen's relationship to Pestalozzi was a complex one, quite tendentiously rendered in his autobiography. The cornerstone of Owen's interest in the famous school established by Pestalozzi at Yverdun in Switzerland was the inclusion in its philosophy of a concentration on the educational needs of the very young. Pestalozzi had clearly formulated this approach out of his reading of Rousseau and Rousseau's hallowing of the importance of infancy and early childhood in the development of healthy adult individuals. The philosophy also echoed Owen's long-held adherence to the Enlightenment principle of environmental determinism and the growing conviction in his thought that effective education had to engage with the lives of children at the very earliest stages of their development if it were properly to shape their future adult personalities. Owen was gratified to see in the day-to-day routines of learning and teaching at Yverdun a strong resemblance to his own emphasis on vocationalism and civic responsibility, as well as on the interaction of young children with the natural world. He was also heartened by Pestalozzi's stress on the emotional care of children, rooted in the sympathetic relations between teachers and pupils (Podmore 1906, pp. 126–138).

From out of these fundamental ethical principles Pestalozzi had crafted his characteristic version of the curriculum for infant and early years education, founded upon the 'object lesson.' Stressing sensory learning, the method of the object lesson involved the process of forming clear concepts from sense impressions. Lessons then planned and guided by teachers taught children to examine the shape and number of varieties of objects placed before them, naming and interpreting them only after direct acquaintance with them. Pestalozzi designed an elaborate series of graded object lessons, by which children examined minerals, plants, animals, and manmade artifacts taken from their surroundings. Following a careful sequence, instruction moved from the simple to the complex, the easy to the difficult, and the concrete to the abstract. The emphasis on sense experience encouraged the inclusion of natural science and geography, two hitherto neglected subjects, in the Yverdun curriculum. On field trips, children explored the local countryside, observing the fauna and flora, topography and economy of the areas in which they lived. Object teaching of this kind was the most popular and widely adopted element of Pestalozzianism and it seems clear that Owen imported a version of it into New Lanark after meeting its creator (Silber 1960; Silver 1965, pp. 150–153). He was less enamored, however, with other important aspects of Pestalozzi's approach, particularly its repeated use of memorization and its pedantic requirement that older children report precisely to younger ones the discoveries they had made – a feature Owen saw simply as disguised monitorialism. Behind Pestalozzi's innovative and often exciting strategies, Owen shrewdly discerned an almost mystical view of childhood and a quasi-liturgical understanding of how young children verbalized their perceptions of the world around them, which, left unchecked, might easily stultify learning. As his own cast of mind on these matters was becoming less rather than more religious, the space provided in Pestalozzi's schools for children to nourish their supposedly instinctive longings for the divine presence in nature left Owen singularly unsatisfied.

His journey through France and Switzerland, and his meetings with some of the great minds of the age, further fortified Owen's belief that the work of New Lanark held an almost prophetic originality for a world obviously embarked upon a historic reorientation of its inherited understandings of education and society. Forever a man of commerce and industry, Owen eschewed what he saw as some of the unrealistically romantic perceptions of childhood informing some of the European educational experiments he had witnessed, skeptical of their real cognizance of the conditions in which the young would have to grow up and earn their livelihoods in a rapidly changing economy. He nevertheless shared their general judgment that the older ways of organizing educational provision were hopelessly unsuited to the challenges of the social order emerging from the Industrial Revolution. The task of New Lanark, he concluded, was to demonstrate that a renewed vision of educational possibility was fully realizable from within the given material conditions of labor and production. The unprecedented wealth and energy derived from the fruits of industry could provide the means for humanity to regain control of the processes shaping its existence. The same principles of rational planning that had transformed the production of commodities could be applied to the emancipation of minds, releasing untold creativity for the building of a better civilization. As we have suggested, the opening of the Institution for the Formation of Character in 1818, placed right at the heart of the village complex, came to symbolize Owen's belief that New Lanark could match anything offered by the continental reformers, while remaining firmly rooted in all that was best and irreversible about industrial living.

Owen, then, quite deliberately spent the next several years turning New Lanark into a showpiece: an example of his 'Village Scheme' in action and a magnet to many thousands of visitors who flocked to the site from all over the world and from almost every conceivable stratum of early nineteenth-century society. We shall examine the intellectual merit of this 'classic' phase in the story of education at New Lanark later in this book, with a close focus, especially, upon some of the key documents in which Owen recorded and publicized it. Inevitably, as the work of education had always meshed in Owen's mind with the goals of successful manufacturing, and as the interest in his Village Scheme quite legitimately focused upon the inextricable continuities in all of his initiatives between educational improvement and social reform, Owen found his national profile once again attracting the support of groups preoccupied with the problem of deepening social division in Britain. Owen of course consistently saw his own celebrity with various pressure groups as a perfect opportunity to advocate the Village Scheme as a solution to the conflict and distress that were seemingly becoming endemic to industrialization. In an extraordinary series of sponsored journals, illustrated pamphlets, subscription lists, national petitions, speaking tours, motions before parliamentary commissions, letters to royalty, lobbies to MPs, fundraising dinners, public debates, and even a failed attempt at securing the Linlithgow seat in the House of Commons, Owen pursued relentlessly the possibility of his scheme receiving a national endorsement. These breathtaking efforts produced no more than a few near misses and the consolidation around him of a more formal structure of disciples and followers interested in everything from his views on education to his ideas for reforming the Poor Law. They nonetheless sustained Owen in the certainty of his outlook and his growing sense that he was ahead of his time and needed only more propitious circumstances in order to vouchsafe his solutions to the difficulties facing society. In a whirlwind tour of Ireland in 1823, he boldly if naively sought to repeat his feats in England and Scotland in mobilizing a broad liberal consensus around community-building as a remedy for the plight of the poor. Shocked by the conditions of near barbarism and starvation he found in Ireland, and appalled by the deleterious effects of sectarian strife, the tone of Owen's radicalism sharpened as he moved through the country. His attacks on the Anglo-Irish elites became more outspoken, introducing for possibly the first time in his polemic a class rhetoric closely allied to a more explicit anticlericalism. Once again, he found as a result that he won disciples and opponents in just about equal measure. Plans for the creation of model villages in Ireland almost reached the point of fruition (and were later attempted again by his followers there), when injudicious public criticism in Dublin of the role of the legal profession in unjustly preserving corrupt Irish property laws brought a storm of protest and sent Owen home frustrated and defeated (Donnachie 2005a, pp. 190–195).

Part of the backwash from his expedition to Ireland came in the form of renewed disquiet about Owen's vexed attitudes to religion. In actual fact, his views on religion were fairly typical of Enlightenment responses to the claims of religious faith, and his approach to the sectarian issue in Ireland had been sincerely conciliatory, seeking to build charitable links between the antagonistic Christian Churches around the support of the Village Scheme. Undoubtedly, however, his skepticism and rationalism had become more pronounced in his writings and speeches and this renewed the unease of his partners and the fears of some of the religious authorities in and around Lanark. The work of the schools and the Institute came in for more searching scrutiny, some of which spilled over from the examination of religious instruction to other alleged eccentricities of the New Lanark curriculum such as the neglect of the use of textbooks and the inclusion of dancing. At first, Owen's standard tactic of citing the endorsements of assorted prominent religious figures to relieve tensions with his partners succeeded as it had done for years. In a number of visits to New Lanark, William Allen took the opportunity to preach to the population and interviewed local ministers, leaving generally assured of the integrity of Owen's treatment of the Christian faith and his good standing with the leadership of the Church of Scotland. In 1823, however, Owen made one of his few errors of judgment in his oversight of the school, proposing that formal religious instruction might be reduced to make way for new subjects such as geography and science. When news of this reached the Lanark Presbytery, Owen was subject to a concerted hate campaign by the local press, which was only abated by the hasty return of his partners and the striking of an emergency agreement to rein in some of the peculiarities of the curriculum, replace some of the visiting teachers, and reinstate the role of religious instruction in the education of the children. Owen balked at the agreement, and continued to resist calls for the school to be inspected by the Church, and significant damage had been done to his reputation with believers (Donnachie 2005a, pp. 196–197).

The experience with Lanark Presbytery was only one of several fronts in which Owen was beginning to incite more concerted opposition, some of it in the form of published attacks on the system at New Lanark. It may have been this important shift in the climate of opinion in the mid 1820s that then drew Owen towards a quite remarkable rethink of his plans for the future extension of his program. In 1824, Owen received two influential visitors from the United States. The first was William Maclure, an extremely wealthy Scottish merchant who had made his fortune in Philadelphia. Maclure was a freethinking disciple of Pestalozzi, with access to the elites of East Coast American society and ambitions to lead major reforms of the then highly disorganized US education system. When Maclure arrived, Owen was also about to welcome a representative of an American religious fraternity with which he appears to have been in correspondence for several years. The fraternity was the Rappites and their agent a man named Richard Flower. The Rappites were a Christian congregation of Moravian decent that had been settled in the United States for several decades and which had arrived at a version of agrarian community living in Harmonie, Indiana, by a route not dissimilar to that which had brought forth David Dale's theological-industrial experiment in New Lanark. The founder of the settlement, a strange German religious visionary by the name of Father Johann Georg Rapp, had shown interest in Owen's writings some years previously and had then made overtures to Owen in early 1824 to inform him of his intention to sell his foundation on the banks of the River Wabash and move with his followers to a new location (Harrison 1969, pp. 105–106). Aware of Owen's desire to disseminate the New Lanark system, Rapp had contacted Owen to enquire if he might be interested in purchasing the Rappite settlement as a possible location for a counterpart to New Lanark in the United States, with many of the elements – including a profitable agricultural turnover – already in place. Strengthening his ties with Maclure and other potential investors intrigued by the opportunity, and consulting with associates in the expanding network of Owenite groups in Scotland and England, Owen quite without warning made arrangements for the governance of New Lanark to be conveyed temporarily into the hands of his son and proceeded to set sail for America and the next phase of his extraordinary career.

New worlds and otherworlds

Owen's rationale for his American expedition is in many respects difficult to fathom. It seems likely that the mounting opposition to his ideas in the United Kingdom had at last begun to dull even his apparently boundless optimism. The realization that even his most loyal partners had found it necessary to distance themselves from aspects of his work may also have contributed to his momentary disillusionment with Britain as a setting for his plans. Viewed more positively, the decision to explore prospects in the United States was perfectly consistent with the inner dynamic of his beliefs, particularly his urge to extend the progressivism of New Lanark to other locations across the globe. Owen must certainly have been struck by the parallels between the opening Fr Rapp was offering him and the potential he had seen in the invitation from Dale years before. He must surely also have recognized the recurrence of certain key themes in this latest opportunity, including the existence of an established and seemingly economically viable commercial concern and the presence of Christian utopianism descended from the same broad tradition of dissenting Moravian piety that he had seen in Dale's work at New Lanark. Early nineteenth-century America had become a haven for such nonconformist and inner light religious groups, fleeing persecution and drawn by the pioneer allure of the wilderness. In its own near-mythic self-understanding, America was the archetypal Promised Land in which all sorts of versions of the perfect society might be pursued in the spirit of equality and freedom from state interference.

Following swiftly on a lavish series of receptions arranged by the enlightened elites of New York, Philadelphia, and Washington, at which, predictably, Owen wined and dined with some of the leading figures in the US establishment, his party at last completed their journey to Harmonie in Indiana. Here Owen was received by Frederick Rapp, adopted son and nominated successor of Johann Georg Rapp, with whom he speedily concluded negotiations for the purchase of the settlement on the Wabash on behalf of himself and Maclure. After a brief survey of the site and its facilities, Owen quickly returned again to the great cities of the east coast, pressing forward with an awareness-raising drive, principally to attract new settlers and investment as the Rappites decanted, while fulfilling a diary of high-profile appointments, including meetings with the new President, John Quincy Adams, with Thomas Jefferson, and with James Madison. In contrast to the often depressing situation in Britain, it appeared to Owen that democratic America was hungry for the new system and for the example he would bring to the fledgling republic of the habits of rational living at the beacon community in Indiana.

Although New Harmony appeared to get off to a promising start, with the mixed population of ex-Rappites and idealistic incomers responding well to Owen's plans, serious problems began to emerge almost immediately (Harrison 1969, pp. 75–77, 172–180). The main difficulty was one that Owen, with his immersion from his Welsh childhood onwards in the deep-seated rhythms of established working communities, really ought to have foreseen. New Harmony was essentially an invented community founded upon an agriculturally-minded refugee Christian sect and lacking a sure material foundation in the patterns of occupational life. It might be replied to this that New Lanark was an equally 'invented' space, built from the ground up by Dale and his partners. New Lanark, however, was rooted in the manufacture of cotton and from its inception embraced modern technologies of industrial production. This attracted to the village highly skilled artisans and craftsmen, motivated by a common language of labor and predisposed to the formation of a collaborative community. New Harmony lacked almost all of this material and symbolic capital, inclining towards a much more backward-looking, pastoral conception of life held together by the charismatic authority of a quasi-religious, even priestly leader. It is interesting that New Harmony came closest to a functional existence whenever Owen was physically present to sustain its inspiration and to galvanize its low-skill, transient workforce. Whenever he left – and his celebrity combined with his continuing responsibilities in Scotland meant that he left often – it swiftly fragmented, producing factionalism and emigration. Owen's principal effort to combat this instability was to work at the formulation of some sort of written constitution for the village, which would then be embraced and administered by the residents through a species of popular democracy. Ironically, the cooperative, redistributive, and egalitarian elements of this blueprint went well beyond anything he had dared attempt at New Lanark, but it still failed repeatedly to win the hearts and minds of the Harmonists, forcing Owen into the role of shepherd-king to his confused and leaderless flock – a position he eventually came to loathe for its echoes of a regressive political, almost theocratic, authority he felt modern, enlightened people must surely have transcended.

The approach to education at New Harmony illustrated these dilemmas. Owen had originally intended education to be 'the base upon which the future prosperity of the community must be founded'

(Johnson 1970, pp. 61–62) and he accorded it the highest importance amongst the various 'departments' or functions into which the village was schematically divided. He had to contend, however, with two difficulties unknown at New Lanark. The first was the generally low rates of enthusiasm for learning among the indigenous population and the marked preference for work in the fields and workshops over sitting in classrooms. The second was the presence of Maclure, who was a convinced Pestalozzian with strong views on the importance of rigid routine, memorization, and the discrete subject disciplines of the new European curriculum (Harrison 1969, pp. 38–41). The result was an uneasy compromise in the design of educational policy in the village, with Owen once again compelled personally to set out in a summary checklist of documented procedures the structure to which learning and teaching was expected to adhere in the day and infant schools. There were undoubted achievements in education at New Harmony despite these difficulties and some of these will be discussed later in this volume. Owen had learned from the successes and setbacks at New Lanark, and New Harmony gave him the chance to integrate into the curriculum some of the best of the innovations he had observed in Europe in areas such as vocational and technical education. Under the directorship of Joseph Neef, the schools became for a brief period exemplary in the teaching of science and technology to children, attracting the so-called 'Boatload of Knowledge' to the Wabash – a vessel containing an impressive lineup of scientists and artisans responding to Owen's earlier invitation and stirred by the unusual prominence he and Maclure accorded technical skill and scientific knowledge in their schools (Pitzer 1989).

Despite these gains, it was essentially upon the issue of education that Owen's partnership with Maclure finally foundered (Bernard 1988; Royle 1998, pp. 166–181). The difference in their outlooks, undoubtedly exacerbated by the more general failure of the community to achieve proper self-governing stability, and even decent levels of prosperity, led rapidly and inevitably to an estrangement over fundamental questions of pedagogy, assessment, and discipline. Maclure became disillusioned with Owen's plans and impatient with his 'wild theories,' angrily alleging that he had 'not the smallest idea of a good education and will not permit any to flourish within his reach.' (Bestor

1948, p. 385). Tensions were especially acute between the two men over the matter of adult education, which was low on Maclure's list of Pestalozzian priorities yet integral to Owen's conception of the formation of character. Maclure thought it impossible that Owen would ever realize his dreams for altering 'the confirmed habits of adults in 10 times the length of time his enthusiasm allots for it' (Bestor 1948, p. 382), while Owen bitterly lamented this damaging obstacle placed by the Maclure faction in the way of a program vital to the marshalling of the type of social solidarity that New Harmony so palpably lacked. The gap between the two partners widened over operational details of the schools such as the permanent assignment of teachers to particular classes and the procedures for testing pupil attainment. Maclure embarked upon an expensive arbitration lawsuit, asserting that key terms of the partnership had not only been breached, but had never in fact existed. Owen vigorously contested this account of the partnership and meanwhile began actively to sell, at a considerable financial loss, portions of the land of New Harmony to its occupants, who in turn often parceled it and sold it on as smaller sharecropper units, thus contributing to the steady disintegration of the community. While the arbitration exercise found for the most part in Owen's favor, the quarrelling with Maclure drove a deeper wedge between the two owners.

The collapse of the New Harmony experiment was by no means immediate or total. The more the community seemed to fragment, the more extravagant became Owen's plans to reorganize and revive it. Rescue packages and bold attempts at relaunches were tried month after month, along with sincere efforts to heal the growing rift with Maclure. All of this was punctuated by Owen's dashes back to Scotland to reassure his partners at home and raise fresh capital. In one of his most audacious moves, Owen agreed with Maclure to implement plans for the creation of what he grandly termed a 'Community of Equality' – a complete revision of the system of ownership, labor, and decision-making at New Harmony, bringing forward a stage he had originally envisaged as one at which the community would arrive only after several years of consolidation (Harrison 1969, p. 165). The hurried imposition of the constitution for the Community of Equality was at least in part forced upon Owen by the declining finances of New Harmony and the drain it was placing on his personal fortune. It laid emphasis on stout republican virtues such as hard work and frugality, requiring the Harmonists to live within their means and develop much more transparent forms of self-government. At first these austerity measures appeared to stabilize the situation and it seems that some of the original optimism returned to the community, with the cycles of education, work, and recreation assuming for a time some of the purposefulness for which Owen had longed. This superficial improvement, however, disguised ongoing structural and environmental problems and beguiled Owen into concluding that a turning-point had been reached, when in fact the town continued to rely on his presence and continued to break up into separate zones with quite distinct views of the meaning of property and equality. Maclure's fears of the worryingly despotic character of Owen's personal authority in the running of New Harmony deepened and, as the financial situation worsened, a permanent split between the two men became inevitable. Still assured that the community could weather the transitional difficulties through which it was toiling, Owen nevertheless concluded that his own individual governance of the project was no longer consistent with its egalitarian objectives and on 1 June 1827, before setting off on yet another return visit to Scotland, he formally renounced his role in its leadership (Donnachie 2005a, pp. 222–223). The allure of the New World remained strong with him in the immediate aftermath of this decision. Within three months he was back in New Harmony, unable to resist the hope that his vision would somehow miraculously be realized. Further, extraordinary expeditions ensued to Texas and to Mexico as his enduring fame with liberal opinion in the United States, together with the burgeoning across the expanding American frontier of a plethora of mostly fanciful utopian ventures and speculations, served to sustain Owen as an important figurehead in the quest for alternative communities. Increasingly, however, these travels settled into a pattern familiar from earlier phases of his career. Ostentatious treks to exotic locations, accompanied by high-status meetings with national leaders and rousing mass rallies of enthusiastic but frequently fickle supporters, were invariably followed by putatively ground-breaking reports to governments on the untapped potential for rational living present in their own societies. These reports were repeatedly received with fanfares and high-flown promises of action, by everyone from Martin Van Buren to Lopez de Santa Anna, very few of which ever came to fruition. It remained a peculiarity of Owen's personality to be undaunted by setbacks of this kind no matter how often the sequence repeated itself. He returned from unfulfilled schemes with still more complex and outlandish proposals for social transformation that he was certain would succeed whenever the next opportunity presented itself.

As the centre of gravity of his activism steadily shifted back to Britain, despite the constant shuttling to and from America, several harsh realities began to set in for Owen and his long-suffering family. In the first place, it became clear that his New Harmony adventures had taken a severe toll on his finances, depriving him of a large proportion of the personal wealth he had devoted to his various causes. He was by no means impoverished, but possibly some three quarters of his personal fortune had been lost and he was in considerable debt. Secondly, it became increasingly obvious to Owen that his de facto leadership of New Lanark had ended and it would be sensible for him to extricate himself from the existing partnership and reduce his stake in the company. This disengagement from New Lanark took some years to conclude, but operational control of the plant and the village had, in effect, passed from Owen's hands to his managers since the onset of the New Harmony project and his removal of himself and his family from the site served only to confirm what was already an inescapable reality on the ground.

By no means all of the developments around the phenomenon of Owenism in Britain had been negative while its author's attention had been diverted by the lure of America. Owen was heartened to discover that several of the local associations set up to lobby for the Village Scheme had acquired a self-organizing infrastructure of their own and were developing a collaborative ethos responsive to the new challenges facing poverty relief campaigns in the United Kingdom. This was the embryo of the Cooperative Movement and looked forward to the self-help and voluntarism that would mark later Victorian approaches to charity and social welfare in Britain. In a similar vein, some of the energy Owen had expended with the Lanark County authorities in pushing for the extension of the Village Scheme to other parts of

Central Scotland had borne fruit in the creation of a new community at Orbiston near Motherwell, under the direction of an Owen disciple, Abram Combe. Orbiston was fated to recapitulate the story of New Harmony, excessively reliant on the personal charisma of its founder and insufficiently capitalized to cope with the first major downturn in demand for its textiles. Owen had little direct involvement with it, but he took heart from the initial progress it made and from the milestone he felt it represented in the adoption of the Village Scheme by the Scottish political leadership.

From 1829 until around the mid 1830s, a new spirit enveloped Owenism in Britain. It had a paradoxical effect on Owen himself, because it quickly acquired a life of its own and relied much less heavily than in the past on his personal authority and his inexhaustible production of ideas and projects. Owen's individual stature in the movement named after him inevitably receded somewhat, to be replaced by something approaching a genuinely democratic ethos fuelled by the working-class organizations that were beginning to advocate certain key dimensions of his program as a solution to social inequality. Aspects of this response to Owen will be analyzed when his educational legacy is considered later in this volume. From the perspective of Owen's own intellectual biography, the nascent struggle of the owning and producing classes had always been a method of understanding social change from which he had recoiled, afraid of the uneducated ignorance of the masses as he saw them and convinced of the merits of responsibly exercised privilege. Even in America, where his attitudes to wealth and property had become more egalitarian, he pursued an essentially classless vision rather than one based upon the inevitable antagonism of the rich and the poor. The prolonged common education of all in the same school and in the same values would be the key, he believed, to the arrival of social and economic equality. When he returned to the Britain of the early 1830s, embroiled as it then was in the historic contest around the passage of the Great Reform Act, Owen found that his ideas had been annexed to a quite differently-accented political campaign orchestrated by the newly emerging trade unions with their much more confrontational critique of the ownership of wealth and the control of political power (Claeys 1989, pp. 174–183).

To his lasting credit, Owen worked hard over a full five-year period to respond pragmatically to this new appropriation of his thought. He collaborated enthusiastically with the many organizations that had grown up around the themes of cooperation and solidarity, proposing and even attempting to launch new initiatives in the exchange of labor for the unemployed and in support of the new confederations of working men's associations. He found himself once again thrown into the centre of a mass movement, which, if no longer dependent upon his personal authority, still drew sustenance from his inspirational rhetoric. In it he believed for a time that he had found the sort of elusive popular following that would unify the central themes of his thought and translate them into a compelling political platform. Always hesitant about the aggressive agitation of the unions for improved factory conditions and increases in wages, and wary of the use of the strike weapon as a means to secure these objectives, Owen nevertheless strenuously opposed the Whig government's attempt to make an example of six laborers from the village of Tolpuddle in Dorset, who had been found guilty in 1834 of using illegal rituals and oaths as part of their union activities. In the wake of the turmoil caused by the harsh sentences meted out to the Tolpuddle Martyrs by the courts, Owen assented to assumption of the office of president of the fledgling and volatile Grand National Consolidated Trade Union (GNCTU), principally as a kind of national unity figure attractive to the fissiparous membership of the organization yet difficult for the government to label subversive. It proved an unwise decision. The GNCTU was an alliance of convenience and even Owen proved incapable of holding it together in the face of government harassment and the loss of confidence among members from a wide variety of frequently competing guild and craft organizations. The rapid collapse of the GNCTU permanently undermined Owen's always uncertain acceptance of the class analysis, rekindling his instinctive suspicions of the purposes of radical politics and driving him and his closest adherents back to their roots in an essentially reformist, moralistic view of social change (Claeys 1989, pp. 194–199).

From this important juncture onwards, Owen entered the phase of his career that Ian Donnachie has perceptively termed his 'Social Fatherhood,' from a phrase used by one of the several reformist

organizations patronized by him (Donnachie 2005a, p. 250). The
central Owenite body went through a number of changes of name,
each one grander and more all-embracing than the last, while smaller
pressure groups and fraternities began to operate semi-independently
under its wide umbrella, pursuing disparate initiatives connected with
community-building, education, labor relief, retail cooperation,
secularism, radical journalism, and even birth control. In an echo of
the displaced religiosity that somehow always seemed to haunt Owen
and Owenism, the movement called its local organizers 'Social
Missionaries' and began to imitate organizational features of the
highly successful grassroots Churches such as the Methodists and the
Southcottians active in the urban centers. This included the building
of meeting houses named 'Halls of Science' in which large assemblies
of middle- and working-class sympathizers would gather for popular
lectures or readings from Owen's work. For a time, this structure of
Owenite activism represented a genuine alternative to the nascent
trade union movement, offering a subtly different approach to the
quest for social change and individual self-improvement, and
appealing to the aspirations of large sections of the artisan classes in
the major towns and cities. Only with the rise of Chartism in the
1840s and the revitalized local networks of the trade unions
themselves, more systematically embedded in the needs of workers
in factories, mills, mines, and dockyards, did the quaint routines of the
Owenite movement – if not its ethical principles – begin to appear less
relevant and more outdated to many working-class people (Chase
2007, pp. 87–88). Even then, devotion to the person of Owen endured
for some considerable time, as he moved majestically around the
various initiatives bearing his name, while the substance of his views of
civil society and the purposes of inclusive education continued to be
taken up zealously into the political agendas of many of the trade
union organizations themselves.

Throughout the 1840s and into the 1850s, as the remainder of his
wealth mostly hemorrhaged away servicing his various projects, Owen
continued steadfastly to champion the vision he had first formulated in
Manchester and New Lanark and which he remained convinced was
the answer to the unique problems of the modern, industrial epoch.
He continued also to write and publish, editing or sponsoring a

succession of periodicals for the promotion of his ideas to his followers. When he became involved in yet another failed village scheme at Queenwood in Hampshire, which miscarried yet again owing to inadequate capitalization and the inability to retain a coherent workforce, Owen retreated into one of his most eccentric endeavors – the building of Harmony Hall, a lavish institute for the training of his disciples in the correct interpretation of his environmental philosophy. Harmony Hall also bled resources and there was a sequence of unseemly spats with his associates leading ultimately to the Owenite Congress of 1842 requiring his removal from the institute (Donnachie 2005a, p. 261). Undeterred, Owen continued his ceaseless international missions, tours of the United States, and voluble petitions to Parliament. His language in these later ventures became increasingly strident and apocalyptic, as he proclaimed the coming of a new secular millennium in which labor and rationality would be transformed and a host of pernicious evils including religion, war, and class privilege would be abolished. Audiences for these various pronouncements were never hard to find, but increasingly Owen had become a curiosity, especially to those in power, and his ideas began to sound like a worthy but wearisome throwback to a lost age of romantic self-deception and political naïveté.

In 1854, Owen was converted to spiritualism, a religious craze of the time originating in the United States and brought to Britain by traveling mediums and disciples of its founders, the sisters Margareta and Catherine Fox. This epilogue to Owen's glittering career has been a source of embarrassment to many of his biographers, explained away by his great age and his lifelong fascination with novelty (Browning 1971). Yet it seems clear that his embrace of spiritualism – which, typically, saw him assuming an executive role in the movement in which he claimed to have had the principles of the new Church dictated to him from the beyond and to have held conversations with the ghost of P. B. Shelley – was in many respects consistent with important vectors in his intellectual biography. As we have seen, despite his declared rationalism, there was a markedly religious register to many of Owen's utterances throughout his public career and an unmistakably prophetic edge to his critique of the moral shortcomings of industrial society. Radical Christian revivalism of one kind or another was never far from his inspiration, even if he implicitly rejected the claims of confessional faith more or less consistently throughout his adult life. To its sincerest adherents, spiritualism was the ultimate 'rational religion': a strictly materialist creed offering 'scientific' evidence for the existence of an afterlife that required no revealed truths or divisive sacred scriptures to guarantee it (Gomel 2007). Its appeal to Owen lay precisely in its apparently public, irrefutable demonstration, as assuredly as the vindication of the Owenite New System had lain all along, he insisted, in the incontestable achievements of New Lanark under his beneficent tutelage.

Owen's almost legendary energy persisted to the end of his life. In 1857, flush with his belief that spiritualism portended a major revolution in the scientific understanding of man in the universe, he convened a 'Congress of the Advanced Minds of the World' in London. He then attended an educational conference held at the Willis Rooms in June of the same year under the presidency of Albert, the prince consort. He went on to read a paper at the inaugural meeting of the Social Science Association held at Birmingham in October of the same year. Exactly one year later, he was attending another Owenite meeting in Liverpool. Though now extremely feeble, he was placed on the platform and was introduced to the audience to say a few words before being carried to bed. Two weeks later he asked to be taken to Newtown in the company of his eldest son, Robert Dale. He went there, but made another journey back to Liverpool to deliver yet another speech, finally returning to Newtown for the last time to die quietly on 17 November 1858 in a local hotel not far from his birthplace. Only his son and a few loyal followers attended him. A few days later, he was buried in the grave of his parents in the ruins of St Mary's Church, Newtown, following the rites of the Church of England.

Robert Owen's lengthy and astonishing career had taken him from provincial Wales to the swamps of Mexico, from his father's shop to the offices of the President of the United States. He had met some of the most brilliant minds of his age – politicians, scientists, philosophers, industrialists, and educators from all across Europe and America. He had taken the commercial operation of small isolated textile village in a remote part of Central Scotland and made it a symbol of the human potential for the building of a better, fairer world governed by the principles of reason and limited only by the powers of the imagination. By the end of his frequently controversial life, he had established a vibrant, varied movement determined to preserve his legacy and renew its relevance to the needs of a future society the lineaments of which, Owen knew, could only be dimly observed from the vantage of the mid nineteenth century. It is the merit of this legacy, and the key documents in which Owen's thought was set forth, that now seem worthy of a fresh evaluation.

Part 2

Critical Exposition of Owen's Work

Chapter 2

Key Principles of Owen's Educational Thought and Practice

New Lanark in context

In order to understand the character of the educational reforms introduced at New Lanark by Robert Owen, it is necessary to appreciate something of the educational context in which the village was situated at the point of his acquisition of it and in the years that immediately followed. We have seen that Owen's educational and social theories emerged very distinctively from his direct experiences and from the practical improvements over which he presided as a factory owner. These were eventually set down in writing as a quite sophisticated, if markedly derivative, philosophical credo, but they remained forever rooted in the shifting material circumstances of New Lanark and its various successor sites. We have also observed that Owen's inadequately acknowledged debt to his father-in-law, David Dale, illustrated something of the mixed pedigree of his educational thought. The unfolding over several decades of the program of first Dale's and then Owen's reforms highlights, however, two other highly important historical factors of major significance for the understanding of educational change within the New Lanark project.

The first of these is the specifically *Scottish* setting of the village and its educational outlook. In several of the standard accounts of New Lanark, the relationship of the village to broader trends in Scottish education is generally downplayed or ignored. This is in some ways surprising, because the period of New Lanark's incubation as a center for educational experimentation also coincided with the rising reputation of Scottish education throughout the expanding British Empire as a much-imitated model of academic excellence (Mirayes 2005). Perhaps because of its relative novelty, compounded by the 'incomer' status of its champion – an expatriate Welshman and Lancashire entrepreneur – the 'Scottishness' of New Lanark as a manufacturing community and educational laboratory was even in its own time overshadowed by a repeated emphasis on its uniqueness. This appeared entirely to detach the site from its cultural and political surroundings, raising it to an imagined European benchmark of enlightened educational practice discontinuous with anything seen previously or elsewhere in Scotland. Certainly, important aspects of Owen's globetrotting self-promotion colluded with this perception, but it is equally clear that Owen expended considerable quantities of energy striving to establish the indigenous credentials of his work and agitating with the regional political and commercial elites for the wider adoption of his philosophy in Central Scotland as a legitimate expression of long attested national values.

Owen himself was perfectly well aware of the lineage of the dominant Scottish system of education, the backbone of which was the celebrated parish schools network. This was an institutional arrangement dating back to the first days of the Scottish Reformation of the 1560s whereby the Church of Scotland administered through local Kirk Sessions an elementary school in every parish in the country, funded principally by local landowners, or 'heritors' as they were known. In a poor and frequently divided nation such as early modern Scotland, the goal of a school in each parish was not realized anywhere other than the most populous parts of the Lowlands, but it retained an important symbolism as a shared national ideal and helped establish an approach to the education of the general population that was certainly more inclusive than almost any to be found elsewhere in Europe (Paterson 2000). Important parliamentary Acts of 1796 and 1803 had sought to reform the parish system in response to the social and economic changes beginning to overtake Scotland in the early industrial period. Financial arrangements were overhauled and abuses of patronage purged. Fee structures were updated to try to ensure that schools accumulated sufficient income from better-off families in order to maintain the widest possible clientele. Legislation of this kind made some modest progress towards modernization of existing patterns, but it was clear that the scale of demographic change and wealth disparity in industrializing Scotland – most seriously evident in the rapidly expanding towns and cities where the parish structure was least stable – was stretching the old Reformation system to breaking point. Even in its heyday, the parish system had succeeded in educating to basic levels of literacy and numeracy perhaps a third of the juvenile population (well above, it should be noted, the European average). By the end of the eighteenth century, it was obvious, however, that vast sections of the new and impoverished working classes were receiving no appreciable education of any kind (Houston 1985; Anderson 1995, pp. 1–7, 24–26).

Consistent with the spirit of the industrial age, the 1803 Act introduced an element of deregulation into the provision of schooling, encouraging, for example, the development of semi-academic 'side schools,' where non-tenured teachers could be employed by parishes for lower wages based on fee income alone. This was further supplemented by various types of voluntary or 'free market' facility such as 'adventure schools' staffed by unsalaried (and frequently unqualified) itinerant teachers, 'dame schools' for female pupils to learn domestic crafts, and also 'minding schools,' where elderly or retired teachers looked after the children of workers and laborers. The last of these foreshadowed the concept of the workplace nursery that was to prove of such interest to Robert Owen, though little is known of what was actually taught in these early establishments. The 1803 Act also helped usher in a new era of charitable school foundation, supported by the affluence and benevolence of both the old landed elites and the first generation of merchant-industrialists beginning to accumulate considerable fortunes from the new systems of production and trade (Scotland 1969, pp. 95–114, 204–224). Charity schooling tended on the whole to be concentrated in the expanding towns and cities, resulting in the development a broad variety of school types. At its pinnacle sat the city academies, most of them created in the decades before the 1796 Act and directing their charity somewhat disingenuously towards the education of the children of the newly-emerging middle classes. Included in the urban charitable mix, however, were more sincerely philanthropic endeavors such as the first proper Sunday Schools and a patchwork of endowed day schools for the poor, in each of which genuine efforts were made to extend the teaching of reading and writing to the offspring of the most deprived sections of society (Smout 1979, pp. 448–450, 423–424).

Deregulation of even this relatively modest and improvised kind inevitably raised the issue of control. One of the principal aims of the 1796 Act was to confirm the role of the Church of Scotland as the chief regulator of all schools in the country. The system became so fragmented, however, that it swiftly became impossible for the Church adequately to police the organization and governance of schools. As a consequence, the question of control came to haunt the Church's approach to education for most of the nineteenth century. The matter was further confused by the increased presence in the more open market of schooling of providers drawn from dissenting sects and fraternities towards which the Church of Scotland was often implicitly suspicious. Historically, the main reason for the Church's involvement in education had been to ensure the teaching of sound doctrine and to guarantee access to the vernacular Scriptures for all of the faithful. Doctrinal differences between the national Church and dissenters usually fell within the margins of Protestant tolerance, allowing a somewhat grudging acceptance of the new establishments on the part of overstretched ecclesiastical authorities. Nevertheless, even limited diversification of schools offered the possibility of alternative forms of curriculum and pedagogy, particularly where the schools and their teachers had origins subtly distinct from the Scottish mainstream. This posed dangers for the idea of an integrated nationwide system subject to the scrutiny of the Church (Withrington 2000).

There seems little doubt that both Dale and Owen exploited the openings created by stresses within the national system to pursue distinctive approaches to the planning and organization of education at New Lanark. In this they each followed routes pioneered by other, often anonymous, experimenters motivated by the opportunities created as the older Scottish models began to falter. At the same time, their populist objectives can be said to sit squarely within a tradition of common schooling which, despite the sometimes exaggerated claims made for it, reflected an enduring set of cherished national educational values. Indeed, at the height of his fame, Owen tried to assuage Scottish ecclesiastical anxieties about the allegedly secular complexion of his schools by appealing to these same national sentiments. While previous innovators altered the prevailing model on the basis of religious principles, or because a simple lack of expertise or resources meant that the curriculum in their schools had necessarily to be trimmed, Dale and then Owen were able to draw upon another set of educational precedents which, taken together, form the second major contextual influence for the overall understanding of education at New Lanark. This was the tradition of industrial schooling, which had been an accompaniment to the emergence of the factory system almost since its inception.

For reasons of prudence as much as principle, David Dale began at New Lanark by imitating the curriculum of the nearby parish schools, with its emphasis upon basic literacy, numeracy, and religious instruction (McLaren 1999, pp. 55–76). Conscious, no doubt, of his own technical status as a religious dissenter who had seceded from the Church of Scotland, Dale tacitly agreed to a formal oversight of the school by the local Kirk Session. His own Christian commitments were never in doubt, but he appears to have steered with some diplomatic skill between the jurisdiction of the Church and his enthusiasm for some of the more radical options introduced into the schoolrooms linked to other factories and industrial communities in various parts of Britain. The most obvious of these was the promotion at these early sites of technical and vocational education, deemed more appropriate for children and young people whose future employment almost certainly lay in factory work. Some parish and charity schools had also recognized this reality and made alterations to their curriculum – for example, abandoning Latin in favor of a greater emphasis on mathematics. It was, however, in several of the early cotton mill complexes that substantial departures from the national norm began to become evident in the last quarter of the eighteenth century. The prehistory of this provision remains poorly researched, but under the inspiration of the nonconformist businessmen involved in their founding, cotton mills at places such as Cromford (Arkwright) and Belper (Strutt) developed, first, Sunday Schools for religious instruction and then day schools for more practical education in literacy, numeracy, and craft skills (Fitton and Wadsworth 1958, pp. 101–103). As David McLaren has shown, it is even possible that in Scotland David Dale was pre-empted in his creation of a factory school by a competitor, William Gillespie, who appears to have had a school operating at his North Woodside cotton mill in the early 1780s (McLaren 1999, p. 56).

Dale went further than his peers by introducing to his mill schools at Catrine, Blantyre, and finally New Lanark an unprecedented level of formal curricular planning upon which Owen was later very successfully to build (Donnachie 2005a, pp. 108–109). This included careful provision for the education of girls and for their craft training in skills such as sewing and tamboring. It also stretched to the more advanced organization of age-bandings, school uniforms, academic progression, and even agreed schemes of work for individual classes. The recruitment of better qualified and more highly paid teachers, together with the improved synchronization of the school and factory timetables, further enhanced the status of education offered at the mills, persuading children and their parents that seemingly unproductive labor was, in the longer term, contributing meaningfully to household earnings and security of employment, even if it entailed some modest family outlay to send children to school. Dale made no attempt to disguise the pragmatic calculations involved in these educational decisions: the objective, he averred in 1790, was to fashion young people equipped to serve in a highly competitive labor market, armed with functional literacy and numeracy, but also trained in the transferable skills and work habits advantageous for profitable factory employment. In this sense, Dale's efforts – closely followed and elaborated by Owen – may represent the first concerted attempt to integrate the processes of industrial and knowledge production, importing into the schools practices and perspectives seen as intrinsic to successful manufacturing. Unlike Owen, Dale made no moves to codify his approach as a fully articulated philosophical system, and he kept his improvements well within the confessional orthodoxy safeguarded by the parish schools. Nevertheless, in the combination of a curriculum expressly attuned to the needs of industry and commerce, a welfarism designed to mitigate some of the harshness of the laboring life and an overall educational methodology unashamedly imitative of the production management regimes perfected in the mills and factories, Dale may be said to have raised industrial schooling to a new level of sophistication, presaging the arrival of modern state education later in the nineteenth century. As the direct heir of this enlightened agenda, it was left to Owen not only to extend the range and raise the quality of the educational experience available at New

Lanark, but also to embed its principles in a rationale that was at one and the same time an endorsement and a subtle revision of the industrial model favored by his father-in-law.

A Statement Regarding the New Lanark Establishment (1812)

As the economic historian John Butt once pointed out, Owen's *A Statement Regarding the New Lanark Establishment* of 1812 is essentially a business plan canvassing for new partners for the exciting commercial venture upon which its author had embarked and which was then facing a renewed crisis of ownership (Butt 1971, p. 186). It is also Owen's first published pronouncement on the village and its social-industrial ethos, very much reflective of the forces summarized above and which had been shaping the development of the village since Owen's initial acquisition of it more than ten years previously. Lacking the philosophical depth of the essays which were to be published by Owen soon after as *A New View of Society* – and which had clearly been in preparation for some considerable period before that – the *Statement* nevertheless goes straight to the heart of the interlace of financial and philanthropic motives driving with increasing urgency some of Owen's most ambitious designs. We have noted that the first decade of his residence in the village seemed an unexpectedly sluggish period in the unfolding of Owen's social and educational vision, hampered by the shadowy presence of somewhat reluctant partners and distracted by the many challenges involved in raising the productivity of the plant at a time of economic recession to levels that would successfully and sustainably fund his schemes. The *Statement* is Owen's first attempt to set out explicitly in pamphlet form, for a wide audience of potential investors, the coherence of a development strategy in which commercial profitability and social philanthropy are presented as a single, mutually-reinforcing program for economic growth. In adopting this stance, Owen openly acknowledged the precedents set by his father-in-law's improvements, tacitly identifying himself with the wider movement of factory reform and aligning his efforts with the more moderate elements of progressive opinion across

Britain, most especially with their desire to neutralize potentially revolutionary unrest through a humane response to the legitimate grievances of the laboring classes. According due recognition to some of its genuinely radical propositions, the *Statement* can nonetheless be quite reasonably interpreted as a natural expression of the enlightened impulses at work in various areas of the early factory system and to which David Dale had probably given as yet the most credible shape in his first version of New Lanark.

The intellectual seriousness of the pamphlet is immediately obvious in the manner in which it blends cool commercial calculation with the succinct communication of complex philosophical and psychological propositions. These are the same classic Enlightenment doctrines that would be defended at length in *A New View of Society*. Though expressed more concisely than in the longer work, Owen makes no attempt in the *Statement* to minimize their centrality to his argument. 'The plan' for New Lanark, he boldly informs his readership, was originally founded not upon a financial determination, but on the

> evident principle, that any characters, from the savage to the sage or intelligent benevolent man, might be formed, by applying the proper means, and that these means are to a great extent at the command and under the control of those who have influence in society [...]
>
> (Owen 1993a, 1.14)

Resolute adherence to the abstract view that man's character is shaped by his circumstances is the initial empowering step, Owen argues, in the moral reform of the neglected laboring population, replacing vice with virtue and fostering the attitudes and dispositions conducive to good governance and industrial prosperity for owners and workers alike.

This core conviction of course quickly opens Owen's argument in the *Statement* to the potential of education as the principal medium of character formation: 'to give [...] children the most beneficial education for their station in the community, and effectually to train them to the habits which could not fail to make them valuable members of society' (1.16). The proto-behaviorist attitudes in evidence here might be interpreted in either progressive or instrumental terms and it seems clear that Owen was ready, like many of his contemporaries, to embrace both judgments. They reflect on the one hand the generally enlightened belief in the human potential for perfectibility, a doctrine which challenged the supposed moral pessimism of the Christian past and which in Owen's time had inspired much of the movement for social and political reform in which he had himself begun to become active. At the same time, they point unmistakably to the disciplinary tendencies visible throughout Owen's thought, and present also in the broader rationalist propensity to regulate the inner lives of, especially, the lower classes in the interests of capital and the preservation of a tranquil social order. The dual intention of securing 'the further improvement of the community, and ultimate profit to the concern' (1.17) is set forth in the *Statement* quite candidly, with active education of the working population from infancy to adulthood openly advocated as the most efficient means of achieving this end. The chief symbol of the centrality of education to the program of character development at New Lanark as Owen here envisages it is also one of the main objects of the *Statement*'s financial prospectus and its rallying call for fresh investment: the building at a freshly capitalized village complex of a '*New Institution*¤, situated at the centre of the establishment, with an inclosed area before it' (1.17). These were the premises destined in Owen's thinking to become the Institute for the Formation of Character, already presented in this early document as crucial to the village's distinctive philosophy of education. The *Statement*'s detailed description of the intended institution and the various educational purposes assigned to it prompts some of Owen's so far most extended reflections on the content of learning and teaching in the ideal industrial settlement. It serves also to set up the lifelong association in his mind between the architecture of imagined spaces and the careful zoning of activities and pastimes presented as integral to the flourishing of individuals and communities.

These reflections provide the basis for Owen's perspective on the school curriculum, underlining both the continuity with Dale's earlier work and the departures from it. In the sketch offered of the New Institution, the dedication of a large room to what Owen terms 'general education' prompts a brief yet revealing description of that peculiar synthesis of the academic and the functional for which early industrial schooling had already become well known, but which also receives at Owen's hands some distinctive refinements and amendments:

> In this it was intended, that the boys and girls were to be taught to read well, and to understand what they read; to write expeditiously a good legible hand, and to learn correctly; so that they may comprehend and use with facility the fundamental rules of arithmetic. The girls were also to be taught to sew, cut out, and make up useful family garments [...] and to clean and keep a house neat and in order. And the boys were to be taught in the drill-ground the manual exercise [...] to render the most effectual defence to their country.
>
> (1.18)

In this summary, it is possible to discern several of the key features of the Owenite approach to education, including its sharp separation of the spheres of male and female responsible action and its strongly vocational justification for the acquisition of academic skills. There is, however, much more than a performative or reductive view of technical competence at stake here. 'By the arrangements formed for the education of the children, they will be trained regularly for their employment,' Owen acknowledged. But 'all their habits, bodily and mental,' he continued, will be 'formed to carry them to a high state of perfection; and this alone, in its consequences, will be of incalculable advantage to the concern [...]' (1.20). The ambitious commitment to general character formation penetrates every aspect of the rationale Owen offers here, evident in the stress on the availability of educational opportunity from infancy to adulthood and tangible also in the repeated assertion of the links between effective education and the attainment of happiness and perfection. These of course were social objectives characteristic of much Enlightenment moral philosophy of the preceding century, but Owen's assimilation of them to the practical operations of a leading-edge industrial community was unique in its optimistic insistence that the interests of capital and labor, and group and individual, could be made to converge around the collaborative pursuit of material prosperity.

The phrase Owen used in the *Statement* for this synthesis was 'domestic economy' (1.20) and, once again, it was very clearly identified in his mind with an emblematic space or room. Here formal educational instruction would eventually blossom, he believed, into a wider desire within the population for rational recreation and ongoing self-improvement. In the 'lecture-room,' which would also serve on Sundays as the community's interdenominational church, the benefits of enhanced education would be further reinforced by evening classes in parenting, in household thrift, and even in music and dance. The resultant blurring of boundaries between formal academic instruction, vocational training, and rounded self-development – even the suggested relaxation of interactions between younger and older generations – represented, Owen clearly felt, the heart of his vision of education and the area where it advanced most palpably on anything achieved by previous entrepreneurs, including David Dale. The combination of philanthropic idealism and commercial incentive is not opportunistic or cynical within the ethical framework Owen sets out in the *Statement*. Rather the special synthesis of place, work, and education is presented as the most obviously rational context in which to materialize abstract principles as fully realizable and edifying social goals beneficial to all of the members of society, so that 'our entire population will gradually change its character' (1.20). At this stage in his thought, the potential of education actually to question or even overcome the economic and political asymmetries of class and wealth is undeniably remote from Owen's schemes – and it is at least arguable that it remained this way throughout his career. However, the rhetorical style of the pamphlet and its high-minded efforts confidently to persuade readers and investors that the correct combination of place and education would without doubt redound to 'the general happiness of society' (1.20), sets the tone for much of his later and more seasoned polemic on behalf of popular mass education. Similarly, the attention in the pamphlet to specific examples of effective education in action typifies Owen's concern with evidence and his impatient desire to see abstract principle translated into viable classroom practice.

Learning and teaching in New Lanark

For Owen, the new system of education to be implemented at New Lanark under the aegis of the third, definitive partnership of 1812 would advertise itself as nothing less than the principal means of resolving many of the serious problems afflicting British society. 'Only by education rightly understood,' he wrote in *Report to the County of Lanark*, '[...] communities of men can ever be well governed and by means of such education every object of human society will be attained with the least labor and the most satisfaction' (Owen 1993b: 1.320). Owen's daughter and disciple, Jane Dale Owen, later offered a powerful summary of her father's vision of education as he had zealously carried it through when the success of the third partnership appeared finally to grant him the license for which he had spent a decade waiting. In Jane Dale's eyes, her father's system was to be properly understood only

'in an extended sense [...] ...as signifying a general superintendence of the individual from birth to maturity; thus including the cultivation of all his powers, physical, mental, and moral, and the placing of him under such circumstances as are best suited for the development of his character.

(Owen 1968, p. 178)

In his autobiography, Owen revealingly borrowed a banausic metaphor to isolate the potential he had grasped in this moment, seeing in the scope given him by his new partnership access to a unique 'moral lever' whereby 'ignorance, poverty, disunion, vice, crime, evil passions and misery' (Owen 1993e, 4.302) could finally be eradicated from society. The ultimate goal, he subsequently stated in one of his later works, *The Revolution in the Mind* of 1849, was to prepare the young 'to receive from birth the best cultivation of our natural powers – physical, mental moral and practical – and to know how to give this training and education to others' (Owen 1991b, p. 368).

The relationship of 'training and education' to the moral reformation of 'our natural powers' in important respects captures the essence of the educational program at New Lanark as Owen began to administer it. It was once again in the symbolic and functional spaces of the Institute for the Formation of Character (also called the New Institution for the Formation of Character; Owen used both terms) that this was most comprehensively disclosed. Donnachie and Hewitt point out that in this period 'most of the descriptions leave us somewhat confused about which activities were pursued in the Institute and which in the school. To all intents and purposes they were probably interchangeable as far as the instruction of children was concerned.' (Donnachie and Hewitt 1993, p. 97). The two-storey Institute, formally inaugurated with some ceremony by Owen in 1816, possessed five rooms and housed at its largest extent as many as 600 children. The two rooms in the upper storey, fitted with double rows of windows quite different from design of badly-lit parish schools, were each sufficiently spacious to accommodate a large section of the New Lanark community. The main room was initially furnished on the standard Lancastrian template, with desks separated by a central aisle, a teaching lectern or pulpit at one end and galleries for visitors or observers on the three remaining sides. By this stage in his thinking, Owen had begun to distance himself from orthodox Lancastrian methods, disillusioned by some of the excesses of the monitorial system, such as the reliance on pupil-teachers to teach huge numbers of children, and inclining more readily to the formal employment of teachers who might then be better suited to additional training in his own ideals.

The second room on the top floor was used for public lectures, music, and dancing, just as has been imagined in the *Statement*. Unlabeled maps were displayed at one end of the room, encouraging children when it was being used as a teaching space to investigate for themselves the names of countries, cities, and stretches of water rather than simply memorizing facts imparted by an instructor. This was another subtle rebuke to the Lancastrian method and also to the parish school preference for the rote learning of scripture and the classics. It was continued into the ground floor rooms, which were assigned by Owen to the teaching of reading, natural history, and geography. Here the pupils took part in small-group activities, with class sizes ranging from 12 to 40. The under-7s were taught coeducationally, while older boys and girls were segregated, meeting on average for two hours per day for music and dancing. One teacher was allocated to each broadly age-banded class. The main teaching staff were frequently supplemented by the recruitment of peripatetic specialists drawn from further afield for the teaching of singing, dancing, and physical exercise. Pupils attended classes for approximately five hours, usually beginning at 5.30 in the morning. Parliamentary records for 1816, the year of the Institution's formal opening, indicate a quite astonishing figure of 444 children enrolled at the school, ranging from 3 to 10 years of age, and reflecting in their sheer numbers something of the ambition with which Owen approached the task at New Lanark once the issues of ownership and funding seemed to have been resolved in his favor (Erickson and McPeck 1964, p. 242). The inauguration of a separate school building the following year served only to confirm Owen in his self-assurance.

Instructional methods at New Lanark quickly became for pupils and visitors alike one of the sources of greatest distinction (and, later, greatest controversy) for the school and its owners. From the outset, Owen urged his teaching staff to provide intellectually absorbing objects and resources as the stimulus materials for lessons, adapting pedagogy to what he saw as the natural appetites of the young when faced with the diversity of the natural world around them. Pictures, charts, plants, animals, and inanimate man-made objects such as wheels and engine parts formed the bedrock of classroom learning and teaching, underlining Owen's conviction that the cognitive development of the young progressed organically from the familiar to the unfamiliar, from the particular example to the general rule, and from the sensory concrete to the symbolically abstract. This was a view promoted widely in Enlightenment associationist psychology and it is conceivable that Owen had been first exposed to it through the reading and deliberations of the Manchester Society. There can be no certainty of this, however, and the fact that Owen had formulated many of these ideas before his first meetings with some of the great European educators of the age suggests that the ten years of seemingly intellectually fallow occupation of New Lanark had been employed somewhat more experimentally than Owen was prepared to acknowledge. Indeed, it may well be that in taking forward the strongly vocational bent of Dale's methods, with their emphasis on practical, experiential learning, Owen discovered his own, semi-independent route to an enlightened theory of classroom pedagogy (Carlson 1992, pp. 18–26).

The practice of moving from the consideration of concrete objects to the codification of abstract conclusions was not confined to natural history. In the study of society, teachers were encouraged to examine the social and economic order by placing before the pupils a pyramid of wooden blocks signifying the arrangement of the social classes. By virtue of this visual aid, Owen intended to spark 'an animated conversation between the children and their instructors, now themselves acquiring new knowledge by attempting to instruct their young friends, as I always taught them to think their pupils were and to treat them as such.' (Owen 1993e, 4.194). While instances such as the use of the pyramid have often been cited to reproach Owen's seeming political naïveté, and his ready acquiescence in an unjust economic system of which he and his commercial peers were the chief beneficiaries, less acknowledgement has been given to its far-sighted view of the teacher as a professional who *learns from* his pupils; or the perception of the instructor as an adult rooted in a relationship of mutual trust in which the child's freshness of sensation is affirmed as a potential form of critical understanding in its own right. In a deep sense, an interactive pedagogy of this kind can convincingly be seen as much more radical in outlook than anything likely to emerge from the simple didactic instruction of the young by their teachers in the patent injustices of the surrounding social order. The child's life experience is validated here, opening on to a perception of the knowledge and the authority of the teacher as dynamic terms in a much more fluid and unpredictable understanding of collective classroom enquiry that sets few theoretical limits on the capacity to imagine other ways of ordering the world, including its current distributions of political and social power. The teachers at New Lanark, Owen recorded in one of the numbers of his quarterly *Journal* of 1850–1852, were expected consistently to follow this open-ended understanding of the natural processes of learning in accompanying children on the path towards truth:

[...] it is proposed that the mode of communicating knowledge by means of sensible signs and of conversations with the teacher, shall supersede, for a considerable period, the usual practice of learning from books, which if commenced before the child can have acquired an adequate number of correct and useful ideas, is calculated [...] to fill his head with mere words, to which either no ideas or very erroneous ideas are attached, and thus materially to injure his faculties and retard or prevent his intellectual improvement.

(Owen 1852, pp. 119–120)

The suspicion of books, for which this passage and others like it have become famous in Owen's writings, diverts attention from its deeper pedagogical insight, which lies in the commitment to the 'conversations with the teacher': the joint construction of meaning by pupil and teacher through the dialogic exploration and evaluation of ideas validated by reason and experience rather than merely custom. It is plain from this judgment that Owen is not opposed to books as such, but to particular and premature uses of books in the lives of the young to vouchsafe the merit of ideas and opinions on the basis of nothing more than the prestige of the print text as a repository of uncontested truths. Once again, the radicalism of this perspective on the authority of the text is too easily submerged in the oversimplified fixation on its recommendation about the place of books in the classroom. Owen's cumbersome tone here perhaps diverts attention from the underlying originality of his argument.

Many visitors to the New Lanark schoolrooms were struck by their general hospitality to talk and discussion. In part this surprise stemmed from the contrast with the pedagogic norms of most other schools of the time and their usually strict insistence upon silence as a precondition of effective learning. It was also, however, as Owen's statements confirm, as much a reaction to the observed direction of such talk and the unsettling nature of the social relations it seemed to imply. Aside from the unexpected informality of teacher-pupil interactions, Owen's methods encouraged frequent and unusual levels of cooperation between the sexes in the day-to-day activities of the classroom. While, as we have seen, a separation of the spheres undoubtedly continued at New Lanark, and young women were prepared conscientiously for their future roles as housewives and mothers, the strongly vocational emphasis of the school, and its link to the factory, incentivized mixing of the sexes and levels of academic education for females that were well in advance of the standards of the period. The practice of collaboration and mutual assistance held a strongly moral appeal for Owen, especially when it was applied to groups of human beings with a pronounced history of antagonism or misunderstanding. Divisions of gender, generation, or religious faith seemed to him fertile contexts for the application of teaching strategies rooted in the experience of dialogue or sharing. From this beginning, he believed, children could be encouraged to absorb the principle of cooperation as part of their lifelong motivation, 'as though they were literally all of one family' (Owen 1993b, 1.317). The analogy here is revealing. As a social category, 'family' occupied throughout Owen's thought an ambiguous position reflective of the shifting social and economic realities of early capitalism and their frequently corrosive impact on traditional domestic structures. From certain perspectives, it is clear that Owen regarded the institutions of marriage and the family as divisive and repressive: obstacles to the building of resilient community bonds (Harrison 1969, pp. 59–60; Chase 2007, pp. 250–251). Nevertheless, commitment to the values of family ran deep into Owen's own psychobiography and his first-hand experience of the transitional forms of industrialization. A nostalgia for the emotional resources of the *extended* family, in particular, is an enduring feature of his thought, suggesting that many aspects of his mature community-building were efforts to recapture the cooperative kin networks that capitalism seemed ordained to dissolve, but to the virtues of which Owen had remained resolutely attached from his Newtown upbringing onwards. If there is a continuing social radicalism about this view of human solidarity, and the place of education in promoting it, then it is often expressed in a paradoxically conservative language, wedded to an older, organic understanding of the nature of the social fabric somewhere between kin group and civil community. It is indeed conceivable that the recurrence of this sentiment in Owen's thought allies him to the vigorous eighteenth-century criticism of political economy that David Eastwood has memorably termed 'romantic conservatism' – a view to which we will return later in this book (Eastwood 1989).

Owen knew that the radicalism of his educational goals, and the moral feelings around which it revolved, would require a redefinition of the role of the teacher if the essential climate of conviviality were to flourish in his classrooms. In some respects, the initial expectations placed upon his teaching staff were more concerned with conduct and manners rather than academic qualifications. Owen needed younger, more flexible teachers than was common in Scotland if his understanding of the classroom as a place of gracious rational enquiry was to be realized. New Lanark teachers were required to be more resourceful than their parish counterparts, committed to outdoor education, for example, and continually open to the unexpected in their dealings with young children. This was a particularly acute issue in the area of pupil discipline, where some of the methods favored by Owen seemed to invite the forms of misbehavior on which the established system came down so harshly. The Lancastrians had tried to mitigate the often violent practices of the parish classrooms by the introduction of their trademark schedule of rewards and penalties, moving away from excessive physical chastisement to a more complex reinforcement routine of praise and admonishment. Owen, however, grew vehemently opposed to the underlying psychology of this approach, arguing that rewards and penalties simply bred in children a prudential calculation incompatible with the enthusiastic embrace of education for its own sake. Recalling as an adult the atmosphere of the New Lanark classrooms of his youth, Owen's son, Robert Dale Owen, stressed the centrality of this principle to the whole ethos of the school. Rewards, Robert Dale argued, were rejected because of their dangerous tendency to breed in their recipients 'pride, vanity and inordinate ambition.' Penalties were equally unacceptable because of their effect of 'debasing the character, and destroying the energies of the individual' (Owen 1824, p. 11). In their place, Owen boldly asserted that 'every child will always be treated kindly, whatever his natural character, physical or mental, may be' (Owen 1852, p. 119). Misbehavior, he argued, was the product of miseducation, and the words and actions of tolerant, compassionate teachers were much more likely to produce amenable children than any measures, physical or emotional, taken against them. Referring in his autobiography to the first teachers he had hired, Owen recalled that 'The first instruction which I gave them was, that they were on no account ever to beat any one of the children, or to threaten them in any manner in word or action, or to use abusive terms.' When a response to inappropriate behavior became necessary, it was to be offered, Owen insisted, 'in the spirit of kindness and of charity, as from the more experienced to the less experienced' (Owen 1993e, 4.193–194), avoiding any hint of retribution likely to induce feelings of guilt or humiliation. The rationale for this fresh approach to the motivation of the young stemmed from Owen's fundamental belief that the repugnant behavior for which sections of the impoverished working classes were rightly feared in his society originated in a cycle of intergenerational deprivation and despair from which only education held the prospect of release: 'The infants and children of every generation have been the mental slaves of the preceding generations [...] they have been compelled to become – what their fathers had been previously compelled to be – slaves to the most gross and inconsistent errors' (Owen 1993d: 3.49).

Gradually, Owen came to recognize that the scale of the educational reforms he was contemplating would entail special courses in his own distinctive methods for the teachers in his employ and that these courses in turn highlighted a need for teachers to be properly trained professionals from the outset of their careers. This was a position far removed from the parish approach to teacher recruitment and even from the relatively enlightened policies of the Lancastrians, who were moving increasingly towards the employment of the better educated, including graduates of academies and universities. By the time of his composition of *A New View of Society*, Owen had concluded that the whole platform of popular educational reform depended upon the preparation of a better educated teaching force, confidently equipped with knowledge of the natural and human sciences and morally committed to the tenets of the new rational pedagogy:

At present there are not any individuals in the kingdom who have been trained to instruct the rising generation as it is for the interest and happiness of all that it should be instructed. The training of those who are to form the future man, becomes a consideration of the utmost magnitude; for, on due reflection, it will appear, that instruction to the young must be, of necessity, the only foundation upon which the superstructure of society can be raised.

(Owen 1993f, 1.93)

In later life, these views were to lead Owen into strongly supporting the 1830s campaign of the Glasgow educationalist, David Stow, in whose 'Normal School' in the city the first systematic attempts were made in Scotland to formalize teacher training and to link the academic education of student teachers to field placements in model schools where enlightened methods were being regularly practiced (Cruickshank 1966). In the absence of such facilities and linkages, Owen's own first experiments in the hands-on training of his teachers at New Lanark were, to say the least, erratic. James Buchanan and Molly Young, Owen's first employed teachers, were initially hired by him precisely because he perceived them to be free of the taints of the parish and monitorial systems. Buchanan, who became the first headmaster at the Institute, proved a controversial choice, but eventually established a positive working relationship with Owen and winning admirers among the pupils and their parents for his assiduous efforts to implement the new curriculum. In later life, however, departing from Owen's service, Buchanan's supporters began to claim for him a much greater role in the original creation of the ethos of the New Lanark school, while his involvement in the early infant schools movement in England grievously disappointed Owen when he visited Buchanan and witnessed what he took to be a return to the old punitive attitudes. For Owen, an important vindication of the New Lanark philosophy actually came in the wake of Buchanan's resignation, when Owen felt confident enough to appoint to the leadership of the school 'one of the new trained pupils' and someone who in Owen's eyes had 'imbibed the true spirit of the system' (Owen 1993e, 4.196–197). The idea that New Lanark had begun so effectively to form the characters of its members that they were assuming as adults positions of authority within it represented for Owen a further confirmation of his insights and a vital testimony to their relevance for wider society.

The New Lanark curriculum

We are fortunate to possess, in the form of Robert Dale Owen's short memoir, *An Outline of the System of Education at New Lanark*, an illuminating guide to the curriculum of the New Lanark school in the period of Owen's greatest autonomy as its owner and manager. *An Outline* was published in 1824, shortly before Robert Dale and his father became involved in the New Harmony project. It therefore represents a distillation of the best features of the New Lanark ethos, while also cleverly setting out a series of objectives for the American venture. Its general reliability is corroborated by accounts from visitors to New Lanark around the same period, including those who left the village singularly less impressed by its educational content than was Robert Dale.

Steadfastly opposing the dominant teaching methods of the parishes and the Lancastrians, with their reliance upon the memorization of what *A New View of Society* termed 'precept upon precept, line upon line' (Owen 1993f, 1.63), Owen made the central driver of his curriculum a special synthesis of applied knowledge (clearly inherited from Dale) and spontaneous discovery. To some cursory observers, the impression created was of an essentially utilitarian approach to practical learning, embedded in the vocational needs of a manufacturing community. It is clear, however, from Robert Dale's account and from Owen's own pronouncements that the economic foundation of the New Lanark community in no way restricted the curriculum to a functional or attenuated understanding of educated rationality. In a later work of 1841, *A Development of the Principles and Plans on which to Establish Self Supporting Home Colonies*, Owen itemized the subjects, skills, and – most importantly – *dispositions* that should inform the schooling of the young in the ideal society. As well as emphasizing 'Reading, writing and accounts,' *Principles and Plans* also lists 'mechanics and chemistry' and 'A practical knowledge of agriculture and domestic economy' as important subjects of study. Even the stress on 'knowledge of some one useful manufacture, trade, or occupation' is highlighted for its contribution to self-fulfillment as well as to employability, undertaken by the pupil 'for the improvement of his mental and physical powers.' Technical mastery is carefully subordinate in Owen's thought to what he here terms 'knowledge of himself and of human nature, to form him into a rational being, and render him charitable, kind, and benevolent to all his fellow-creatures' (Owen 1993g, 2.399–400). This integrated understanding of the purposes of education shaped decisively the day-to-day content of learning and teaching at New Lanark.

On the vexed question of literacy, actual practice at the village school revealed a deeper appreciation of the motivation to read and write than the conventional Owenite skepticism of books seemed at first glance to suggest. Owen's determination was to avoid literacy becoming an end in its own right, to ensure that the ability to decode print text was wedded to the capacity to comprehend and derive satisfaction from the act of reading. Reading was, in effect, an exercise of the liberated reason and the reason required an incentive to read akin to the instinctive human appetite for discovery and the pursuit of fresh experience. Hence the exclusion from the school of books for children under 6, especially of those over-complex, didactic texts favored by the parish schools since the Reformation and condemned by Owen as generally 'worse than useless' (Owen 1993e, 4.230). In their place, younger children were encouraged to explore their environment in order to recognize its many information-rich sources of meaning, directly fitted to the human inclination to enquire and make sense of new experience. According to Robert Dale, this preparatory method led in turn to an initial encounter with books such as travelogues and natural histories, continuing in print form the journeys children had made with their teachers around their local surroundings. Popular 'educative' novels, such as those by the celebrated children's writer Maria Edgeworth, also suited this stage of literacy, prompting children quite naturally to compare, contrast, and ask questions. Even for the children over 10, books were used sparingly and always at the service of the core interaction with the teacher. Texts were read aloud by the teacher and the sharing of them was routinely accompanied by discussion and the expression of personal responses to the themes present in them. 'The general principle,' Robert Dale recorded, 'that children should never be directed to read what they cannot understand, has been found to be of the greatest use' (Owen 1824, p. 36).

In common with the Lancastrians, Robert Owen delayed the

teaching of writing until the basic principles of reading comprehension had been laid down in the child's mind, in the belief that, once again, the desire to produce print text would issue from a natural urge to communicate. Unlike many of his contemporaries, however, Owen did not dwell on the formalities of copperplate handwriting, but on the acquisition by pupils of 'a good legible hand' (Owen 1993f: 1.64) practised by them as they responded to the ideas discussed in the classroom. This served in typically Owenite terms to subordinate the tool of writing to larger educational aims while also developing in pupils a practical skill for working life. The teaching of mathematics and arithmetic was approached in a very similar fashion, eschewing the memorization of tables, proofs, and rules in favor of a method based around the kinds of problem-solving and mental arithmetic calculations that would encourage the young to seek underlying mathematical explanations and patterns. Robert Dale goes so far in his commentary to record the impact of Pestalozzi's view of mathematical reasoning on the changes introduced by his father into the teaching of numeracy at New Lanark, noting how this was combined with incentives based around explicit links to the skills required for future employability. In the study of maths, for both Owen and Pestalozzi, emphasis was laid on the understanding of general mathematical concepts and the command of transferable computational and deductive procedures based upon the growing knowledge of the rules of arithmetic, algebra, and geometry (Owen 1824, p. 40).

The natural and social sciences enjoyed a particular prominence in the New Lanark curriculum, almost as if their position at the cutting edge of 'modern' rationality resonated especially aptly with the larger social and intellectual objectives of the school. It was to Buchanan and Young's celebrated lessons in natural history and geography that visitors were most often invited by Owen, allowing him to showcase the discovery methods of these disciplines in ways that echoed the increasingly scientific procedures by which they were beginning to be pursued in the wider community of scholars. There is a clear connection to be made between the late Enlightenment enthusiasm for experiment as the cornerstone of scientific investigation and the classroom strategies advocated by Owen and his staff. It is indeed hard to avoid the broader parallel with New Lanark and its sister sites as themselves essentially 'experiments' in the shaping of a new model of society. In the study of the physical and life sciences, the pupils at the New Lanark school were introduced to a way of seeing the world free of superstition and subject only to the application of educated rationality (Stewart 2008). The classrooms were decorated with colorful posters of the animal, vegetable, and mineral orders of the natural realm to reflect this sense of open-ended learning and curiosity. In the study of geography, pupils were presented with the latest findings of travelers and explorers, assiduously disclosing to the minds of the young a world infinitely more diverse and surprising than earlier systems of classification, based upon subservience to classical or biblical models, had proposed. Much class time was as a result devoted to the handling of maps, almost as if the cartographic mentality had become somehow emblematic for Owen (himself, of course, a prodigious traveler) of the new empiricism by which proper education was now to be characterized and which placed inherited lore and dogmatic assertion very firmly below the fruits of guided but independent scientific scrutiny in the hierarchy of truths. This approach to geography was, for Owen, vital to the defeat of prejudice and to the promotion of the insight that no cultural or social system, whether at home or abroad, was to be regarded as immutable or beyond the reach of human dominion, provided the relationship of place to behavior was properly understood. It is easy to see how aspects of this philosophy seemed in the eyes of some of Owen's more traditional critics to orient education at New Lanark in an unduly secular or even 'relativist' direction, incompatible with the eternal verities of the Christian Gospel and the proper recognition of the obvious superiority and historic destiny of the European races, then rapaciously extending their empires across the globe. 'It was surprising to hear,' noted one famous visitor, Dorothy Wordsworth,

> with what readiness Boys of from seven to ten years old gave the names of rivers with uncouth names, of distant seas and countries, at the pointing of a Wand over a large map of the world placed on a frame near the head of the room, the class standing in a semi-circle before it. The room is hung round with materials for study – paintings of beasts and birds, fossils and flowers.
>
> (Wordsworth 1941, pp. 343–344)

In an intriguing adaptation, Owen also applied the 'cartographic' method to the teaching of history. Historical facts were arranged in a chronological sequence, so that events recorded in them could be studied in conjunction with the geographical locations, resources, and conditions against which they took place. Behind this approach lay yet again Owen's perception of the role of environment in the shaping of behavior and the corresponding need for education to accord more significance that in previous eras to the constraints placed by time and circumstance on the destinies of human societies. The culmination of this approach to the appreciation of the past was the resource Robert Dale called the 'Streams of Time,' its form in all probability borrowed from a teaching tool devised by the scientist and philosopher Joseph Priestley in 1765: the Chart of Biography:

> Seven large maps or tables, laid out on the principle of the Stream of Time [...] are hung around a spacious room. These, being made of canvas, may be rolled up at pleasure. On the streams, each of which is differently coloured, and represents a nation, are painted the principal events which occur in the history of the nations. Each century is closed by a horizontal line drawn across the map. By means of these maps, children are taught the outlines of Ancient and Modern History, with ease to themselves, and without being liable to confound different events or different nations.
>
> (Owen 1824, pp. 50–51)

This is in many respects a classic Enlightenment teaching aid, with its obvious appeal to the Owenite zeal for charts and diagrams. It is also, of course, a potentially radical instrument for the promotion of the faculties of comparative judgment and the due discernment of the achievements (and shortcomings) of other civilizations. In this capacity it served the broader Owenite ends of 'democratizing' the study of the past by subjecting the historical narratives of diverse peoples and societies to objective appraisal, challenging cultural and racial elitism while at the same time underscoring the potential of human beings to comprehend and alter the circumstances in which history might arbitrarily have placed them. Robert Dale's explanation of the rationale for the approach is astonishingly progressive in the ambitions it sets for the study of both history and geography when cross-disciplinary knowledge is deliberately organized in such a non-hierarchical structure:

> The minds of the children are thus opened, and they are prevented from contracting narrow, exclusive notions, which might lead them to regard those only as proper objects of sympathy and interest, who may live in the same country with themselves – or to consider that alone as right, which they have been accustomed to see – or to suppose those habits and those opinions to be the standard of truth and of perfection, which the circumstances of their birth and education have rendered their own. In this manner are the circumstances, which induce national peculiarities and national vices, exhibited to them; and the question will naturally arise in their minds: 'Is it not highly probable that we ourselves, had we lived in such a country, should have escaped neither its peculiarities, nor its vices – that we should have adopted the notions and prejudices there prevalent?' [...] A child who has once felt what the true answer to such a question must be, cannot remain uncharitable or intolerant.
>
> (Owen 1824, pp. 47–48)

These statements underline the extent to which the individual subjects of the curriculum at New Lanark – whatever their long-prized intellectual merits or august academic pedigrees – were placed by Owen and his teachers at the service of a broader overarching vision of education. Moreover, we can also see here that the moral logic of this perspective on knowledge does not stop at this point. Education is itself, in Owen's system, an activity closely allied to a still more comprehensive project of cognitive and social emancipation, beginning in the minds of individual children, perhaps, but with a craving to forge new forms of social belonging for the reform of an unjust world. It may be anachronistic simply to label this a version of 'Education for Citizenship' – still less *global* citizenship. But Owen's work reminds us that the key concepts of this way of imagining education and its place in the world originated with Enlightenment thought and that from their inception they entailed a vital role for popular schooling in the building of a new society. Owen's embrace of these values ranks among one of the first concerted efforts to reproduce in ordinary classrooms the sense of common humanity upon which the great *philosophes* had argued the future peace and fulfillment of civilization would depend. That it was undertaken at a time when the social and economic order had shifted in ways which even the most prescient Enlightenment minds could barely have foreseen, underlines the boldness and optimism of its vision.

The social harmony and renewed sense of the common good for which Owen wished New Lanark to be acclaimed was most publicly expressed in the school's celebration of the arts of music and dance. Many visitors commented favorably on this, including the American physicist John Griscom, of the New York Institute:

> I found there a music school. Half a dozen or more little fellows had each a flute, and were piping away in notes that did not preserve the strictest tunefulness [...] From this we went into a large room above stairs where there were fifty or sixty young people, both boys and girls, attending to the lessons of a dancing-master. These young students of the 'merry mood' were not equipped in all the gaiety of a fashionable ball-room; though there was a great diversity in costume.
>
> (Griscom 1824, pp. 250–251)

As well as diverging from the censorious gender divisions prevalent in the surrounding parish schools, which never would have countenanced such contact between boys and girls, the prominence of music and dance at New Lanark was a potent metaphor for Owen in conveying his passionate understanding of the contribution of education to the cultivation of the good life. In music and dance, individual talent and self-expression were celebrated (even, importantly, if the outcomes did not always attain classical standards of excellence!), but always inseparably from cooperation with the group. In the children's dancing, Robert Dale pointed out, 'Their own improvement is not their only source of enjoyment. That of their companions they appear to witness with pleasure, unmixed with any envious feeling whatever [...] ' (Owen 1824, p. 73). The accentuation in these remarks of the principles of pleasure, satisfaction, and reciprocity made the imagery of the dancing bodies of the young an abiding representation in Owenite thought of the transformed society to which progressive education might vitally contribute.

Chapter 3

Education, Work, and Community

The 'Principle Regarding Man'

A New View of Society is essentially a manifesto by which Owen sought to circulate his ideas for social and educational reform among influential political and cultural elites likely to promote the expansion of his achievements at New Lanark to wider British society. Its overall prose style reflects Owen's emphatic view that the social and economic crisis through which he and his contemporaries were living demanded more than the salon-room debates of the *philosophes* and the pamphleteering of public intellectuals defending either tradition or reform. The urgency and breathlessness of Owen's writing in *A New View* reflects the same convictions that had produced his bold commercial coup at New Lanark: that the time had come for action rather than words; for intervention rather than extended philosophical reasoning; for a direct appeal to power rather than an incremental consolidation of public opinion around gradual change. The four essays that make up *A New View* are consequently comparatively short, even when drawn together into a single volume, but they do contain in its most succinct and concentrated form the kernel of Owen's social and educational worldview, packaged as a series of propositions organically attached to which is an outline program for the renovation of the fragmented, superannuated educational systems of the British Isles. As several commentators have suggested, the key to Owen's economy of expression in *A New View* may reside in the background editorial guidance of Place and Godwin in condensing the manuscript. Despite the importunity of their polemic, the four essays do generally avoid the overblown rhetoric and repetitiousness that can be such distracting mannerisms of Owen's subsequent writings. While some of the underlying ethical and epistemological assumptions of the essays are simply asserted rather than demonstrated, or taken to be unquestionably self-evident to right-thinking observers, the argument is presented with the kind of compelling simplicity often associated with critical reflection upon first-hand experience. The reader is left with no doubt that the remedies proposed for the nation's ills in *A New View* are the fruits of a mind directly and practically engaged with finding solutions to the myriad social and economic problems it documents. It is perhaps this tone of pragmatic authenticity that lends the essays their peculiarly modern sense of social purpose, situating them prominently in the annals of progressive educational advocacy.

The first essay, which in its stand-alone form carried the title 'On the Formation of Character,' lays out some of the main philosophical foundations upon which the remainder of the argument is to be raised. Chief among these is Owen's classical insistence that *'Any general character, from the best to the worst, from the most ignorant to the most enlightened, may be given to any community, even to the world at large, by the application of proper means'* (Owen 1993f, 1.34). Behind this carefully-italicized proposition lies the still more fundamental doctrine, articulated most succinctly in the Third Essay and heard like a clarion throughout all of Owen's work: *'that the character of man is, without a single exception, always formed for him* [...] *Man, therefore, never did, nor is it possible he ever can, form his own character'* (1.62). The roots of this idea are as deep and as ancient as philosophy itself, emerging out of two profoundly contrasting accounts of human existence which contend with one another in many of the world's major philosophical and theological systems, from the conflicts of the pre-Socratics through to the claims of twenty-first century neoDarwinism. The question of whether the individual character – and, indeed, the dispositions of whole societies – emerge entirely as effects of the material and cultural conditions of existence, or, by contrast, unfold in accordance with certain interior human impulses central to which is the exercise of individual will and personal agency, represents a controversy of monumental proportions in western thought. It has been known by several names across the spectrum of the humanities and social science disciplines down the centuries. It can, in fact, on closer inspection, be seen to embrace a series of distinct but interlocking disputes about the underlying bases of human understanding and the sources of human behavior. It is often referred to in modern popular educational psychology, for example, as the 'nature-nurture debate,' while sometimes discussed in more philosophically elevated parlance as the dispute between 'free will' and 'environmental determinism' (Wood 1992). It remains as potent a controversy in contemporary thought as it was in Owen's time and it continues to play an important role in the shaping of educational values and the making and unmaking of educational policies in accordance with the changing political judgments formed in response to it (Pinker 2002).

Despite its abiding and distinguished lineage, the debate as Owen almost certainly encountered it had assumed a central place in the civic deliberations of his time largely as a result of the influence of certain key thinkers associated with the early European Enlightenment. We have seen that the haphazard quality of Owen's own education, and the unsystematic, autodidact profile of his reading, makes it very difficult accurately to reconstruct the precise pedigree of his key concepts. Nonetheless, the climate of ideas into which Owen plunged from his Manchester years onwards undoubtedly immersed him in the struggle between rationalists and empiricists, which dominated European philosophy from the late seventeenth until the late eighteenth century. As Owen and others correctly intuited, there was much more at stake in the rivalry of these two schools than idle philosophical speculation. In 1690, the philosopher John Locke, in his *Essay Concerning Human Understanding*, had launched a wide-ranging attack on the rationalist assumption that human nature was shaped in large part in accordance with certain innate ideas, concepts, and categories. These categories, rationalists stated, come to us as part of an irreducible core or natural endowment of human qualities, which then go on to shape our primary apprehension of the world and our capacity to give meaning to our experience. Against this view, Locke famously proposed that human nature was to be more accurately regarded as a 'tabula rasa,' or blank slate, accumulating almost all of its knowledge and understanding from perception of the world around it from infancy onwards. In the *Essay*, Locke develops a theory of experience as the source of all human ideas, offers an account of the mental faculties that can be brought to bear on these ideas, and applies these materials to precisely the notions of infinity, number, space, substance, causality, and so on, which rationalists had insisted were the abstractions that could most definitively *not* be derived from perceptual experience alone. Locke strove to demonstrate that such ideas and principles *can* be acquired without the need for any innate mental infrastructure, arguing that the key to our sense of intelligibility and understanding lies in a proper assessment of what the powers of reason can accomplish when applied to the impressions received through experience (Moseley 2007, pp. 60–65). Nearer to Owen's time, the Scottish philosopher David Hume had taken Locke's defense of empirical experience a dramatic stage further by arguing audaciously that the assumption that the mind can make the world intelligible through the application of abstract categories is itself a doubtful philosophical presumption. In its place, Hume advocates a *naturalistic* account of how human beings impose sense on their primary perceptions of the world – collating, combining, and associating the results to guide future judgments and to construct a dynamic, provisional yet basically functional picture of reality. Our grasp of this reality is reduced, in Hume's view, to something the rationalists would barely accept as understanding at all: colored by our sentiments, our emotions, our sympathies, and benevolence, our prejudices and every haphazard mode of experience opening us out to the shaping influence of our surroundings as thinking and acting beings (Kail 2007, pp. 56–75).

It is, of course, doubtful whether Owen was fully cognizant of the complex, deep-seated philosophical conflict out of which the seemingly conclusive empiricist triumph of his own time had emerged. Much more importantly, *A New View of Society* shows Owen's thought operating within a broader climate of ideas centered upon the victorious empiricist construction of human nature but also ranging out from this into broader perspectives on knowledge and society. In its Lockean and Humean interpretation of the ways in which the external world gave rise to human behavior, empiricism resonated powerfully with the other important influences in eighteenth-century thought. The most important of these was the Newtonian, scientific worldview, with its expanding appreciation of the mesh of causes and effects by which, experiment had irrefutably demonstrated, the laws of the physical universe seemed everywhere to operate. The sheer explanatory power of Newtonian physics, combined with the technological feats accomplished by its application, suggested to many that the laws of nature identified by Newton and other experimental scientists operated consistently in every dimension of the natural order including, quite probably, the sphere of human action and behavior itself. The empiricist idea, therefore, that the shape of the human character was *caused* by the operation of the external world on individual awareness possessed for many an almost scientific prestige, echoing the integrated understanding of the universe of actions and reactions, causes and effects, depicted so eloquently in Newtonian mechanics. If man were fully a part of material nature, then his inner psychology and his external societies almost certainly operated in accordance with the same fundamental laws codified elsewhere as part of the proper taxonomies of nature. It was the principal task of a revived 'science of man' to identify the ways in which these laws extended into the human domain, and empiricism offered itself as the most compelling candidate framework on which to found this endeavor (Janiak 2008, pp. 25–32).

In Owen's time, the term used to describe the integrated, systematic conception of the place of the human within the natural order was *necessitarianism* (Harris 2005). Given classic expression in the philosophical theology of David Hartley's *Observations on Man* of 1749, necessitarianism was rooted in an empiricist associationist psychology that stressed the invariable succession of cause and effect in the continuum from external world to human individual, highlighting the deterministic role of this causal sequence in the molding of human personality (Hartley 1749). Hartley's 'science' of human character drew upon Newtonian principles to speculate that the sense impressions central to empiricist theory were recorded on the brain through the vibration of nerves in response to external stimuli. In this way, Hartley seemed to close the gap between the experimental understanding of the natural world and a materialist theory of mind. His argument further explicitly emphasized the role of social institutions (especially, for Hartley, the Church) in reforming human motivation in order to align it with a universal order disclosed by God in the laws of nature. In the hands of skeptical thinkers such as Nicolas de Condorcet and William Godwin, the residual religious infrastructure of necessitarianism was quickly discarded, leaving a compelling naturalistic philosophy of human behavior in which immense influence was attributed to the external social and cultural environment in determining individual motive and character (Claeys 1989, pp. 115–119). The word 'environment' had yet to appear in the English language in Owen's time, but Owen's preferred term – 'circumstances' – carried much of the same charge. Almost certainly guided by his reading and subsequent encounter with Godwin, Owen had arrived at a position, by the time of the composition of *A New View*, where he regarded the contest between innateness and the new, empiricist doctrine of necessity as the central issue of moral and social existence. If individuals and groups were the product of their circumstances, their behavior could only be expected to improve as and when their surroundings were altered to deliver that improvement. In the same vein, if it could be proved 'scientifically' that certain sets of circumstances could produce more advanced individuals, then immersing everyone in the same environmental stimuli looked likely to create what Owen was to term in a later text a 'new moral world.'

Owen's implied understanding of 'character' is the least elaborated feature of his psychological theory in *A New View*. On the one hand, he seems to favor the more ancient, almost literal definition of 'character' as 'inscription,' consistent with the empiricist doctrine that the human mind is an entirely blank slate on which external stimuli can etch almost any identity. Conversely, there are aspects of the essays that point to some sort of core utilitarian conception of basic 'drives' or 'desires' motivating human beings at an almost animal level to pursue pleasure and avoid pain, and constituted in some fashion by their fundamental nature. The phrase Owen uses for this property is 'happiness of self' (Owen 1993f, 1.36) and for all the hesitation with which it is expressed, it undoubtedly sits in some degree of tension with the absolutism of his radical necessitarianism. It is, indeed, the primary interior impulse on which he believes the intended reform of external circumstances will most fully act, prompting men and women to take up new, shared ways and habits of living because the changes then embraced so manifestly and rapidly conduce to their individual and collective happiness: 'experience will soon teach us how to form character [...] so as to give the greatest happiness to the individual and to mankind' (1.38).

Recognizing this seeming paradox signals the extent to which the attack launched by Owen on what he regarded as false and pernicious constructions of human nature has a specific target in mind. For strategic, political reasons Owen proves reluctant to name his opponent explicitly, but it is clear upon a close reading of the First Essay that it is nothing less than the Christian doctrine of free will that he wishes to overthrow. The principle of free will, or the assumption that individuals possess a God-given responsibility for their choices and actions and can be rewarded or punished for their behavior accordingly, lies at the root, Owen suggests, of the corrupt systems of education and government of his day, particularly as these bore down upon the seemingly reprobate conduct of the poor who were thereby always held culpable for their own every misfortune. Owen's opposition to the concept of free will – which he refers to indirectly as a 'ridiculous and absurd mystery' (1.36) – and to the institutions founded upon it, is part of his wider effort to provide an alternative explanation for the pervasive presence of poverty and misery, and an alternative remedy for their removal from society. The depth of hostility evinced towards free will in the First Essay, especially, is part of a wider antireligious slant in *A New View*, which, however obliquely expressed, is perhaps more germane to Owen's campaign than most commentators have hitherto admitted. In order to maintain his standing with the political elites at which his essays were aimed, Owen refrains from outright criticism of the Church, or of Christian theology. His juxtaposition of reason and truth against 'falsehood and deception' (1.47) remains nevertheless a revealing one, emphasizing that the exercise of a properly applied critical rationality soon exposes the philosophical incoherence of free will as the grounding of human behavior and proposes in its place a fresh way forward for raising the ethical standards of the masses. The secret of this revised approach to the improvement of the moral and intellectual life of society is, of course, education, and the First Essay ends in a typically Owenite call for a renewal of the nation's educational institutions on the basis of the transformed rationale held out by the theory of necessity:

the governing powers of all countries should establish rational plans for the education and general formation of the characters of their subjects. These plans must be devised to train children from their earliest infancy in good habits of every description [...] They must afterwards be rationally educated, and their labour be usefully directed.

(1.38)

It will be through education, Owen urges, that the theory of necessity will confirm with 'mathematical precision' that man 'may be surrounded with those circumstances which must gradually increase his happiness' (1.38). Proper education is thus the ultimate vindication of empiricist determinism in action, while also functioning as the principal means by which the existing, deleterious 'circumstances' of society – and the bogus justifications for their existence – can be most comprehensively eliminated. Owenite thought wrestled with an obvious difficulty here that has confronted all necessitarian accounts of subjectivity from the Enlightenment onwards: if the influence of circumstances is so total in the determination of human behavior, by what means do groups and individuals emerge equipped with the rational insight to challenge and change these circumstances? Later political science was to offer several resolutions to this problem. Owen's own answer is an indirect one suggested in his claim that the crisis occasioned by industrialization had irretrievably broken the hegemony of earlier systems of belief, and disclosed the underlying reality of the human condition for those with the discernment to see it. While this is perhaps a philosophically unsatisfying response, it creates the required space for Owen to extend his argument in *A New View of Society* from philosophical first principles to the inception of a social and educational program in which these principles will be given self-validating substance.

Owen was not the first to take empiricist psychology and necessitarian social science and draw forth from the combination of the two a set of vital conclusions about the potential of education. That accolade almost certainly belongs to the French philosopher Claude Adrien Helvétius (1715–1771). Helvétius had embraced Locke's theory of the tabula rasa, but took it much further, arguing that the untouched human mind was free from *all* innate dispositions and susceptibilities. Each of the perceived inequalities in the capabilities of individuals arose, Helvétius argued, not from natural inheritance or mental organization, but from the unequal desire for knowledge produced entirely by the influence of external circumstances on the individual passions. 'No nation,' Helvétius claimed, 'has reason to regard itself superior to others by virtue of innate endowment [...] All men have an equal disposition for understanding' (Helvétius 1759, p. 21). In view of this shared natural potential, every human being possesses the same underlying capacity to learn. Education can hence be rationally defended, according to Helvétius, as the principal method by which to reform society, and there are few constraints on the scale of the social change it might then, if properly directed, effect. Helvétius saw immediately the dangerous political repercussions of this belief, arguing that all of the apparent inequalities between individuals and classes stem from the corrupt operation of law, government, and education. 'The art of forming men,' he concluded, 'is in all countries [...] strictly connected to the form of the government' (p. 325). It therefore becomes the moral duty of government to manage a just and equitable system of popular education in order to equalize opportunity for the whole polity. Exactly if and when Owen took up these ideas of Helvétius has been much debated by several of his biographers (Silver 1965, pp. 97–98). Certainly, Helvétius' principal text on education, his *Treatise on Man: His Intellectual Faculties and his Education*, was available in English translation from 1777 and it seems to have made a profound impact on William Godwin, even if Godwin finally dissented from Helvétius' view of the relationship of government to the system of national schooling (Helvétius 1777). There is, however, only indirect evidence of Owen's acquaintance with the writings of Helvétius and it may well be that he knew no more of them than was paraphrased by Godwin or summarized at discussions in the Manchester Society. The presence of Helvétian thought nonetheless provides another important element of the intellectual backdrop to the argument Owen then pursued in his principal work.

Principles and practices of learning

Remaining in an openly persuasive and declaratory mode, Owen in the Second Essay of *A New View* sets out to elaborate a theory of learning derived from his philosophical assumptions. As always with Owen, the lineaments of such a theory are inseparable from his first-hand experience as an educational reformer and the narrative of the New Lanark experiment is never far from his attention in this phase of his argument. He begins, however, by drawing out a key educational implication of the necessitarian theory of character first hinted at by Helvétius, which is 'that children [...] are [...] impressed [...] by the circumstances in which they have been, are, or may be placed [...]' by 'parents and instructors' (Owen 1993f, 1.41). Of course, theorists from Locke to Rousseau had recognized that the empiricist account of human understanding and the necessitarian description of the social order combined to render infants and children uniquely impressionable, while at the same time lending to their adult mentors a prodigious capacity to influence and shape their personalities and attitudes. Children, it was repeatedly asserted, could be seen as the test case of the naturalistic philosophy in action (Musgrove 1962; Woodley 2009). Owen is heir to an essentially optimistic interpretation of this Enlightenment doctrine, seeing only hope in the power thus accorded to educational interventions in the lives of the young:

> Children are, without exception, passive and wonderfully contrived compounds; which, by an accurate previous and subsequent attention, *founded on a correct knowledge of the subject*, may be formed collectively to have any human character. And although these compounds, like all the other works of nature, possess endless varieties, yet they partake of that plastic quality, which, by perseverance under judicious management, may be ultimately moulded into the very image of rational wishes and desires.
>
> (Owen 1993f, 1.41)

The stress on the 'plastic quality' of the child's mind draws together in Owen's thought an empiricist epistemology with what might be termed a much more Romantic view of the potential of the properly educated child to bring about a much needed transformation of society. If the First Essay argued that this was the entitlement of all people, and that all people would respond positively to improvements in their material circumstances, the Second Essay, in a more visionary

Romantic style, spotlights the uniqueness of the child. This is the child implicitly configured as the ultimate educable subject, while at the same time hailed as a wellspring of promise and social redemption. From the well-established empiricist metaphors of 'impression,' 'molding' and 'plasticity,' Owen extrapolates an essentially *ethical* conception of the place of education in the creation of temperament and sympathy. Confronting the realities of human conflict and mutual incomprehension to which Christians, especially, pointed in their skeptical rejoinders to the moral idealism of the progressive necessitarians, Owen argues passionately for the role of reason and imagination in harnessing the energies of childhood to the renewal of relations between all of the members of society:

> The child who from infancy has been rationally instructed in these principles, will readily discover and trace whence the opinions and habits of his associates have arisen, and why they possess them [...] The pleasure which he cannot avoid experiencing by this mode of conduct will likewise stimulate him to the most active endeavours to withdraw those circumstances which surround any part of mankind with causes of misery, and to replace them with others which have a tendency to increase happiness.
>
> (1.42)

Owen's analysis here combines several distinct but related elements of the empiricist theory of mind. Supplementing the almost infinite malleability of the child's capacity to learn from the environmental influences to which he is exposed, Owen argues that the operation of that environment upon the child's inherent instinct for pleasure produces not the competitive individualism of the capitalist mode of production (or, indeed, the Christian theology of inherited self-ishness), but a species of compassionate rationality. The effect of this is to foster in the child a natural sympathy with those forced to inhabit debilitating social circumstances and a desire to work in solidarity with others for the removal of all impediments to the collective happiness of society. The presence of key terms such as 'pleasure' and 'happiness' in an otherwise almost classically empiricist thesis underlines some of the genuine subtlety of Owen's critique and his essentially organic understanding of the processes by which learning progresses from a simple stimulus-response stage of character formation to genuine, reflective moral and social action.

The Second Essay in *A New View* also seeks to examine further the causes of the 'circumstances' currently constraining the human capacity to grow in rationality and conditioning the fundamentally punitive culture in which the very poor and the very young find themselves trapped. For Owen, the errors of the present moral order are inherited and replicated in precisely the manner predicted by the empiricist template. While this exonerates each generation from any sort of underlying culpability of the kind represented in, for example, the Christian doctrine of Original Sin, it also highlights the essentially educational task by which false belief and irrational attitudes are in Owen's view to be combated. Owen's optimism here consists in the opinion that the integrated coherence of truth presented in all its fullness to the minds of the very young can dispel the incoherent falsehoods of rival explanatory systems, be they philosophical, theological, or merely the prejudice of tradition. In an important sense, this argument represents an anticipation by Owen of a rationalist moral objection frequently leveled at the 'blank slate' philosophy of mind: that its insistence that the content of mental life is simply a reflection of the circumstances in which the individual personality is placed deprives us of any criteria for adjudicating between candidate models of the good life; in other words, that there is no meaningful ground for judging between the merits of one arbitrary construction of character and another. If man is in his entirety the product of his circumstances then there is no procedure for discriminating between better and worse circumstances or better and worse characters. Owen's solution to this problem in the Second Essay is to propose a coherence theory of the truth and a voluntaristic concept of moral assent which is essentially heuristic in complexion:

Let truth unaccompanied with *error* be placed before them; give them time to examine it and to see that it is in unison with all previously ascertained truths; and conviction and acknowledgement of it will follow of course. It is weakness itself to require assent *before* conviction; and *afterwards* it will not be withheld. To endeavour to

force conclusions without making the subject clear to the understanding, is most unjustifiable and irrational, and must prove useless
or injurious to the mental faculties.

(1.43)

This is Owen's most agile move in averting the accusation of
indoctrination often laid against empiricist and necessitarian theories
of education such as his own. Conviction can only precede assent when a
principle of freely-exercised rationality is motivating the educational
activities of dominant character-formers such as parents and teachers.
The overwhelming coherence of the truth presented to the young will
then compel the commitment of learners not because it is more perfectly
mediated than its rivals, but because its sheer explanatory power excels
anything offered by alternative descriptions of reality regardless of the
penumbra of authority or tradition attaching to them. 'The errors of the
systems of our forefathers' (1.26), as Owen calls them, are then exposed
to the tests of critical scrutiny *and* moral authenticity. When they are
then seen obviously to fail on the grounds of both intellectual
consistency and contribution to the promotion of happiness and well-
being, they will quite naturally be discarded and the historical progress
of rational education will have advanced another vital stage.

Owen's conception of the role of formal schooling in this process –
based upon an extended reflection upon his New Lanark experiments –
is incremental and ameliorative. In keeping with his wider affinity with
progressive necessitarian politics of the sort championed by Godwin,
Owen recounts, and then generalizes from, the story of New Lanark and
the approach to education adopted in the village very much in terms of
the steady removal of obstacles to human fulfillment rather than the
revolutionary installation of a new moral and educational order:

In this progress the smallest alteration, adequate to produce any
good effect, should be made at one time; indeed, if possible, the
change should be so gradual as to be almost imperceptible [...] By
this procedure [...] the inclination to resistance will be removed,
and time will be given for reason to weaken the force of long-
established injurious prejudices.

(1.52–53)

The appeal of such gradualism, according to Owen, lies not merely in the avoidance of conflict, but in the reinforcement of a rational practice thereby rendered all the more effective at comprehensively neutralizing the corrupt legacy of the past and then sustaining itself within each individual learner as an ingrained habit of independent critical enquiry. The term Owen uses repeatedly in the Second Essay for this pedagogical style is 'training' – a concept the instrumental connotations of which have seen it long exiled from the vocabulary of liberal educational thought. Owen's repetition of 'training,' however, reminds us of the behaviorist backdrop to his theory of learning, with its dogged, formulaic emphasis on the deterministic role of circumstances in the making of character. It also serves to underline the ambition of his educational program at local and national levels for the repair of both social circumstances and personal character. Such is the scale of the challenge, the depth of the error to be corrected, that nothing less will suffice than 'a reform in the training and in the management of the poor, the ignorant, the untaught and untrained, or ill-taught and ill-trained, among the whole mass of British population [...]' (1.53). For Owen, children and the populous at large are never in fact free of 'training'; they are always inevitably trained either explicitly or implicitly by the material and cultural conditions in which consciousness and character first arise and then are formed. It is from the misguided training of the past and the confused training of the present, with all of their attendant social evils, that rational education will deliver society, Owen argues, by establishing optimum social and pedagogical conditions for the creation of an entirely transformed generation of young people afforded access to a convincing vision of the truth.

Education, recreation and moral development

The central design of the Third Essay of *A New View of Society* is to set out the moral and developmental implications of the collection's perspective on the acquisition of enlightened rationality and to examine further the role of education within this. With his New Lanark experience once again providing the context for his reflections,

Owen turns his attention to themes such as infancy, family, recreation, and sociality in an effort to capture the full, lived possibilities of his vision of reformed community seen in something approaching its totality. In considering the part played by infancy in his scheme, Owen's purpose is to reiterate that the formation of character is a process embedded in the most fundamental ties of family and community interdependence.

> It must be evident to those who have been in the practice of observing children with attention, that much of good or evil is taught to or acquired by a child at a very early period of its life; that much of temper or disposition   is correctly or incorrectly formed before he attains his second year [...]
>
> (1.57)

The Third Essay quickly sets up a powerful resonance between the processes of character formation from infancy onwards and the resultant moral climate of the wider society in which the child lives. In highlighting this quite 'primordial' understanding of the relationship of self to environment, where the origin of almost every feature of the individual temper can be traced to the shaping influence of adult society, Owen is at pains to locate the institutions of education within a wider interactive ethical economy. Disordered, error-based societies produce maladapted individuals who in turn perpetuate these same corrupted institutions of socialization, of which formal schooling is probably of the foremost significance. If this cycle is to be broken, then the potential of a large-scale educational intervention of the kind attempted at New Lanark can only succeed when the other institutions of the social fabric act in moral concert with it. Educational reform alone, Owen seems to suggest, will not succeed in the task of renewal because the development of character is already so well advanced even before schooling begins.

In certain respects, the radical solutions Owen advances in his analysis of the scale of the problems confronting his society entail intrusions into the private spheres of domestic and family life from which modern mainstream liberal thought habitually recoils. These intrusions were later to become a source of hostility towards Owenism on the part of the leading philosopher of liberalism, John Stuart Mill. Owen in general refrains from articulating a detailed theory of the state in the course of *A New View*, but when in the Third Essay he proposes that 'The child will be removed, so far as is at present practicable, from the erroneous treatment of the yet untrained and untaught parents' (1.58), in order to guarantee its formation free from false belief, it is possible to see the specter of the coercive state oppression that was destined to assume sometimes monstrous proportions in the totalitarian politics of the twentieth century. Certainly, it is difficult to see how Owen imagines such removals taking place without some illiberal intervention on the part of highly dictatorial state agencies. The latent authoritarian inclinations in Owen's educational thought can nonetheless be too easily exaggerated and it is important to set his remarks about parents and families in the Third Essay within the broader context of the existing regulated, industrial pattern of which the community of New Lanark was a part. The ominous comment about confiscating children from their inadequate parents can then be understood in relation to the extended sequence that follows it in the text on the requirement of any rational community to break down barriers of prejudice and suspicion through a species of shared corporate socialization acting in harmony with the rights and responsibilities of parents. Owen's essentially incremental view of social reform presupposes a general benevolence on the part of parents towards their offspring living in healthy, functioning communities even where elements of the parental influence on children may be rooted in the inherited and erroneous worldviews of the past. Parents delivering their smallest children into the care of their community institutions do so for fundamentally pragmatic reasons associated with the labor routines of industrial production. In the enlightened climate of which Owen hoped New Lanark was a harbinger, they do so also in the assurance that their children will be afforded opportunities to progress intellectually and morally beyond the confines of the past in which the parents themselves have been penned. The politics of this model – such as they are – are undoubtedly hierarchical and paternalistic, but they function on the basis of a rational communitarian consensus, Owen insists, rather than legalistic duress. While hardly liberal in the later sense of that term, they represent a major advance on the norms of pre- and early industrial society.

The wider imagining of community life and domestic relations attempted in the Third Essay is perhaps most clearly revealed in Owen's comments on the place of recreation and leisure in the formation of character across the generations. Ratcheting up the subtle yet pervasive anti-Christian sentiment that runs throughout *A New View*, Owen is typically scathing about the hypocrisies of the Christian Sabbath, which he boldly condemns for its entirely ineffective contribution to working-class rest as well as for its production of 'superstitious gloom and tyranny over the mind' (1.59). In its place, he advocates what he argues is a much richer philosophy of recreation, securely integrated into the textures of working and domestic life. While fully enlightened in its conception – and, indeed, quite possibly one of Owen's most genuinely original contributions to educational thought and practice – Owen's understanding of recreation must again be seen in its industrial context. Casually acknowledging, for example, that even in the relatively benign conditions of New Lanark, his employees were expected to work 'ten hours and three-quarters every day in the week except Sunday,' Owen describes 'rooms for innocent amusements and rational recreation' (1.60) as part of the management of community space and the regulation of the cycles of community time. Instead of a desiccated sabbatarianism, he recommends regular participation in recreational and self-improving activities set within the established rhythms of work and rest. Recreation is for Owen not simply abstention from labor, it is part of the endless, inescapable formation of character; an education for adults beyond 'the proper season for instruction' (1.66), understood in expressly moral developmental terms: 'It has been and ever will be found far more easy to lead mankind to virtue, or to rational conduct, by providing them with well-regulated innocent amusements and recreations, than by forcing them to submit to useless restraints' (1.60). There is perhaps an unavoidable tendency for contemporary critical hermeneutics to interpret these proposals as part of the coming of what Frederic Jameson has called the 'bourgeois cultural revolution' (Jameson 1981: 152–153) with its complex internalization of the disciplinary regulation of potentially subversive subjectivities through the intimate technologies of the self, such as recreation and entertainment. Lifelong education combines with a ration of leisure in this structure to reproduce the docile, compliant, consuming subjects upon which the free market system would soon come to depend. It is perhaps inevitable that a veil of some such suspicion is cast repeatedly over the New Lanark experiment, and the intended Owenite programs distilled from it, particularly in view of the subsequent evolution of the sinister instruments of social control in later industrial society (McGillivray 2005). It is nevertheless possible for this vigilance towards Owen's account of recreation to exist alongside a more optimistic appreciation of his theory of community, especially when contrasted with the dismal alternatives with which Owen had in his own era to contend. The centerpiece of Owen's understanding of leisure is, of course, the Institute for the Formation of Character, with everything this implies about community self-organization, intergenerational communication and lifelong learning to repeal 'ignorant association and erroneous instruction' (1.66). Owen's comments on recreation in the Third Essay include perhaps his sternest denunciations of the perpetuation of error by the existing institutions of government and Church. The rescue that children may be offered from this malaise by a reformist education is not readily available to their parents, he suggests. But if filial harmony is to be maintained and estrangement avoided, then the practices of recreation must be organized in such a manner as to broaden adult horizons in ways parallel to the liberation afforded children by properly enlightened schooling: '[. . .] an education for the untaught and ill-taught becomes of the first importance to the welfare of society; and it is this which has influenced all the arrangements connected with the New Institution' (1.63).

Interestingly, the juxtaposition Owen makes of adults and children, education and recreation, work and leisure, the ill-taught and the untaught, operates in each case in two directions. Hence in concluding his observations on recreation, Owen translates some of the key insights derived from the ongoing formation of adult rationality and well-being through the constructive uses of adult leisure time, back to the domains of the child and the school. Just as the Institute for the Formation of Character is not simply a school for adults, so also the school, operating within the orbit of the Institute's experiments in recreation, acquires by its proximity to the Institute further insights into the practices of effective learning and teaching and successful moral development beyond any narrowly performative conceptions of learning and teaching. This explains many of the departures in the New Lanark curriculum and methodology from, for example, even the standard, relatively innovative Lancastrian styles of pedagogy. One important consequence of this subtle cross-fertilization of recreation and education in the Third Essay is the enhancement of the status of children as full members of the community:

> It is much to be regretted that the strength and capacity of the minds of children are yet unknown [. . .] if they were never taught to acquire error, they would speedily exhibit such powers of mind, as would convince the most incredulous how much the human intellect has been injured by the ignorance of former and present treatment.
>
> (1.65)

It is not an exaggeration to suggest that the much-vaunted traditions of child-centered education stretch back, at least within the British tradition, to this passionately-held belief of Owen in the potential of the unencumbered intellect of the child, placed in an enlightened community of learning, to reach the highest levels of academic achievement and emotional and moral fulfillment. No teaching strategy, no curriculum content, no assessment system, no matter how enlightened, can by itself, in Owen's view, fully exhaust the wealth of this insight into the truth of human nature. It demands, instead, a wholesale realignment of the resources of society to eradicate the damaging legacy of the past and to surround the young with people and practices unswervingly committed to a rational understanding of their needs and susceptibilities. When this is accomplished, 'there is not one member of the great family of the world, from the highest to the lowest, that will not benefit from its public promulgation' (1.69). For it is through the young that a future can most confidently be forged untainted by the mistaken dogmas of history. Nothing less than the thoroughgoing transformation of society, Owen declares, will result from this discovery. In a concluding declamatory restatement of his central claims, rhetorically crafted as a resounding series of propositions purposely soliciting from his readers either immediate acceptance or refutation, Owen recapitulates the entire moral and educational psychology of *A New View*. His intention at this juncture is to take the abstractions of the empiricist and necessitarian worldviews with which he began and condense them into a succinct, persuasive account of human nature and a viable program of educational and social reform within the capabilities of his elite readership to implement. All through the Third Essay, Owen has been in the background cleverly refining his idea of a target audience, which now emerges from the shadows of his argument to be complemented on the foresight and imagination it shares with the author: '[…] those individuals of every rank and class and denomination of society, who have become conscious of the errors in which they exist […] who are ardently desirous of discovering and following truth wherever it may lead […]' (1.75). This is the alliance of the politically courageous and the intellectually informed to which Owen then proceeds to direct his concluding address, in a final sustained effort to bridge the gap between aspiration and realization in the building of his new system.

Political economy

Owen's intention in the Fourth Essay of *A New View of Society* is to bring to its culmination a theme present throughout the work: galvanizing the decision-makers and opinion-formers among his readership in order to secure the sorts of changes in government policy that will enable the expansion across Britain of the social and educational innovations introduced at New Lanark and urgently needed by the whole country. In one respect, this attempt by Owen to win influential allies repeats a pattern familiar from all of his efforts as a businessman and philanthropist. But it is fair to say that Owen's outstanding commercial triumphs, and even his achievements as a local social reformer, were never matched in his lifetime by a corresponding political success. There were many reasons for this, not least the inherently corrupt character of the political systems of his age. Only marginally less significant, however, in explaining his relative political failure is what is perhaps best understood as a lack of political judgment in his many engagements with the realm of public affairs. Owen's essays, pamphlets, and civic exhortations can often sound shrill in tone, browbeating his readership into agreement with what he repeatedly maintains are self-evident truths and often impatiently dismissing the benighted beliefs of those obtusely incapable of seeing the obvious sense of his analyses and his solutions. As a result, the eventual effect of prolonged exposure to Owen's energetic and ornately rhetorical style as a writer and agitator can too easily turn to exhaustion and not the assent he craves – a response often associated with the effects of propaganda rather than persuasion. The Fourth Essay for the most part evades the defects of tone and register which mar his later work, largely because its political aspirations are so openly indebted to the ideas of William Godwin and to a general trend in reformist English writing which commanded the respect of much mainstream opinion of the period by navigating skillfully between flattering the political elites and admonishing them (Richardson 1994, pp. 48–64). There are nonetheless intervals throughout *A New View*, not least in its thinly-disguised contempt for Christianity, where its hectoring, repetitious reproaches come close to robbing the argument of genuine moral force, as a result alienating key sections of its intended readership.

The tenor of direct address to government apparent in the Fourth Essay is a reflection of Owen's conviction that the self-evident truths of his system required only statutory endorsement in order quickly to achieve all of its goals. Owen is typically vague on the precise legislative actions needed to put his principles into wider national practice, opting instead to win the support of politicians by entreating them, somewhat indistinctly, to respond courageously to a moment of supreme historic opportunity:

The important knowledge to which we allude is, 'That the old collectively may train the young collectively, to be ignorant and miserable, or to be intelligent and happy' [...] Fortunate will be that government which shall first acquire this knowledge in theory, and adopt it in practice.

(1.77–78)

In keeping with the styles of radical prose circulating in progressive British movements of the time, Owen carefully combines this exhortatory tactic, with its appeal to the supposedly enlightened instincts of policy-makers, with a more genuinely portentous language, warning the elites of the dire consequences of inaction and the likely outbreak of serious social unrest if nothing is done. In a pervasively revolutionary era, this discourse, when properly applied, undoubtedly possessed real political purchase. Britain had moved through a decade of extreme social tension, exacerbated by a prolonged war with a revolutionary opponent, and countered with often fierce domestic repression. Owen's perspective on the pressures of his age diverges in key respects from the standard radical or progressive analyses of his contemporaries by returning again and again to the central hypothesis of *A New View*: that the causes of, and the solutions to, the present crisis lie not in electoral change but in the proper understanding of character development and the role of national education in reforming it.

It is easy to see how this was interpreted by some as a naïve and simplistic assessment of the problems confronting the systems of representation in Britain. It is also easy to appreciate why it provoked the ire of those who felt that it lacked any serious insight into the nature of economic inequality in the early capitalist mode of production. Accepting the gravity of these reservations, however, ought not to compromise entirely our recognition of the radicalism of Owen's demands. Owen is uninhibited in pointing to both the severity of the threats facing the social order and their origins in 'ignorance, proceeding from the errors which have been impressed on the minds of the present generation by its predecessors; and chiefly by that *greatest of all errors, the notion that individuals form their own characters*' (1.78). There is little deference to tradition in this claim, still less an obvious respect for hierarchy. Owen blames unreservedly the existing structures of moral and political authority for the present crisis of poverty and injustice in Britain and is scathing in his denunciation of the role of cherished British institutions such as the establishment of the Church of England and the Poor Laws in perpetuating want. Similarly, the tasks Owen sets in the Fourth Essay for his imagined system of national education have their own marked and particular radicalism, difficult to resolve fully into conventional models of economic amelioration and social reconciliation. 'Human nature,' Owen declares in one of his boldest statements of empiricist universalism, '[...] is one and the same in all; it is without exception universally plastic, and by judicious training *the infants of any one class in the world may be readily formed into men of any other class* [...]' (1.84). Owen's educational thought is often accused of lacking any credible class analysis, but comments such as these show a recognition that all forms of social organization are arbitrary and acquired, reinforcing his idealist view that effective education could remedy the asymmetries of social power merely by exposing their baselessness (Claeys 1989, pp. 170–174). This belief places Owen's educational thought squarely in a materialist understanding of culture, in which one of the purposes of learning is to unmask the ideological maneuvers by which arbitrary, unjust social arrangements are made to seem inevitable and immutable. This particular illusion of culture is to be dispelled, Owen argues, by the introduction into the education of the young of a '*system without mystery*,' from initiation into which future generations will learn to apply to the ordering of society an untarnished critical rationality, 'equal to the accomplishment of the most grand and beneficial purposes' (1.85). There is, arguably, incalculable revolutionary potential in this.

The 'system without mystery' is to be realized, Owen urges, only by government accepting its responsibility to provide a structure of national education covering all classes and stations of children. Once again, Owen largely sidesteps consideration of the difficult legislative procedures by which such an ambitious goal is to be achieved, preferring to dwell upon the strengths and limitations of the existing progressive initiatives of Bell, Lancaster, and the Quaker, Samuel Whitbread. While acknowledging 'that these new systems are an improvement on the modes of instruction that were formerly practised' (1.86), Owen sternly reprimands Bell and Whitbread because of the obviously Christian underpinning of their movements for national popular education. This leads Owen into some of his most daring (if unguarded) criticisms of orthodox Christian doctrine, on the basis of its fundamental incompatibility with the empiricist truths of character formation:

Let us then in this spirit openly declare to the Church, that a national unexclusive plan of education for the poor will, without the shadow of doubt, destroy all the errors which are attached to the various systems; and that, when this plan shall be fully established, not one of the tenets which is in opposition to facts can long be upheld.

(1.90)

Controversial assertions of this kind seemed hardly likely to win support for Owen's program for a still largely Christian House of Commons, regardless of the token gestures made in the essay to a kind of deistic ecumenism, prepared – but only reluctantly – to see the merits in all religious denominations provided their tedious and delusory creeds were stripped away.

Even Lancaster, however, despite Owen's preference for his marginally more secularized model, is rebuked for what Owen considers to be the unnecessarily rigid and sterile aspects of his methods, including the excessive emphasis on rote learning and the accumulation of facts, a 'mockery of learning' (1.87), 'debasing man to a mere irrational military machine which is to be rapidly moved by animal force' (1.92). The rejection of these elements of Lancaster's pedagogy does not lead Owen towards an exclusively process-based concept of learning of the type prized in much subsequent twentieth-century 'child-centered' educational theory. On the contrary, the responsibility for character formation demands, Owen restates, that education address the 'matter of instruction' (1.93) ahead of the 'manner,' because 'the first is the means only; the last the end to be accomplished by those means' (1.87). While the content of learning and teaching must for Owen extend well beyond the leaden positivism of memorization for its own sake, it must nevertheless maintain an irreducible core of curricular knowledge, founded upon empirical truth, if the goal of liberated rationality is to be attained. The indisputable facts of humanity's condition, the modes by which it apprehends reality and the potential in all of this for building personal autonomy and a heightened form of fraternity across classes and cultures, constitute the curricular heart of education. Taken together, they require a quite prescriptive organization of the forms of knowledge for subsequent mediation to schoolchildren. It is on the basis of such knowledge that future generations will be released from the superstitions of the past and molded in ways that maximize the human potential for perfection. The main role of government in the realization of these ambitious, multifarious goals is to provide the resources not simply for a national system of schools, but, much more importantly, for a national network of training institutions – or what Owen revealingly terms 'seminaries' – in which a new breed of teachers will be prepared for the delivery to pupils of the radical new philosophy of learning:

> The training of those who are to form the future man, becomes a consideration of the utmost magnitude; for, on due reflection, it will appear, that instruction to the young must be, of necessity, the only foundation upon which the superstructure of society can be raised. Let [...] the instruction to the young be well devised and well executed, and no subsequent proceedings in the state can be materially injurious.
>
> (1.93)

His comments on his intended 'seminaries' represent what is probably the single most practical suggestion to emerge from *A New View*, one which Owen subsequently, if fruitlessly, spent much of his energy and resources trying to bring about. In certain respects, it prefigures the initiatives in teacher education which emerged later in the century, some of them with the older Owen's full endorsement. In other respects, however, the sheer scale of the anticipated undertaking, and its departure from the confusion of existing practice, place it among Owen's most utopian ideas, highlighting the ironic ways in which the system promoted in *A New View* mimics the organized religions that Owen otherwise so scornfully disparages. It was perhaps Owen's fate in the essays and elsewhere to underestimate the disorder of the early industrial educational system, trapped as it was in a transitional phase between two thoroughly irreconcilable conceptions of society, and to overestimate the resources and reach of government in a still only nascent technological age.

In the closing stages of the Fourth Essay, the powerful theme of necessitarian optimism running like a current through all of Owen's reflections, assumes its greatest prominence. Owen's devotion to the 'wonder-working power' of a population educated in 'unlimited benevolence' (1.93) engages forcefully in these breathless passages with some of the most pessimistic, regressive political philosophies with which the London radicals such as Place and Godwin had been locked in decades of conflict. The key oppositional figure in these disputes was the legendary Thomas Malthus, the father of the science of political economy and the target of much radical antagonism. Malthus had defended implacably the untrammeled laissez-faire free market economic system, explaining it as a complex, optimally self-regulating mechanism which, by uncompromising laws such as the starvation of excess populations, perpetuated its own existence and maximized the wealth of the nation. By Owen's time, Malthus had become an almost stereotypical hate-figure for progressive opinion; caricatured as a fierce critic of Godwinian optimism and as an allegedly heartless apologist for the economic and social logic of the capitalist mode of production (Hilton 2006, pp. 342–346). Of course, part of the hostility excited by Malthus' ideas stemmed from his cunning use of precisely the same principles of empiricist psychology and deterministic ethics employed by Godwin and his followers. It is often forgotten in the standard histories of British political economy that Malthus initially presented himself as a radical and a materialist, bravely disclosing to squeamish public opinion the important, hitherto overlooked roles of basic physical human needs such as nourishment, reproduction, and sexual instinct in the determination of all motivation and behavior (Dean 1995). Indeed, it is no small irony that the sternest critics of Malthusian determinism, including distinguished literary figures such as Robert Southey and William Hazlitt, also subsequently turned their withering skepticism on Owen's schemes and for precisely the same reasons – their dismay at the mechanistic view of human behavior underpinning each.

Owen's treatment of Malthus in the Fourth Essay of *A New View* is much more measured than either that of Godwin himself or that of the later Romantics who attacked Godwin and Malthus in equal measure. Owen's reference to Malthus is brief, and it may reflect his reading of the MP and political economist, David Ricardo, with whom he maintained a correspondence and towards whose labor theory of value he grew increasingly sympathetic as a corrective to Malthus' relentless laws of supply and demand. Owen's response is to recognize that Malthus is:

> correct, when he says that the population of the world is ever adapting itself to the quantity of food raised for its support; but he has not told us how much more food an intelligent and industrious people will create from the same soil, than will be produced by one ignorant and ill-governed. It is, however, as one to infinity. For man knows not the limit to his power of creating food.
>
> (1.96)

The secret, once again, in this subtle reworking of Malthus, is education. It is, for Owen, education that is the missing term in the sometimes brutal analysis offered by political economy. Owen is perfectly willing to endorse an assessment of social conditions that points unequivocally to 'circumstances' as the major determinants of human choice. He also warms to a boldly materialist definition of the character of man. But he is not willing to see the given circumstances of the age as anything other than the arbitrary products of diminished versions of human possibility, reproduced across the generations, and perfectly susceptible to transformation under the influence of properly directed education. It is not simply the capacity for food production that the educated polity has the ability to revolutionize beyond the limits set by Malthusian economics, it is every feature of the bounded, circumscribed, fatalistic understanding of the world and humanity's place within it:

> All men may, by judicious and proper laws and training, readily acquire knowledge and habits which will enable them, if they be permitted, to produce far more than they need for their support and enjoyment: and thus any population [...] may be taught to live in plenty and in happiness, without the checks of vice and misery.
>
> (1.96)

The vocabulary of this passage near the end of *A New View of Society*, with its Romantic economics of abundance, and its telling references to 'training,' 'habits' and what 'may be taught,' serves to underscore not only the huge measures of hope invested by Owen throughout the work in the practices of popular education, but also to confirm his absolute faith that the embrace of education as he uniquely understood and defended it would extend human capabilities beyond anything imaginable to his own or previous generations.

Chapter 4

The Education of Citizens in the Just Society

The production of knowledge

Despite the comparatively limited impact of *A New View of Society* on its intended readership of politicians and business leaders, it is clear that the four essays placed Owen and his thought for a time in the mainstream of the volatile intellectual debates surrounding the future direction of industrial Britain. There is no doubt that Owen sincerely believed that his key claims in *A New View* had come to him from first-principle reflections upon experience and from his practical decision-making as a commercial manager and reformer. Some of his contemporaries scoffed at this, including several of his sympathizers, and the roots of his thought in general long-term trends of Enlightenment philosophy – however obscurely these had actually been mediated to him – seemed plainly visible. The most obvious continuities appeared to be with the writings of William Godwin and, through him, with the ideas of earlier eighteenth-century necessitarians such as Condorcet and Helvétius. Harold Silver has pointed out that the evidence of Godwin's influence on Owen is paradoxical. While there are passages in *A New View* in particular that strongly echo the phrasing of Godwin's most important text, *Political Justice* (some of which may actually be attributable, of course, to Godwin's editorial hand in Owen's manuscript), there are significant differences between the two men (Silver 1965, pp. 84–90). Godwin was firmly committed to the view that:

> We bring into the world with us no innate principles: consequently we are neither virtuous nor vicious as we first come into existence [...] From these reasonings it sufficiently appears, that the moral qualities of men are the produce of the impressions made upon them [...]
>
> (Godwin 1993, 3.10, 13)

However, he retained from his critical reading of Helvétius a stronger sense of the irreducible characteristics of the self on which these circumstances must operate. Similarly, while remaining passionately committed to the ideals of mass popular education, the strongly anarchist tendencies in Godwin's thought saw him oppose a system administered by government, on the grounds that 'Government will not fail to employ it, to strengthen its hands, and perpetuate its institutions' (3.359). The prospect of lifelong learning – repeatedly highlighted by Owen as a cornerstone of his scheme – Godwin had earlier reviled in *Political Justice* as a device by which the plutocracy running Britain would defuse revolutionary tension by retaining the population in 'a state of perpetual pupillage' (3.358). While sharing wholeheartedly Owen's belief in the untold potential of unfettered rationality, Godwin remained much more of an individualist than Owen, fearful of his younger disciple's domineering inclinations, and much more convinced than Owen that the motivation to learn sprang from the deepest desires of the human heart and required always to stay in touch with those appetites if education was to succeed in its aims.

Ironically, there is some circumstantial evidence that the specifically political dimensions of Owen's educational thought may have been shaped more by the writings of Godwin's remarkable wife than by Godwin himself. Mary Wollstonecraft's *A Vindication of the Rights of Woman* of 1796 appears along with *Political Justice* in some of the bibliographical notices of the Manchester Philosophical Society. We cannot be certain even from this that Owen had any detailed knowledge of it, but we do know from correspondence of Fanny Imlay, Wollstonecraft's daughter by a previous relationship, that Owen esteemed Wollstonecraft's ideas and, had she been alive, believed she 'would have warmly [...] entered into his plans.' (Stocking 1995: 56). Fanny's remark references something typically self-aggrandizing about Owen's relationship to possible precursors, but it is fascinating to note that in two important chapters of *A Vindication*, Wollstonecraft refracted the standard Helvetian perspective on education very much in terms with which Owen would have identified. 'So ductile is the understanding,' she noted, rejecting even rationality as an innate idea, 'that the associations which depend on adventitious circumstances [...]'

can seldom be disentangled by reason' (Wollstonecraft 2008, p. 192). Her defense of the extension of the educational entitlements of girls also takes her deep into territory Owen would have considered the heartlands of his argument, denouncing the rote learning or 'parrot-like prattle' (p. 247) conventionally offered to females in schools and demanding that their education be enlarged to include proper social interaction, recreation, and moral deliberation (Laird 2008, pp. 109–138).

The proximity of these great thinkers to Owen's ideas depends less upon a notion of direct influence – which it seems all but impossible to map – and more upon a larger sense of the climate of opinion into which the composition of *A New View of Society*, in particular, had plunged Owen and at the center of which he for a time assumed a genuine importance. Alignment with figures of the stature of Godwin and Wollstonecraft may have gratified Owen, but it was no substitute for the political recognition for which he yearned and which he believed would be the cardinal means of achieving his ends on a truly national platform. As we have seen from a recurring pattern in his biography, disappointments at a national level did not deter Owen for long, however, and he drew considerable esteem from the groups and networks in early nineteenth-century Britain that did respond positively to his ideas, conscious that the movements among which his writings were starting to circulate had longer-term ambitions and were beginning to find openings for their initiatives in alternative extra-parliamentary organizations such as the fledgling trade unions and friendly societies. The effect of this pattern of response to his ideas was undoubtedly to radicalize Owen, while at the same time urging him on to the redoubling of his efforts to find sympathetic collaborators for the actualization of his plans. His educational thought, in consequence, entered more fully and challengingly into what he revealingly termed 'the science of political economy' (Owen 1993b, 1.288) foreshadowed at the end of *A New View of Society*.

The occasion for Owen's use of this pregnant phrase was his 1821 document, *A Report to the County of Lanark*. This was the result of Owen's protracted exchanges of 1819–1820 with the hard-pressed Commissioners of Supply of the County of Lanark, the body responsible for trying to deal with the intense post-war pressures of poverty, crime, and mounting social unrest among the working classes of the wider county in which New Lanark was itself located. Ian Donnachie has rightly described the *Report* as Owen's 'most famous economic thesis' (Donnachie 2005a, p. 186) and it is therefore illuminating to see how the increased sophistication of Owen's economic analysis shapes the specifically educational elements of his proposed remedies for the ills confronting the region of Scotland in which he lived and worked. The shift of focus from national, centralized political planning to a more locally-based and indigenous form of sustainable community of course retains at its centre the experience of New Lanark, reinforced by Owen's enthusiasm for the then fashionable 'spade-husbandry' form of intensive agriculture, a measure introduced into several areas of Britain after the Napoleonic Wars in order to provide work for the long-term unemployed. Despite the primary purpose of the *Report* being economic rather than strictly educational, Owen makes it clear in the third 'head' of his text that the management and functioning of the self-sustaining communities through the adoption of which the Lanark County authorities might hope to mitigate the present economic crisis must include at their heart 'arrangements [...] for training and educating the children' (1.304).

Owen's commentary on education in the *Report* appears at first sight to commence from the same fundamental principles articulated in *A New View*: that 'all human knowledge has been acquired, through the evidence of the senses' and 'that men may now possess a most extensive control over those circumstances which affect the infant after birth; and that, as far as such circumstances can influence the human character [...] the rising generations may become [...] whatever men now desire them to be [...]' (1.316–317). Almost immediately, however, Owen introduces into his theory a modulation of his core hypothesis that accords significantly greater prominence to the 'natural qualities' of infants than anything in his previous writings. In a quite startling – and to modern temperaments, perhaps disturbing – departure from the empiricist purism of *A New View*, Owen goes on to argue that the identification of these qualities in the very young 'will give to men the same kind of control over the combination of the natural powers and faculties of infants, as they now possess over the formation of animals.' He then proceeds to anticipate a time 'not perhaps far distant' when it may be possible 'to improve the breed of men, more than men have yet improved the breed of domestic animals' (1.317). The radical naturalism of these statements is, it must be acknowledged, not central to the overall educational argument of the *Report*, which swiftly resumes its standard Owenite logic in insisting that man 'does not possess the smallest control over the formation of any of his own faculties or powers' (1.318). It is also perfectly conceivable that the unprecedented concession Owen makes here to a kind of bedrock of animal innateness at odds with strict empiricism can be traced both to his interaction with Godwin and, more calculatingly, to his reading of the predispositions of his audience, always likely to be suspicious of 'blank slate' theorizing. Nevertheless, the observations undoubtedly resonate with other trends in Owenite social experimentation, such as its controversial encouragement of birth control and the later indirect association of Owenite socialism with the science of eugenics. (Waller 2001).

Owen, of course, would have balked at any suggestion that his perception of the relationship of nature to environment could be used to sanction the elimination of unfit populations or coercively to breed racially superior forms of human beings. Indeed, the direction of his argument in the *Report*, beyond these passing conjectures, inclines heavily towards his entrenched view that 'circumstances can influence human character,' while the biological imagery moves once again towards a familiar Owenite metaphor in its suggestion that the education of the young ought to ensure that 'the children shall be trained together as though they were literally all of one family' (1.317). This understanding of family solidarity held immense power for Owen, partly because of what he considered to be the role of flourishing family units in the commercial and social success of New Lanark and partly because of his wider, instinctive defense of the extended kinship network as a preindustrial bulwark against the ethically corrosive effects of the factory system. This was true even at those junctures where Owen rejected the perceived inertia and oppressiveness of the patriarchal family institution. The continuities between family, infancy, education, and work are more pronounced in the *Report* than in *A New View*, largely because of the later text's overarching concern with questions of economic and labor reform.

Alongside a restatement of the principles of character formation, the *Report* emphasizes the acquisition of 'useful knowledge through the means of sensible signs' as the most effective means to cultivate the 'powers of reflection and judgement' in the young:

> This mode of instruction is founded in nature, and will supersede the present defective and tiresome system of book learning, which is ill-calculated to give either pleasure or instruction to the minds of children [...] [who] will, with ease and delight, acquire more real knowledge in a day, than they have yet attained under the old system in many months.
>
> (1.320)

The citation of 'real knowledge,' in contrast with learning derived from academic study, is here accorded its strongest bond yet in Owen's thought with the experience of work, including the requirement for children to 'be trained to fill every office and to perform every duty that the well-being of their associates and the establishments can require' (1.320). Again, it is possible that there is a strong element of premeditation involved here, as Owen seeks cleverly to sell his educational proposals to local political and commercial interests preoccupied by the social dislocation brought on by economic recession and unemployment. This is not to diminish the genuine affinity Owen saw between education and the broader patterns of community life such as labor, productivity, and recreation, but it does place this connection firmly within the ambit of his overriding view of the formation of character and, indeed, his deepening understanding of the role of education in remodeling a failed political and economic system seemingly bound to endemic poverty and cyclic recession: 'It is only by education, rightly understood, that communities of men can ever be well governed, and by means of such education, every object of human society will be attained with the least labour and the most satisfaction' (1.320).

While 'It is obvious' to Owen 'that training and education must be viewed as intimately connected with the employment of the association' (1.320), this is for him inseparable from the *transformed* understanding of work that will result from a proper recognition of its relationship to character and learning. Rejecting the prevailing view inherent in the factory system – and derived from Adam Smith – of 'a minute division of labour and a division of interests' (1.320), Owen also dismisses any narrow vocationalism satisfied with nothing more than the attainment of basic literacy and numeracy preparatory to employment. In its place, he advocates an enriched and integrated conception of education in which labor and learning interact dynamically with one another, constantly extending the frontiers of knowledge and critical rationality within the individual and the community as whole. Book learning is spurned in this context, it must be stressed, not out of a hostility to books as such, but because of the crippling uses made of books by ineffective teaching methods implicitly designed to induce in learners mindless memorization and uncritical submission to received opinion.

The fresh synergy of education and work envisaged by Owen promises by contrast to confer upon the laboring poor, he declares,

> giant powers compared with those which the working class or any other now possesses. There would at once be an end of all mere animal machines [. . .] Instead of the unhealthy pointer of a pin [. . .] without understanding or rational reflection, there would spring up a working class full of activity and useful knowledge, with habits, information, manners and dispositions that would place the lowest in the scale many degrees above the best of any class which has yet been formed by the circumstances of past or present society.
>
> (1.321)

The repudiation of 'animal machines' represents one of Owen's sharpest criticisms of the dehumanizing effects of the capitalist mode of production at its most mechanistic. It is also an angry reproach to pedagogical methods that deliberately replicate the procedures of the factory system in the schooling of the young of almost all classes. Owen brings out clearly here his view that education as a social practice cannot be isolated from the wider values of a culture, or from the other institutions of political economy through which these values are expressed (Gallagher 2009). An economic philosophy impassively reliant upon the reduction of human labor to the functioning of 'animal machines' is likely to engender an education system premised upon parallel calculations of performative efficiency, in which the measurement of input-output ratios entirely effaces the humanity of the producing class in the schoolroom as on the factory floor. Many decades into the nineteenth century, Marx and Engels were to draw similar conclusions about the deleterious effects of capitalism in precipitating the 'alienation' of the proletariat from the fruits of its own labor and in similarly blighting every social institution rooted in such a dysfunctional process of production. The challenge issued at the end of *A New View* to resist the minimalism and fatalism of the Malthusian version of political economy in many respects presages Marx, disavowing Malthus' definition of both the limits to growth and the restrictions on the human potential to master the brute facts of nature. Owen pursues it with still greater energy in these concluding arguments of the *Report*, where the key audience is precisely the owning class most likely to be in thrall to the seemingly unalterable Malthusian laws of scarcity and surplus, supply and demand. Owen's rhetoric is once more quite deliberately crafted to counter the pervasive defeatism of orthodox political economy as he saw it, without detaching itself unrealistically from the tangible problems of unemployment and deprivation confronting the Lanark commissioners. The discourse of the *Report* tirelessly recapitulates the classic Owenite belief in the untapped potential of new social alignments – most especially new approaches to education – for maximizing prosperity and for planting firmly the powers of 'rational being' in areas hitherto regarded as outside the boundaries of human capability. It is this capacity of enlightened education to prefigure forms of community, morality, production, and knowledge that society otherwise cannot yet fully foresee that perhaps represents Owen's most radical protest against the debilitating social and economic structures by which he and his contemporaries were, he believed, hemmed in.

Visionary rationalism

In the growing social and economic crisis of the 1820s, destined to culminate in the political emergency of the 1832 Great Reform Act,

Owen's thought began to move in what might be termed more genuinely visionary directions. This idealist strain was perhaps always present in his work and it was certainly a vital dimension of the powerfully Romantic sentiments of the revolutionary era, which exercised such an important influence over changing cultural perceptions of childhood, education, and social equality. At the same time, even as Owen's grip upon the New Lanark venture began to loosen, and his audiences became more openly partisan and self-selecting in pressurizing for his policies, he lost little of his awareness of the material realities in which his multiple economic and educational schemes were grounded. The New Harmony project in America, and the time and resources it profligately consumed, is perhaps the clearest illustration of this. It existed, however, alongside other bold attempts to replicate the New Lanark successes, as well as a concerted campaign of publications, public meetings, petitions, and associations designed to advance the case for searching educational reform (Yeo 1971). This peculiar combination of factors is significant to any lasting assessment of the realism of Owen's plans. It is tempting to cast him as a Romantic dreamer, repeatedly projecting impossibly idealistic proposals never likely to take root as enduring practical undertakings. Alternatively, it is sometimes easy to view him as essentially a failure, whose practical endeavors in social and educational improvement, with the conspicuous if relatively short-lived exception of New Lanark, repeatedly proved economically unsustainable.

It is certainly the case that in later publications and pronouncements, Owen adopted an increasingly prophetic register, heavily imbued with a kind of 'secular millenarianism.' This discourse anticipated a sudden transformation of society, already inaugurated, it implied, by the dramatic breakthroughs in science, technology – and even politics – that nineteenth-century people could see unfolding all around them (Harrison 1969, pp. 92–103). It is clear, of course, that millenarianism was a significant strand in Owen's thought almost from his first public appearances, with obscure origins in his evangelical Protestant heritage and its traditions of Christian enthusiasm. It is also true that the more consistently 'vatic' features of Owen's rhetoric made themselves felt most powerfully in his wider estimations of the future of society as a whole rather than in his detailed resolutions for practical educational reform. Here they found an obvious echo in the revolutionary sentiments of the age. Nevertheless, in a classically Owenite text of the 1830s, composed in just this style and ardently entitled *The Address of Robert Owen...Denouncing the Old System of the World, and Announcing the Commencement of the New* (and published in Owen's own newspaper, *The Crisis*, in May 1833), it is again the institutions of education that assume most prominence in the intended program for wholesale social renewal (Owen 1993h, 2.224–231).

The prophetic – even apocalyptic – tone of the *Address* is evident from its outset, with its declamatory language of 'announcing' and 'commencement,' as if Owen had come to believe that his own public speaking had itself become a catalyst for the metamorphosis to which he looked forward. The same attitude, bordering at times on the histrionic, is continued in the series of 'declarations' that form the backbone of the speech and the second of which is Owen's presentation to his audience of the so-called 'Religion of Truth': a faith to replace all previous 'false religions' and 'the only one that can conduct man to the practice of pure charity and real virtue [...]' (2.225). The new religion in fact represents an elaborate consolidation of the empiricist and necessitarian doctrines evident in Owen's social theory from its inception. But there is no doubt that adoption of both the posture of the prophet and the discourse of credal assent (the very phrasing of the speech echoes the cadences of the Christian creed), lends tremendous moral urgency to the demand for change – as well as quite probably fulfilling a hieratic impulse always latent in Owen's personal philosophy and sense of mission. Creeds require catechists and the truths of the new faith are to be imparted to infants by parents and teachers with all the force of 'laws of nature.' Equally, in order 'to new form the general character of the rising generation, and to regenerate the existing adult population,' arrangements must be made for the creation of 'New Institutions' (2.226) through which the entirely refashioned approach to education and society will be implemented and regulated. The template for this particular proposal is obviously the Institute for the Formation of Character at New Lanark, reflecting the increasingly iconic role the building had assumed in Owen's thinking. Owen goes much further in the *Address*, however, quite purposely positioning the anticipated work of numerous such institutions within a boldly religious, indeed biblical, frame of reference, extending so far as to predict that 'the period is near at hand when the minds of men must be born again; when they shall no longer see as through a glass darkly [...]' (2.226–227). The somewhat overblown scriptural allusions in this language would have been manifest to Owen's original audience, perhaps confirming for many of his supporters (not to mention some of his opponents) that Owenism as a broad historical movement was quite self-consciously evolving into a complete post-confessional belief system, a secular or replacement religion apposite to the necessitarian and scientific age, where all previous superstition would be eventually dispelled and the zeal of religious enthusiasm properly directed at last to the material and ethical improvement of humanity. The 'superior education from birth' available in this new, secular era would, Owen promised, 'render the succeeding generations a superior order of beings compared with those who have hitherto lived' (2.227) and deliver the long-sought moral objectives of 'charity, peace and good-will' pursued universally by the higher religions:

The new mode of forming the character of the children of the new world will cultivate, and bring forth to maturity and perfection, all the physical, intellectual and moral faculties and powers which have been given to human nature. Arrangements will be formed to admit and encourage the due exercise of each of these [...] for it is only by all of them being called into action at the period designed by nature, that man can feel satisfied, contented and happy.

(2.229)

We see documented in this important, idiosyncratic text, a revealing transition in Owen's thought, which carries his still essentially Enlightenment convictions forward into the era of nineteenth-century progress, when the strides made in industrial technology and even political representation persuaded many in Britain that a new era of unprecedented material advancement had dawned. The history of ideas rarely falls into easily sequenced phases of development in which any given generation can see its own favored or implicit worldviews transparently anticipated by its forebears. For this reason, historians have in recent decades questioned the whole notion of an unproblematic Victorian belief in progress corresponding to the decline of Christian attachment and fuelled by the rise of science and the extension of the democratic franchise. Commentators have underlined the persistence of religious faith in nineteenth-century British society, as well as the endurance of patterns of association and deference with an ancestry in the deep values of pre-industrial culture. Similarly, although the phenomenon of nineteenth-century religious doubt is widely acknowledged, attention has been drawn to the importance of evangelical revivals and the vitality of religious organizations such as Sunday Schools and temperance movements in preserving the influence of the Christian Churches over the everyday moral fabric of the nation (Von Arx 1985; Smith 2007). A text such as Owen's *Address*, sitting on the cusp of the Victorian age, testifies to the ambiguities in any meaningful account of progress in the first stages of the industrial era. Owen's religious imagery may well be a partial disguise, employed strategically to exploit sentiments still very much a part of the culture in which he lived and to direct them pragmatically to the tasks of social improvement. That said, however, the lecture represents a key shift in the development of a longstanding tradition of dissenting religious protest, quite openly offloading the supposedly superfluous dogmatic theology of the Christian faith while seeking to retain the force of its underlying moral demands and the challenge of its chiliastic call for the total renewal of the world. We might legitimately conclude, then, that despite any serious qualifications we may wish to place around its historical assumptions, Owen's *Address* is indeed an important signpost in the supplanting of orthodox Christianity by the secular doctrine of social progress, recognizing that for Owen a radically reformed education system is to be regarded not merely as a reflection of this historic leap but as a vital engine for its realization.

This judgment may serve to underscore Owen's distinctiveness as a social reformer and assist further in mapping the direction of his educational thought as it became increasingly assimilated into his optimistic vision of a renovated future society. It is important to remember that the body of cherished beliefs that Owen felt confident enough finally to call in the *Address* a 'religion' – even if this choice of vocabulary was rhetorical rather than prescriptive – was at the same time a *rational* religion, underlining the delicate balance he strove to maintain in his mature thought between the virtues of passionate commitment and the systematic pursuit of truths verifiable to reason and experience. The tension between these impulses sometimes overwhelmed Owen's philosophy, bearing responsibility for some of its more hyperbolic claims and overwrought argumentation. It was a paradox also echoed in wider conflicts of the Romantic age, where audacious and highly emotive aspirations for a revolution in individual and societal values too frequently collided with the intransigence of resistant institutions and ingrained modes of living and being. Owen sincerely believed that he had overcome most of the contradictions that might threaten his own particular visionary perspective on historical change by clearly identifying what the earlier *Address to All Classes* of 1832 had termed a 'science of society' (Owen 1832, pp. 3–4) to balance against his more speculative imaginings of future social structures. It was with the discoveries of this 'science' that all right-thinking people, he believed, would swiftly concur, even if the more hypothetical elements of his thought would inevitably continue to cause uncertainty. These 'scientific' breakthroughs would then go on to provide solid, irrefutable grounds for the full mobilization of a popular movement for social renewal.

The dichotomy between the scientific, rationalist dimension of Owen's thought and its increasingly visionary leanings was one that the mature Owen never fully or satisfactorily resolved. It is certainly not the case that, as his anticipation of a future society became more eschatological, Owen dispensed with, or grew less interested in, the role of enlightened rationality and empirical demonstration in advancing genuine and far-reaching social improvement. The Religion of Reason is for Owen both spiritual and material: it will excite levels of devotion exactly commensurate with the truths that it verifies on the plane of direct human experience; it will furnish for its followers a self-confirmatory body of evidence beyond anything offered by traditional religion, guaranteeing to produce incontrovertible benefits to individuals and communities – especially to those classes most completely marginalized by the prevailing economic order. It is this ongoing empirical validation of its truth claims that separates it from 'false belief' and which inspires its adherents to still greater exertions on its behalf. Nowhere is this proof more palpable, Owen argues, than in the practice of educational reform where, as New Lanark so indisputably demonstrated, the results were immediate and transformative and the future prospects they held forth all the more inviting for those participating in the promotion of the venture. At its most consummate, Owen's synthesis of reason and imagination succeeds in purging reason of the restraints of political economy and in grounding imagination in a realizable politics. At its least accomplished, it breaks down into verbose bombast on the one hand and a sterile positivism on the other. When the two elements of reason and imagination are combined successfully – often like a mineral, under great pressure from both sides – the result is close to what M. H. Abrams called, surveying the whole vista of the Romantic era, 'natural supernaturalism': a passionate belief in the power of the collective, concentrated mind of humanity to bring into being a new kind of world (Abrams 1971, pp. 65–71).

The difficulties involved in sustaining his fusion of vision and rationality are evident wherever education is the primary focus of Owen's detailed social thought. In one of his most significant attempts finally to codify all that he had learned about the formation of character through the operation of a thoroughly reconstructed system of education, the lecture entitled 'The Natural and Rational Classification of Society' of 1837, Owen sets out to show that the application of reason to the objective analysis of the human life cycle, from infancy to late adulthood, actually serves to invigorate rather than undermine a visionary hope for future society (Owen 1991a, pp. 344–358). From the title of the lecture onwards, Owen seems determined to prove that terms such as 'rational' and 'classification' need not be held captive to any diminished calculus of human potential of the sort promulgated by the political economists. Although the lecture proceeds with an almost mathematical ordering of its thought, Owen's baseline conviction endures that 'it is yet unknown what are the capabilities of human nature [...] when it shall be taught truth [...] when it shall be educated to acquire the best habits for its own happiness, and the well-being of society.' The open-endedness of the chosen 'oracular' mode of address is here immediately tempered by a firm grounding in what Owen terms the 'self sustaining manners' to be acquired by the educated subject as he 'advances in life' (p. 345). Immersed from infancy onwards in an experience of lifelong instruction, carefully fitted to each stage of development, the desires of the individual and the needs of the community become both harmonized and satisfied, but at levels beyond the initial apprehension of each. Owen here locks education into the Romantic project of the self and self's enlargement of its powers, while striving through the principles of character formation to embed this subjectivism in an organic understanding of the ties of the community, binding and validating its individual members in the pursuit of shared goals (Steedman 1995, pp. 77–96).

'The Natural and Rational Classification of Society' proceeds with typically astonishing ambition to elaborate the developmental sequence by which the phases of a normative human existence are to be 'classified' and supported. The lecture identifies eight chronological stages, the first six of which are of five years duration (0–30), the seventh of ten years (30–40), and the eighth of a length determined only by the individual's eventual lifespan (though Owen speaks of a period from 40–60). At each of the stages, the lecture configures the experience of life between four parameters: education, work, recreation, and participation in society, the proportions of each shifting in accordance with the propensities and rights appropriate to the age-banding in question. The total effect is to articulate possibly Owen's most coherent and ambitious conception of citizenship and to foreground education as perhaps the most important, shaping factor in the human life cycle. Education ceases in this rationale to be simply another presence, however influential, in the formation of character and is instead portrayed as the central source for the fashioning of the self and the forging of the social contract. For this reason, the first 'class,' as Owen describes it in the lecture, 'from birth to the end of the fifth year,' is marked by possibly the strongest sense yet seen in his writings of personal liberty and instinctive pre-rational solidarity. Infancy is to be protected as a special zone of pleasure and exploration where very young children will be 'always expressing their thoughts and feelings' without 'knowledge of punishment or reward' and in a spirit of growing 'charity and affection for all' (p. 346). It is revealing that Owen sees this largely unregulated freedom of the infant class as the place where children will learn to 'think, speak and act rationally' (p. 347), underlining the affinities in his mature thought between the facilitation of the natural, instinctual life of the child and the steady acquisition of reason. Reason is not a faculty to be artificially instilled in the young: it arises organically from the observable facts of our primary inclinations and our inescapable interdependence with others when these elements are permitted their natural growth.

The next two stages of the classification introduce more prominently the role of formal instruction in the shaping of character and aptitude, including a greater emphasis on the active involvement of children with their surroundings, their first acquaintance with the experience of physical labor (including the care and exercise of their own bodies), and their sheltered introduction to the world of work. Intriguingly, Owen's discussion of the needs of the 5 to 15 age range makes a virtue out of the supposed limitations of childhood, which previous generations of educators had often construed as incapacity or as obvious evidence of dependent vulnerability (Martin 2009). Rationality can be advanced by younger children witnessing the ways in which the intellect – and the scientific and technological fruits of the intellect – enable human beings to overcome the restrictions inherent in any given circumstance or stage of life: 'These new operations will be, to them, a continual source of instruction and amusement' (p. 348), inspiring respect for reason as a wellspring of human freedom, a basis for problem solving and a source of enhanced capability. This will also lead, quite naturally for the 12 to 15 age range in particular, to a creative synergy between learning and work, where pupils:

> will be engaged in acquiring a knowledge of the more advanced useful arts of life; a knowledge by which they will be enabled to assist in producing, the greatest amount, of the most valuable wealth, in the shortest time, with the most pleasure to themselves and advantage to society.

> (p. 349)

Even at this more sophisticated point in his overall political thought, Owen is concerned to maintain a critical recognition of the continuities between education and labor, arguing that the much-needed reform of the systems of production will most reliably emerge from a rational reorganization of the economic structures undertaken by those who, through the example of their enlightened schooling, have been introduced to alternative forms of collaboration and personal enterprise in their formative years. Owen's economic theories grew increasingly anti-competitive in the 1830s and this same feeling is evident in his depiction of the schooling of children and adolescents, who are to be carefully instructed by wise adult teachers but who are also to be routinely involved in peer tutoring and the mentoring of younger pupils by older ones. More than in some of his previous writings, Owen stresses the importance of the *culture* of the school in embodying the values of cooperation and shared discovery that he regards as central to the reform of both education and work. Education thereby avoids becoming restrictively functional and vocational and work ceases to be competitive drudgery without obvious purpose or reward beyond the inadequate financial recompense of wage-slavery: 'Under this classification [...] wealth unrestrained [...] will be most easily produced in superfluity; all will be secured in a full supply of the best of it, for all purposes that may be required' (p. 350).

In his discussion of the fourth class, from 15 to 20, Owen departs signally from the norms of industrial society, even from those relatively enlightened authorities who had begun to extend the education of children beyond the previous maximums of the factory system. This age band, in Owen's classification, 'enter upon a most interesting period of human life' (p. 349) marked by increased autonomy, sexual maturity and, it is intended, a completely classless perception of the peers alongside whom they are learning. In keeping with one of the great motifs of the second wave of the Romantic revolution, Owen in these passages invests considerable hopes for the future happiness of society in the emancipation of youth and the dynamism of its intellectual and libidinal energies. Daring by the orthodoxies of the time, Owen's statements in this section of the lecture on the topics such as sexuality and marriage find echoes in important transitions to be seen in the surrounding literary culture, where much of the vitality identified by the first generation of Romantic artists with childhood innocence is transferred to the far more volatile and unpredictable drives of adolescence and youth (Richardson 1999). Owen's careful attention to rationality, of course, avoids the full perils of an unchecked Eros, ensuring that the 'pleasure and enjoyment' (p. 350) of the later teenage years are fully incorporated into the sphere of the social by a more deliberate attention to the civic participation of youth and their increased involvement in the lives of their junior associates in school. Despite this element of caution, it is clear that Owen is certainly one of the first educators to propose a role for schooling, not only in the formation of sexual ethics but also in the active promotion of a more progressive attitude to conjugal love, marriage, and divorce: 'No immorality can exceed that which is sure to arise from a society compelling individuals to live continually together, when they have been made [...] to lose their affections for each other' (p. 351). Once more, the classification of education is held to be inseparable from wider interlocking features of a healthy, functioning society in which free choice and personal autonomy can be perfectly reconciled to the legitimate interests of the community as a whole.

Owen's observations on the fourth class represent for him something approximating the culmination of formal education in his ideal system and he goes so far as to contend that, at the fourth stage, 'such simplified arrangements in all the departments of life [...] will be sufficient to produce a surplus of all the wealth' (p. 351) on which a new model of self-sufficient community can grow. The language of the remaining sections of the lecture turns back, however, to the theme of the surplus and to the compelling, near biblical imagery of abundance which spangles Owen's later writings. It explores this imagery in order to chart additional stages in the life cycle of the individual members of society, imagining the means by which the new community might harness the surplus to the task of extending the range and definition of education beyond anything yet conceived within the standard parameters of the industrial settlement. In pursuing this line of enquiry, Owen revisits themes of lifelong learning and recreation present in his earlier texts and central to the social experiments of New Lanark. It must be remembered that, for Owen, educational provision was to be understood not simply as a beneficiary of the surplus but also one of the keys to the just and effective forms of production through which a surplus of hitherto inconceivable proportions would be created in the first place. This is part of Owen's strategy for removing what he saw as the unnecessary impediments placed on human productivity by the economic models proposed by Malthus and the political economists. Malthusian pessimism was for Owen a failure of imagination, which refused to see the infinite potential of human inventiveness when all of the institutions of a duly motivated society were placed in a new productive alignment geared to the well-being of all. It is therefore no surprise that the later stages in Owen's classification propose an integrated view of society and a self-reinforcing conception of the relationship of education to work, prosperity, and self-realization:

> The great business of human life is, first, to produce abundance of the most valuable wealth for the use and enjoyment of all; and, secondly, to educate all to well use and properly enjoy their wealth after it has been produced.
>
> (p. 352)

In keeping with this quite revolutionary philosophy, the 20 to 25 class (the fifth stage) will, according to Owen, 'form the highest and most experienced class of producers and instructors, and beyond the age of this class, none need be required to produce or instruct, except for their own pleasure and gratification' (p. 352). Owen's view here appears to be that the successful formation of character can correctly anticipate the creation by age 25 and onwards of a population inspired to work by neither the need for subsistence nor the narrow prospect of personal gain, but by a higher ideal of sustainable communal abundance from which all derive benefit. As a consequence, the sixth class (25–30) embodies a turning-point: the first section of the population whose primary responsibility is not to produce but to 'preserve the wealth' and whose education is inseparable from the uses of leisure, or from the consideration by them of 'whether any improvement can be made in them for the general benefit' (p. 352). Owen's interpretation of the purposes of recreation tries scrupulously to ward off any connotation of the narcissism and self-indulgence for which the leisured aristocracy of his own time were often vilified. There are to be no drones in the ideal Owenite society, only sectors of the population for whom work and learning have become indistinguishable from the enlargement of the sympathies and consciousness of a community, the flourishing of which is predicated on limitless growth and improvement free from the taint of personal greed.

The underlying moral vision of the classification is made most transparent in Owen's discussion of the penultimate, or seventh class (30–40). The risk here, of course, is that the momentum built up in the system leads inexorably – despite the author's vigilance – to the depiction of forms of hierarchy and decadence that were everywhere denounced by radical opinion in Owen's time. The imagined occupants of the latter stages of the classification are easily parodied as an effete caste of philosopher-kings dependent upon the labor of others and invested with forms of arbitrary power entirely and dangerously independent of their moral worth as individuals. It seems inevitable that the perception of the seventh class by modern readers will be colored by the twentieth century's unhappy experience of various earnest 'people's party' *apparatchiki* shouldering the burdens of leadership in supposedly egalitarian societies with cynical disregard for the travails of others in maintaining their position and scant observance of even the semblance of democratic accountability. Of course, Owen is not a democrat in any conventional sense of the term and the lecture makes no reference to principles of government, taxation, or representation because it is (rightly or wrongly) not concerned with them. As an essay in educational theory, on the other hand, the profiling of the seventh class does attempt to deal with genuine moral questions and addresses these on the basis of the principles of character formation that run like a leitmotif through all of Owen's ethical reasoning.

Owen defends the 'business of this class,' which 'will be to govern the home department, in such manner as to preserve the establishment in peace, charity and affection' (p. 353) on the basis that it is open to everyone. The system of education envisaged by the classification will not discriminate in assigning the privileges that come with entry into a particular age banding because of the structural assumption that the whole population has been in receipt of the same education from the outset (a strongly Helvétian insight). The model is developmental rather than political or meritocratic and accords greatest authority to the most senior (and, by implication, best educated) members, 'trained and educated from birth to maturity [...] secure of experiencing all the advantages and enjoyments [...] derived from nature' (p. 354). It is the duty of this class to lead for the fixed period of seniority assigned to it. Its credentials for this task come not from occupancy of the class itself, but from the impact of the educational process upon it, which will have ensured its impartiality, its reasonableness, and its probity. Moreover, the ultimate safeguard for the community lies in the nature of the classification itself, which is always dependent upon the natural life cycle of the generations and which will continually propel the occupants of the seventh stage into the eighth (40+), with its accent on disinterested wisdom and detachment from the cares of the world.

As the developmental structure of ages and stages in the lecture progresses into its more speculative phases, least securely anchored in experience, it is fair to say that its educational content becomes inevitably more nebulous and less clearly articulated with the core principles of Owen's bedrock theory and his record as a practical educational philanthropist. The later stages in particular represent at best an extrapolation from the more adventurous New Lanark experiments in character development, socialization, and recreation. At their least persuasive, they typify a social optimism in Owen's worldview unwilling to countenance even fleetingly the possibility of negative or manipulative human inclinations inaccessible to the claims of reason and society. They thus presuppose absolute consistency in the Owenite theory, running from infancy to mature adulthood, and an almost mystical faith in the capacity of education to form personalities who will emerge as unerring moral paragons and secular saints. Owen's rejoinder to the skepticism implied in this judgment would be to point to its dependence upon a conception of 'the human mind in its present and degraded state' bereft of 'the capacity to imagine' (p. 356) genuine alternatives. The 'natural and rational classification of society,' on the other hand, begins from a putatively scientific description of the potential of the human character to evolve, in optimum circumstances, habits of thinking and being which will thoroughly reshape society and relationships at every level of interaction. Even where it shrinks understandably from the idealism of the extreme Owenite position on these questions, progressive popular education gains immeasurably from its intercourse with these aspirations and from the manifold insights they yield into other ways in which the entire practice of education might be conceived and conducted.

The education of infants

The synthesis of visionary optimism and rational planning that is so central to his later writings receives its most extended treatment in Owen's thought and practice around his work on infant education. As a result, Owen's reputation as an educational innovator has become indelibly associated with the origins of British nursery and early years education, even among those skeptical of his larger educational legacy. In the light of classic texts such as *A New View of Society* and 'The Natural and Rational Classification of Society,' it is easy to see that Owen's empiricist psychology and deterministic theory of character formation was likely to privilege the education of the very young, before the blank slates of their minds had been inscribed with the falsehood and prejudice of their surrounding society. Any inclination to interpret Owen's innovations in infant education purely as the unfolding of a predetermined educational program, however, needs to take cognizance of the broader contexts of late eighteenth-century approaches to the education of the very young, especially as these had been shaped by Enlightenment and Romantic views of childhood and by the first popular educational initiatives improvised by the early factory owners.

The chief claimant to the title of founder of the infant schools movement in Europe is the Lutheran pastor Jean Frederic Oberlin, who had created an infant school in Ban de la Roche, France, in 1769 as part of his conscientious efforts to improve the conditions of the rural poor of Alsace (Rusk 1933, pp. 107–113). Oberlin's efforts were little known in his lifetime, to the extent that, in his continental expedition of 1818, Owen mistakenly believed that he had toured an establishment founded by Oberlin when he had in fact visited a later school founded by the Catholic priest Fr Girard. Oberlin's initiative illustrates the close association between the eighteenth-century reorganization of the processes of agricultural and industrial production and the need to provide for the care of very young children. The ending of cottage-based labor and the increased reliance upon women in farms and factories necessitated new approaches to the care of the infants of the working poor, even if these went no further than provision for basic nurture and protection while parents were at work. The intensification of manufacturing output in mills and factories made some of these issues of still more pressing urgency, leading to various attempts at gathering large numbers of babies and infants together under the frequently unskilled care of older women in manufacturing settlements. Some early industrial provision echoed aspects of the Dame School system popular among certain sections of the lower middle classes, in which usually elderly and unproductive women took responsibility for very small children while making some attempt to provide an elementary education to their older siblings. The writer and schools patron Maria Edgeworth was highly critical of these practices in her 1812 novel *Madame de Fleury*, drawing attention instead to Oberlin-inspired ventures emerging in France under the guidance of influential school teachers such as Mme de Pastoret of Paris (Hilton 2007, pp. 120–125). Similar anxieties appear to have prompted Owen's sometime partner, the philosopher Jeremy Bentham, to speculate on the possibility of an infant establishment as part of his famous Panopticon concept. It seems clear, however, that Owen remained unacquainted with Bentham's work in this field.

Understanding something of the cultural and institutional backdrop to Owen's development of infant education helps illuminate the motives that drove him, allowing distinctions to be drawn between what was truly novel in his approach and what simply amplified existing efforts to deal with the care of small children within industrial communities. Robert Dale Owen noted in his memoir that 'The system of education at New Lanark differs essentially from any that has been adopted in [. . .] any other part of the world' (Owen 1824, p. 5). It seems clear that he took the innovations in nursery education to be the epitome of this. The initial purpose of the school as his father articulated it was twofold: to preserve very young children from the harmful influences of their parents and to foster within them the good habits of effective character formation. In his autobiography, Owen claimed impatiently that 'parents are altogether ignorant of the right method of treating children, and their own children especially.' The education of character could not be left to parents, he asserted, but must be provided by specialist personnel trained in the correct methods:

> To form the most superior character for the human race, the training and education should commence from the birth of the child; and to form a good character they must begin systematically when the child is one year old. But much has been done rightly or wrongly before that period. From that age on no child should be brought up isolated.
>
> (Owen 1993e, 4.229)

Owen's first priority as overall superintendent of the affairs of the infant school at New Lanark was to ensure the existence of an appropriate moral and emotional climate for the growth of the children. This was closely identified in his planning with the kind and sympathetic treatment of them by their adult carers and with the cultivation in each child of a persuasion 'never to injure his play-fellows' (Owen 1993f, 1.57). Visitors to the school, such as William de Crespigny in 1819, were struck by the resultant atmosphere of 'harmlessness, of fondness, and of attention to each other, which we do not often witness in this country' (Claeys 2005, p. 234). Central to the ethos was the place of *play* in the routines of the school. The children were permitted long stretches of time outside, with the lightest possible adult supervision and with slightly older children encouraged to help look after the younger ones. The playground was a natural extension to the classroom, facilitating the interaction with the external environment and the enquiry into the operations of nature which, Owen believed, were essential to the developing mind's capacity to discriminate between truth and falsehood, reality and superstition. This was what he called in *The New Moral World* (1838, 3.166):

> the education which alone can fit man to attain a rational state of existence, to know himself and humanity, to acquire useful and valuable knowledge, to be advanced from being the slave of inferior

and vicious circumstances, to a condition in which he will comprehend what are inferior and vicious circumstances, and what are superior and virtuous, how to remove the former, and replace them with the latter, and to enjoy the necessary results of such a change.

In contrast with some of the European Romantic pedagogues and poets, Owen saw early infancy not as an uncorrupted zone proximate to the sphere of the transcendent, but as a phase uniquely susceptible to the nurture of reason through the direct, critical engagement with natural and social phenomena. Play is in this sense for Owen not merely a preparation of the cognitive faculties preliminary to their full exercise in the later, more formal stages of education. Neither is it simply a setting for the perfection of interpersonal skills. It may include elements of each of these purposes, but it is better regarded primarily as a legitimate mode of awareness in its own right, marked by a distinctive epistemology and a unique disposition towards experience from the preservation of which learners at all stages in their development can immeasurably gain (Bloch and Choi 1990).

In recognition of what Jane Dale Owen was subsequently to describe as 'our duty [...] to guard against his receiving any other than the *right* ideas' (Owen 1968, p. 180), the infants in the New Lanark nursery school appear to have received modest but significant elements of formal tuition. There is some ambiguity about this in the sources, reflective perhaps of changes made in methodology as Owen's ideas evolved. The visiting headteacher Henry McNab reported seeing the infants 'taught the letters of the alphabet' (McNab 1819, p. 221), while Robert Dale later maintained that 'no attempt was made to teach them reading or writing' (Owen 1874, p. 90). Owen's firm but flexible view from as early as 1816 was that the children were to be taught 'by example and practice [...] whatever may be supposed useful, that they can understand; and this instruction is combined with as much amusement [...] as to render them active, cheerful, and happy, fond of the school and of their instructors.' (British Parliamentary Papers 1968, 1.240). It is sometimes difficult to distinguish in Robert Dale's testimony between methods that were exclusive to the nursery and those that reflected the presence of Owenite values across the whole curriculum. Certainly, interactive questioning appears to have been used even with the youngest children. Pictures, models, and charts were available in the nursery as elsewhere and the infants were commonly permitted to schedule activities and rest periods for themselves. Books were, of course, eschewed, as were 'useless childish toys' (Owen 1993e: 230). It appears that in certain important instances educational reforms introduced at the nursery level were frequently disseminated to the more advanced year groups of the school, confirming Owen's view that his methodology rested upon fundamental insights into the nature of childhood which could be applied throughout the period of his pupils' growth in maturity and understanding.

In keeping with the Owenite emphasis on the primacy of relationships in effective learning and teaching, Owen set great store on the role of teachers in the lives of the infants. The earliest provision for oversight of the very young in the operations of larger agricultural and industrial communities had relied upon women carers, and Owen appears to have endorsed this without ever excluding male staff from his classrooms. The later career of Owen's first male appointment, James Buchanan, and his part in the controversies surrounding the founding of the infant schools movement in Britain, means that we have more information about Buchanan than about his younger female colleague, the 17-year-old Molly Young. Yet it appears that the main focus of Young's work was the very youngest children, while Buchanan could range more freely across the age ranges. The shifting professional remits of Young and Buchanan in many respects exemplifies the fortunes of nursery educators in the crucial period from the launch of Owen's infant school to the rapid expansion of the movement in England in the later 1820s and beyond. As Karen Clarke has observed, Owen's deployment of his infant staff, though comparatively equitable by the patriarchal standards of the period, nonetheless foreshadowed the later pattern in pre-5 education in Britain, where the day-to-day interactions with the children became the main responsibility of low-status women nursery nurses, while the control and theorizing of the discipline came to be dominated by men (Clarke 1985). This was an imbalance destined to persist into nursery education, and the study of infant psychology, until well into the twentieth century.

In 1819, a consortium led by the radical philanthropist Henry Brougham opened an infant school in Brewer's Green, Westminster. The debt of Brougham and his associates to Owen was immediately obvious in the request they made to Owen for the services of 'a master, J. Buchanan, who had been superintendent of his Infant School' (Pole 1823, p. 8). The transfer of Buchanan to London sparked some controversy because Buchanan soon claimed that in setting up an infant school in an urban metropolis, and in introducing more structured teaching into the curriculum, he had embarked upon an entirely new venture which owed little to the example of New Lanark. Later, he was to acquiesce in claims made by his English admirers that it was in fact he, Buchanan, who was the true founder of the infant schools movement in the United Kingdom. This undoubtedly irritated Owen and his followers and an embarrassed Brougham steadfastly refused to concur with the claim. The ill-feeling surrounding it tended subsequently to obscure the original esteem in which Owen had held Buchanan and helped for a long time to impede recognition of the contribution of Owen to the creation of British nursery education (Silver 1965, pp. 136–141). Much more worryingly, however, when in 1820 – overcoming his annoyance at him – Owen visited Buchanan's school in Westminster, he found himself horrified to discover Buchanan and his wife using corporal punishment on the children and governing the establishment 'in the spirit and manner of the old irrational schools' (Owen 1993e, 4.207), complete with regimented instruction and rote learning of literacy and numeracy.

Owen discerned in these lapses significantly more than a departure from the methods and values he had pioneered at New Lanark. He saw in Buchanan's confusion a genuinely ominous development associated with the appropriation of his nursery education ideals by political and cultural interests closely allied to the old traditions of authority and bent upon the use of early years education for the punitive control of the potentially disruptive lower classes. This was, for Owen, a travesty of his principles. With such a discernible shift in the social climate in which nursery education was required to operate borne in mind, it is possible to read the statements in 'The Natural and Rational Classification of Society,' devoted to the conduct of the first class of education for those under 5, as a rearguard action in defense of values of charity, self-expression, and the subjective motivation to learn, which Owen was convinced were under serious threat. As late as 1838, in an issue of his periodical *The New Moral World*, Owen felt compelled fiercely to condemn the 'abuse' that 'has been the general fate of infant schools.' 'They have been prostituted,' he stated pointedly, 'to the vilest sectarianism' (Owen 1838, p. 321). In this denunciation, Owen conveyed his deep sense of the betrayal of his own original aspirations for nursery education by the steady annexation of the infant schools movement by the forces of educational reaction such as the Churches, the workhouses, and the payment-by-results system. While there is some evidence of the survival of Owenite practices even in this much less sympathetic national climate (Turner 1970; Roberts 1972), Owen's frustration was a personal response prompted by more than the apparent backsliding of the hapless Buchanan. It reflected his quite prescient recognition of the growing influence from the late 1830s onwards of counter-Enlightenment forces in British education, deliberately turning back to more rigid forms of orthodox moral conditioning and religious instruction, and manifest, for example, in the sudden explosion of Robert Raikes' Sunday Schools across the United Kingdom with their evangelical piety and (as Owen saw it) authoritarian attitudes to learning (Hilton 2007, pp. 133–157).

It is important to recognize in Owen's protest against the 'mockery or caricature' of his core principles by later developments in nursery education the continuing centrality to his thought of a quite distinctive vision of childhood and intergenerational relations. A classic Owenite statement such as 'The Infant School was founded [...] to demonstrate to the learned and the unlearned, that man does not possess the power to feel and think as he likes, or to form his own character' (Owen 1993c, 2.156), fully recapitulates the empiricist doctrines that Owen appears never to have disavowed. Yet there is little in mainstream empiricist theory, its attendant associationist psychology, or the necessitarian philosophy with which each was intimately interwoven, that points unswervingly to the practices of infant education defended with such tenacity by Owen. Owen's appeal to sentiment, sympathy, plasticity, sociality, and even the embodied pleasures of an infant state absorbed in the wonder of a prodigal world, moves beyond the rights-based discourse of the Enlightenment to something approximating the

Romantic affirmation of the child as the symbol of all that human beings might imagine themselves to be at their most natural and fulfilled. Owen's work as an early educator, for all its painstaking concentration upon pragmatic questions of learning, teaching, and the care of the young, reiterates the cultural preoccupations of Romantic thinkers from Rousseau to Blake and Wordsworth (Halpin 2007a, pp. 51–71). It lends ethical and social meaning to their poetic defense of childhood innocence as an *entitlement* of the very young and as the signifier of a sophisticated interpersonal psychology in which young children are seen actively to engage with the experiences, conflicts, and opportunities in the world around them (Kennedy 2006, pp. 56–63). Despite the veil of skepticism now commonly cast over this construction of infancy, important elements of it have survived the struggles for control of pre-5 education and it continues to be a deposit of ideas on the basis of which the integrity and independence of nursery schools are defended in the face of manifold attempts to subordinate them to the needs of the more formal stages of elementary or primary education. The example of Robert Owen in this particular domain of popular education draws together distinct but related currents in the changing understanding of childhood and demonstrates the success with which they could be directed to improvement in the lives of the youngest members of society.

Part 3

The Influence and Relevance of Owen's Work Today

Chapter 5

The Ambivalent Legacy of Robert Owen: Utopianism and Rationality

Owen and the Owenites

It is no surprise that the most immediate response to Owen's educational thought and practice – as these evolved in his practical experiments as well as in his writings – arose from his growing band of supporters and sympathizers. As his increasingly strident remonstrations with government seemed to produce less and less practical advantage for the causes he championed, the indomitable Owen quite naturally turned for intellectual sustenance to the radical circles where his ideas had begun to take root, and where agitation for the broader goals of political and social reform was already well underway. This meant, of course, that reception of the specifically *educational* elements of Owen's reforming vision was soon bound up closely with his related objectives for improvements in the factory system, the expansion of cooperation as a principle of ethical production and consumption, and the wider, enduring desire to build new types of communities across Britain based around the lessons of the New Lanark years.

In the turbulent period of British social and political history that followed the ending of the Napoleonic Wars, the debate around the future direction of national educational provision became more heated and more polarized. A general, if sometimes reluctant, recognition among the political elites that existing arrangements were unsustainable and potentially damaging to the considerable international competitive advantage Britain still precariously enjoyed as the world's first and leading industrial nation, found no corresponding consensus on the question of reform. Deep-seated suspicion of the potentially radicalizing effects of the extension of literacy to an already volatile working population still uncomfortably close to the revolutionary events in

France, led some to continue to argue for strict limitations on the education of the poor. As Terry Eagleton has sardonically remarked, the simplest, most effective form of censorship is 'the perpetuation of mass illiteracy' (Eagleton 1978, p. 56). Although this was by 1820 a minority view, conservative opinion nonetheless held fast to the belief that popular education had to be restricted, regulated, and organized around principles of authority and control that would induce in its recipients obedience to and compliance with the established social order (Morgan 2004, pp. 47–49). This meant, in practice, favoring the rigors of the monitorial system of mass teaching, with its use of what one anonymous contributor to an issue of the *Edinburgh Review* of 1825 approvingly called the use of 'the more advanced and intelligent children to teach the rest' (82.321) in the huge, oppressive classrooms typical of the period. It was precisely the model, and the philosophy, to which Owen was unyieldingly opposed and his positive alternatives soon became a rallying point for his allies. One of the most insightful of these disciples, George Mudie, was among the first to recognize that Owenite principles of education could, if properly presented, march at the leading edge of the nascent cooperative movement, which at this time was also acquiring an organizational infrastructure created out of the wider response in radical circles to Owen's writings. Recognizing the growing appetite across the classes for a more just and coherent approach to education, while at the same time appreciating that the incentive of improved schooling for their children might realistically function as one of the new cooperative movement's major sources of recruitment to laborers and artisans, Mudie in 1821 launched a journal, *The Economist*, for the dissemination of Owenite ideas. Immersing himself also in the continental practices of Fellenberg and Pestalozzi, Mudie used the new journal to press for the reform of teacher training, the use in schools of proper subject timetables with specialist teaching, and for a fuller, more intelligent integration of general communal education with vocational training. In this last point, Mudie showed genuine insight into the distinguishing features of the New Lanark methods, which he contrasted favorably with Fellenberg's tendency to stress 'such branches of education' for his pupils 'as shall induce them to prefer the condition of laborers in which they are to be placed rather than aspire to higher stations in society.' By contrast, Mudie praised the

New Lanark emphasis on 'the regular acquisition of knowledge [...] without interruption, for many years' (*The Economist* 1821, 1.8., 123–128) as the key to the emancipation of the laboring classes (Silver 1965, pp. 162–164).

This association of reformed education with both the core values of the evolving cooperative networks, and the increasingly urgent calls for the redesign of outdated pedagogical methods, soon became one of the signatures of the Owenite movement of the 1820s and 1830s. As the movement expanded, some divergences of view arose in the interpretation of Owen's underlying philosophy, most especially in relation to his understanding of character formation and the part it ought to play in the practical outworking of a complex, community-based educational system. Moreover, it seems clear that at certain junctures Owen himself balked at the appropriation of his ideas by some of the increasingly radicalized cooperative organizations, bent upon defining popular education as popular *political* education, to be pursued with equal vigor through activities such as publishing and civil protest as well as through schools. The coherence of the movement nevertheless survived for some considerable period despite these stresses, and the shared commitment to education was one of its chief unifying forces. Devotees of Owen such as Abram Combe, the founder of Orbiston, strove to make 'the war against ignorance' (Combe 1823, p. 8) the primary task of the cooperative settlements they had established, while Brighton physician, Dr William King, instinctively skeptical of Owenite empiricism and by inclination a social and religious conservative, nonetheless concurred that at the heart of every cooperative community there must be a school, 'in order to prove, to the end of time, that knowledge, and knowledge alone, is the true benevolent and omnipotent parent of virtue, religion, happiness and plenty' (*The Cooperator* 1829). King was eventually to emerge as the true progenitor of the modern Cooperative Movement as we know it and his politics diverged sharply at times from those of Owen, but he continued to acknowledge his indebtedness to Owen, especially in the centrality accorded education by the burgeoning local cooperative societies as they fought to establish themselves and attract membership. As the numbers of such local groups across Britain climbed steadily into the hundreds, their public campaigning for the extension of education intensified, as did the elaboration of their plans for a movement-wide integrated educational strategy, encompassing all of the stages from infant schools to trade colleges for young adults and incorporating many of the key values of the New Lanark method.

With his popularity among such pressure groups at its peak, Owen was persuaded in the early 1830s to become more directly involved. He attended the first two Cooperative Congresses in 1831, but chose to retain some distance from the Movement by setting up what he saw as a complementary organization, the ostentatiously titled Association for Removing the Causes of Ignorance, operating out of an entirely new institution at Gray's Inn Road in London. Although he continued to look with some disquiet at elements of the Cooperative Congress, Owen saw in its educational drive a real opportunity to mobilize a mass movement around his ambitions. Besides, as Harold Silver has suggested, it seems that by this period Owen had himself become more politicized, concluding that the prevailing ignorance in British society was an *enforced* or ideological ignorance, which, abetted by structural unemployment, was used deliberately by the ruling classes to maintain 'wretchedness, misery and degradation' (Owen 1832, p. 3) among the poor (Silver 1965, pp. 180–181). These were the terms used by Owen in a major public *Address* issued by the new Association in 1832. Through the Gray's Inn institution, he intended to combat these vices by setting up a new template for industrial schooling, consisting of an infant school, a school for the 5–11s and one for the 12–15s. The constitution he proposed for the new schools complex, and set out in 1834 in an edition of his periodical, *The Crisis*, distilled all of the key features of his educational philosophy and synthesized them with a series of practical principles directly derived from reflection upon the measures implemented successfully at New Lanark. The result was a document that in many respects represents the 'mission statement' of Owenite education and which at the same time functions as a transitional text in the progress from the educational experimentation of the New Lanark years to something approaching an authentic Owenite educational legacy:

1 Every pupil shall be encouraged to express his or her opinion.
2 No creed or dogma shall be imposed on any.

3 Admitted facts alone shall be placed before the pupils, from which they shall be allowed to draw their own conclusions.

4 No distinction whatever shall exist; but all shall be treated with equal kindness.

5 Neither praise nor blame, merit nor demerit, rewards nor punishment, shall be awarded to any: kindness and love to be the only ruling powers.

6 Both sexes shall have equal opportunities of acquiring useful knowledge.

(The Crisis 1834, p. 150)

If the constitution represents any sort of advance on the ideas laid out in *A New View*, it is perhaps in its closer attention to the needs of the individual child – a development in Owen's thought that may well have arisen out his reflection upon the actual operations of the New Lanark classrooms as well as from his closer engagement with the practices of the Cooperative Movement. In part of the text of the earlier *Address*, probably (though not certainly) also written by Owen, it is noted that in the new schools 'Every child shall gradually be made acquainted with his *own nature*.' Instruction is to be 'adapted also to the *peculiar organization* of each child,' in order to foster '*entire confidence and sympathy* between the instructor and the instructed' (Owen 1832, pp. 3–4). It is not too fanciful to see in these statements the germ of what would later be called 'child-centered education,' at last made explicit as a cornerstone of the Owenite pedagogy.

In spite of the flurry of activity and propaganda that yet again accompanied the launch of a fresh Owenite initiative, the Gray's Inn project found it too difficult to raise the necessary capital and the intended schools did not properly materialize. Ironically, the major educational effect of the plan was the creation of the institution itself, which became the London hub for other Owenite educational activities such as public lectures, political discussions and more systematic instruction in Owenite teaching strategies. That said, there was sufficient momentum in the constitution and the ideas that surrounded it for its main proposals to be taken up throughout the Cooperative Movement as local associations and their schools began to proliferate across the country. Predictably, not all of these initiatives either bore fruit educationally or adhered strictly to Owen's founding principles where they did. Owen, however, took enthusiastically to the role of presiding genius of the movement and, as his involvement with British trade unionism also intensified, he became a regular public speaker at, and adviser to, the many locally-based efforts to launch or reform schools and other types of alternative educational facility under the aegis of cooperation. As his public profile as a leading inspiration to the new trade union organizations reached its height, Owen strove to ensure that every constitution, public manifesto, or political platform adopted by the multifarious and fissiparous workers' associations included an express demand for proper mass education as an urgent national priority. Where these groups actually diverted resources into their own, indigenous, attempts at schooling, the presence of Owenite values was often keenly felt.

A similar pattern unfolded in the United States in the wake of Owen's New Harmony venture. Once again, despite the ultimate dissolution of the intended community (in part, as we have seen, because of sharp differences of outlook on the subject of education between Owen and his partner Maclure), important and potent educational values survived, some of which were destined to enter the bloodstream of popular education in America. Perhaps because of the unique pedigree of the Harmonists as an egalitarian Christian sect, reinforced by the democratic ideals upon which the American republic had been so recently founded, the early American Owenites placed a possibly even greater premium than their British counterparts on the role of *community* in the flourishing of progressive education. Owen had sought to capitalize on this himself when he had reminded the Harmonists in calculatedly biblical phrasing that 'a whole community can become a new people, have their minds born again, and be regenerated from the errors and corruptions which [. . .] have hitherto everywhere prevailed' (*New Harmony Gazette* 1826). As one eager follower had written in an edition of the *New Harmony Gazette* of 1825, 'It is on the education of youth, the projector of the new social system relies upon for ultimate success'. 'Ultimate success' was the one outcome that fatally eluded the Harmonists in Owen's lifetime, but there is abundant evidence from the many related educational innovations across the United States, and from the wealth of publications that continued to be disseminated by supporters of the original community's goals, that Owen's fundamental optimism resonated with a deep cultural value in the pioneering spirit of Americans. William Thompson, an ardent American Owenite, defined this in one of his publications as a belief in the 'mental pleasures' (Thompson 1830, p. 205) of education, closely identifying it with the values that had taken so many persecuted minorities to the United States in the first place in the idealistic belief that they could build a better society, leaving the old hierarchies behind (Harrison 1969, pp. 143–147). Even if this peculiarly immigrant aspiration proved to be in its own way as naïve as the dreams of Owen's Harmonists, its capacity to sustain the hopes for educational change in the often dispiriting surroundings created by the fallout from the Industrial Revolution on both sides of the Atlantic could at no time be underestimated.

Rejections of Owen

It was inevitable that a man of Owen's self-belief and single-mindedness, flamboyantly committed as he was to the complete regeneration of some of the most august institutions of British society, would excite hostility as well as acclaim from those around him. Antipathy to Owen and his educational ideas took two main forms in his lifetime. The first might broadly be described as 'cultural.' This is a better term than 'political,' because it encompasses thinkers who sat outside of the conventional political alignments of the day and also recognizes that Owen courted criticism from the Left as well as the Right; sometimes even from among strands of opinion that might have been expected to support him. The second major area of disaffection was religious – a source of endemic controversy that plagued Owen throughout his career and which was to prove of particular frustration for him in his efforts to remodel education.

Even among his admirers, there could often be found widespread aversion to aspects of Owen's manner: his repetitious, hortatory tone and his frequently dismissive attitude to those who might dare to question the validity of the philosophical assumptions upon which his many projects were raised. Francis Place, who as we have seen offered Owen guidance and support in the drafting of *A New View of Society*, nonetheless remained incredulous that Owen could sincerely believe that the views of character formation on which his educational schemes rested were entirely original and that 'on this supposed discovery he founded his system' (Place 1813, p. 268). Place was also shocked by the younger Owen's sporadic disdain for the political aspirations of the working classes, which he felt clouded his perceptions of parliamentary reform and nurtured in him an excessively idealistic view of how the proposed village communities would be organized and administered (Podmore 1906, pp. 121–124; Donnachie 2005a, p. 116). Place, indeed, was among the first to notice that Owen's ambition for the reform of education would soon run into the issues of political accountability to which the Owen of *A New View* for the most part impatiently refused to accord any real significance. Experience at New Lanark and New Harmony was subsequently to prove Place's reservations well founded. The anonymous 1825 commentator in *The Edinburgh Review*, who extolled the virtues of the monitorial system, also attacked Owen's political naïveté, but from a position diametrically opposed to that of Place. Commenting that there was little evidence that 'the extravagances of Mr Owen are making much way in the world,' the writer went on to declare 'an entire unbelief in all projects for regenerating mankind, and giving a new character to future generations, by certain trite or fantastic schemes of education.' The very notion indeed, averred the writer, that schooling of any stripe could effect such far-reaching change in human nature or the providentially ordained structures of society, betrayed the absurdity of Owen's metaphysics: 'the year after the boy has left the school, he will be precisely in the same state [...] as if he had been all the time at home' (p. 316).

This was a fairly typical political reaction to Owen, arguing that his schemes were logistically fanciful and disconnected from the realities of human nature as wisely understood by the ancient institutions of the British constitution and the truths of revealed religion. It was equally interesting, however, that critics of the Left and the Right frequently expressed their concerns in the same language, even where their conceptions of humanity and of the rights of man differed dramatically. It was also noteworthy that their disquiet often focused upon the perceived defects of Owen himself as a personality as well as a thinker. Undoubtedly the most eloquent of those who reproached Owen from out of a broadly radical tradition of skeptical polemic was the renowned essayist and journalist, William Hazlitt. Hazlitt's political position was an idiosyncratic one. While stimulated by the great reformist texts of the 1790s, such as Godwin's *Political Justice*, the violent collapse of the ideals of the French Revolution had bred in him a suspicion of visionary schemes for social transformation almost as profound as his dislike of the corrupt institutions of the old political regime. This stout independence of mind, drawn to reformist aspirations but inveterately wary of the selfish motives they frequently concealed, guided Hazlitt in targeting two elements of Owen's thought with particular vehemence: his utopianism and his alleged monomania.

In an early review of *A New View of Society*, Hazlitt attacked Owen's rhetorical obsession with the 'new' – from new views to New Lanark:

> [...] it is not new. It is not coeval, whatever the author and proprietor may think, with the New Lanark mills, but it is as old as the royal borough of Lanark, or as the county of Lanark itself. It is as old as the 'Political Justice' of Mr Godwin, as the 'Oceana' of Harrington, as the 'Utopia' of Sir Thomas More, as the 'Republic' of Plato; it is as old as society itself [...] The doctrine of Universal Benevolence, the belief in the Omnipotence of Truth, and in the Perfectibility of Human Nature, are not new, but 'Old, old,' Master Robert Owen; – why then do you say that they are new? They are not only old, they are superannuated, they are dead and buried [...]
> (Hazlitt 1998a, 4.92)

Hazlitt was one of the first commentators to identify Owen with a tradition of utopian speculation reaching back to the Greeks. He was also one of the first to see the potential defects in these imaginings, less because of their supposed detachment from reality and more because of precisely the opposite of this: their repeated tendency to bend a resistant reality, by compulsion if necessary, into conformity with their obsessive utopian ideals. Recalling the Terror that followed so swiftly on the hopes of the French Revolution, Hazlitt complained, 'Does not Mr Owen know that the same scheme, the same principles, the same philosophy of motives and actions, of causes and consequences, of knowledge and virtue, of virtue and happiness, were rife in the year 1793 [...]?' (1998a, 4.93). In Owen, Hazlitt concluded, the utopian impulse had met something unique, and something uniquely dangerous: a technocrat with the resources and skills to make his dreams come true, refashioning society through a ruthlessly reorganized education system in accordance with 'the certainty of his principles and the infallibility of his practice':

> His predecessors were clumsy fellows; but he is an engineer, who will be sure to do their business for them. He is not the man to set the Thames on fire, but he will move the world, and New Lanark is the place he has fixed his lever upon for this purpose.
>
> (1998a, 4.95)

In scorning the disingenuous paraphernalia of dedications and encomia in which Owen habitually disguised the menacing social goals in *A New View*, Hazlitt took pains to stress that Owen's schemes had met with the tokenistic approval of the ruling classes precisely because behind their façade of reform the proposals in fact promised to make permanent the unequal systems of production and distribution upon which the present economic order depended. Hazlitt uses Owen's own language against him here, promising to accord the philanthropist the respect he seems to crave as soon as his writings have incurred the persecution suffered by so many of Hazlitt's journalistic contemporaries locked in genuine protest against the government. In the absence of any proper political analysis, Owen's utopian purism represented for Hazlitt an alarming obsession, which, if eventually harnessed by Owen or anyone else to the might of industrial production, held the potential to wreak untold ruin.

Hazlitt's identification of the flaws in Owen's thought with specific traits of his personality, most especially his arrogance and stubbornness, is magnified in an important section of his remarkable essay of 1822, 'On People with One Idea.' Hazlitt's aversion to what he terms people with one idea is essentially democratic in origin. He rebukes a range of thinkers and campaigners who believe themselves to be in possession of an incontestable truth for the healing of society and the betterment of their fellow human beings, but which in each case is by definition to be exempt from proper scrutiny by interlocutors simply too unenlightened to comprehend its obvious validity. This outlook was for Hazlitt fundamentally incompatible with educated rationality even if it often tricked itself out in the clothing of reason. 'Mr Owen,' he states in the essay, 'is a man remarkable for one idea':

> It is that of himself and the Lanark cotton-mills. He carries this idea backwards and forwards with him from Glasgow to London, without allowing anything for attrition, and expects to find it in the same state of purity and perfection in the latter place as at the former. He acquires a wonderful velocity and impenetrability in his undaunted transit. Resistance to him is vain, while the whirling motion of the mail-coach remains in his head.
>
> (1998b, 6.56–57)

Highlighting once again the inescapably technocratic leanings of Owen's mind, with its endless search for simple, expert fixes to intractable social and political problems, Hazlitt shrewdly recognizes that the whole thrust of Owen's thought is educational; that he conducts himself, in fact, with 'the air of a schoolmaster,' an 'expert and sweeping orator' (6.57), unwilling to brook dissent and certain in the truth of his solutions. In spite of the repeated emphasis in Owen's educational writings on the promotion of discussion, Hazlitt sees him as a great silencer of debate, an autocrat whose beguiling benevolence might easily slide into a totalitarianism more pitiless than anything to be found in the old regime because of its superficially persuasive affinity with educated rationality.

Hazlitt's skeptical responses to Owen crystallized perhaps more lucidly than those articulated by others a cluster of anxieties that were felt inchoately across important sectors of radical opinion throughout Owen's career. Perhaps because Owen himself adverted so repeatedly to New Lanark as the obvious vindication of his educational ideas, some of the misgivings harbored by respondents also took New Lanark and the Village Scheme as their principal point of focus, using various impressions of the village and its schools system – either first-hand or reported – in order to express a generalized disquiet towards elements of the style and culture of Owenism as a whole. In his radical newspaper, the *Political Register* of 1817, the reformer William Cobbett fastened on Owen's habitual preference for charts, tables, and diagrams to illustrate the kinds of community and the types of learning he wished to see adopted. Cobbett famously denounced the pictorial representations of the proposed village schemes based upon New Lanark as nothing more than 'parallelograms for paupers,' witheringly repining that Owen:

> is for establishing innumerable *communities* of paupers. Each is to be resident in an *enclosure*, somewhat resembling a barrack establishment, only more extensive [...] I perceive that they are all to be under a very *regular* discipline; and that wonderful peace, happiness and national benefit are to be the result.
>
> (Cobbett 1817, p. 243)

Echoing Hazlitt, Cobbett saw in the Village Scheme not a realization of the radical causes of social and economic reform, but merely another more efficient version of the control of labor by the logic and technology of political economy. The journalist and satirist, William Hone, a stalwart campaigner for press freedom and reform of the franchise, amplified Cobbett's sarcasm the same year in an article in the *Reformist Register*. Hone attacked Owen's village plans for the underlying premise contained in them that:

> all human beings are so many plants, which have been put out of the earth for a few thousand years and require to be reset. He accordingly determines to dibble them in squares after a new fashion [...] Everybody, I believe is convinced of Mr Owen's benevolence, and that he proposes to do us much good. I ask him to *leave us alone*, lest he do us much mischief.
>
> (Hone 1817)

As well as being figures from whose publications Owen might ordinarily have anticipated endorsement, these criticisms from intellectuals of the Left were particularly stinging because of the skill with which they turned the favorite discourses of Owenism against themselves. Owen prized spatial and horticultural metaphors throughout his writings and speeches because they communicated so fluently to his various audiences some of his key concepts and doctrines. Human beings were the product of their circumstances; therefore the creation of utopian environments would indeed promote their perfectibility. The rational powers of most individuals had indeed been poisoned by the toxic dogmas of the past and a 'resetting' in the superior soil of educated rationality would inevitably restore the proper health of individuals and communities. The effect of criticisms such as those of Cobbett and Hone was not to refute Owen's underlying assumptions but to follow them through to much less reassuring conclusions than those reached by their author. This fact made judgments of this complexion potentially much more damaging to the whole Owenite enterprise than the simple self-interested resistance of Old Corruption to altruistic pleas for educational change.

Perhaps the most trenchant direct critique of the New Lanark experiment offered in the period of Owen's tenure by an intellectual born of the same generally enlightened cultural politics as Owen was that recorded (though not published) in Robert Southey's *Journal* after the poet's visit to the Falls of Clyde in 1819. Southey toured the village at some length, including the Institution for the Formation of Character. Impressed by the noise and play he found in the infant school, he was markedly less enthusiastic about the perceived regimentation of the upper school, including his perception of the 'puppet-like motions' of the older children's dancing and marching. The conclusion drawn by Southey and recorded privately in his journal penetrated straight to the heart of the paradox of New Lanark, anticipating the later controversies that would engulf the assessment of Owen's legacy for thinkers across the political and educational spectrum:

Owen in reality deceives himself. He is part-owner and sole Director of a large establishment, differing more in accidents than in essence from a plantation: the persons under him happen to be white, and are at liberty by law to quit his service, but while they remain in it they are as much under his absolute management as so many negro-slaves. His humour, his vanity, his kindliness of nature [...] lead him to make these *human machines* as he calls them (and too literally believes them to be) as happy as he can, and to make a display of their happiness. And he jumps to the monstrous conclusion that because he can do this with 2210 persons, who are totally dependent upon him – all mankind might be governed with the same facility.

(Southey 1929, pp. 263–264)

Once again, Southey had taken classic elements of Owenite practice, trumpeted by Owen and his supporters as the demonstration of the new age of benevolence into which education and society were about to enter, and argued that the veneer of philanthropy concealed despotism of the most ominous kind. Far from emancipating the character of man, Southey suggested, Owen's 'ideal square villages' held forth the prospect that 'the power of human society, and the grace, would both be annihilated.' The key to New Lanark and its blueprint for social renewal was not essentially – as Owen claimed – the empiricist discovery of the infinite plasticity of the human character, to be perfected and made happy by exposure to enlightened education, but a much more sinister secret that Owen, Southey acutely observed, 'keeps out of sight from others, and perhaps from himself [...] that his system, instead of aiming at perfect freedom, can only be kept in play by absolute power' (p. 264). Few subsequent critiques of Owen carried this acumen, even if Owen and his immediate followers never of course became aware of Southey's comments. Cobbett had repudiated the hyper-rationalism of Owen's architectural and educational geometry; Hone had rejected the centralizing interference of Owen's unspoken politics and its infringement of personal liberty; Hazlitt had discerned the potential for coercion in the relentless utopianism of Owen's desire to remake and control the institutions of society and the workings of the human mind. It was as if Southey's analysis had gathered up all of these scruples and combined them into a fundamental disclosure of the hidden, perhaps unconscious, mainspring of the whole Owenite project: its utter dependence upon infinite jurisdiction over the lives and destinies of the industrial population, using the instruments of industrial culture – chiefly mass education – against itself.

These potentially illiberal elements in Owen's thought prompted a final, sophisticated rebuttal in his own lifetime from the son of one of his erstwhile partners, the ex-clergyman and utilitarian James Mill. John Stuart Mill's reaction to Owen implicitly recapitulated many of the objections of the 'Romantic' critics who had engaged with either *A New View* or the operations of the New Lanark settlement. Mill shares several of the anxieties of Hazlitt and Southey about the effects of Owen's system in action. But he goes still further, in questioning the role of the philosophical compound of empiricism and necessitarianism in the shaping of Owen's civic institutions, especially education (Claeys 2005: 25-26; Goldstone 2008). Owen, in Mill's view, is at the heart of his thought prey to levels of pessimism about the potential of human agency as dispiriting as anything proposed by the political economists. In fact, Owen's core doctrine is a still more extreme form of determinism because its assumption that external, ungovernable 'circumstances' condition every human action completely abolishes the value of the personal autonomy it elsewhere pretends to defend, leaving the individual with no genuinely free choices. In this scheme of things, education for the pursuit of happiness becomes an illusion. Employing Owen's own terminology to critique him, Mill argues that:

> though character is formed by circumstances, our own desires can influence those circumstances [...] what is really inspiriting and ennobling in the doctrine of free will, is the conviction that our will has real power over the formation of our character; that our will, by influencing some of our circumstances, can modify our future habits or capacities of willing.
>
> (Mill 1981, p. 176)

The idea of autonomy that Mill affirmed in his *System of Logic* of 1843 and perfected in the classic text of liberal theory, *On Liberty* of 1859, is at its root one of individualistic resistance to the forces Owen had argued fixed immovably the parameters of character development. 'A person feels morally free,' Mill writes in the *Logic*, 'who feels that his habits are not his masters but he theirs: who even in yielding to them knows that he could resist' (Mill 1974, p. 841). Mill accepts many of Owen's strictures about the impact of context and circumstance on individual volition – including the potentially enriching effects of a benign education in the furtherance of happiness – but denies the essential passivity built into Owen's version of the blank slate. Just as Owen in *A New View* severely curtails the capacity of the individual to be anything other than the product of circumstance, Mill by turn portrays Owen's understanding of character formation as equivalent to the fatalism of the old metaphysical order. The true purpose of education, Mill suggests, is to strengthen the exercise of autonomy by providing levels of instruction that maximize the informed individual's capacity to choose and mold the elements of the good life as he or she sees fit. This certainly entails, as Owen had argued, a national civic responsibility for the provision of basic education to everyone, but not in pursuit of the endlessly deferred utopian illusion of perfectibility. Rather, planned rational education should exist for the optimization of diversity and the cultivation within the bounds of liberal tolerance of the interests of all groups and individuals seeking modestly the happiness and prosperity of themselves and others. Mill's rejoinder to Owen, striking at the root of his philosophical worldview, is decidedly anti-utopian in its realism, marking perhaps an end to the millenarian rhetoric of the revolutionary era of which Owen was so obviously a part and introducing a new, more restrained accent to the approach to popular education in modern Britain with possibly less space for Owenism than Owen or his disciples would ever had imagined.

Owen and the rise of mass education

By the closing stages of his life, and in the years that immediately followed, it was possible to discern a major bifurcation in Owen's reputation as an educational pioneer. On one side, his increasingly well-organized followers, directing their energies into a battery of reforming ventures, continued to cherish and develop his core ideas, preserving and enhancing the memory of his innovations. On the other side, the onward advance of mass education in the United Kingdom tilted in a direction quite distinct from the Owenite philosophy, restoring, for example, the role of the Churches and of instruction in faith and morals, to a central role in the governance of schools. National political control and coordination of the expanding education sector did move forward as Owen and his followers had urged, but its growth favored forms of centralization, teaching methods, and attitudes to children for the most part quite inimical to Owen's original designs (Doheny 1991). Partly because Owen had spent so much of his post-New Lanark period linking indissolubly progress in education with progress on a wide front of welfare and community objectives, the intensified official resistance to his grand schemes and his perceived proto-socialism tended to sweep away his educational doctrines along with the whole panoply of his notorious visionary speculations. Even some of his sympathizers within what might be termed mainstream reformist opinion went to some considerable lengths to suggest that the indisputable successes of the New Lanark experiment had less to do with Owen's extravagant theories and more to do with his good judgment as a manager and man of business.

By the 1840s, serious parliamentary efforts to provide rudimentary national structures for the development of basic mass education in England and Wales – and separately in Scotland – had resulted in the considerable enhancement of the powers of the Committee of Council on Education and the production of the landmark Revised Code for Schools (Silver 1977; Gardner 2007, pp. 362–366). In the same period, Owen's influence had been decidedly marginalized. His name is absent from the minutes of the Committee of Council and no reference was made to him in any of the growing number of educational periodicals, such as the influential *Quarterly Journal of Education*, that began to appear in the same decade. Moreover, the teaching methods actively promoted in the Revised Code and related legislation ran counter to everything Owen and his staff had championed at New Lanark and New Harmony, favoring rote learning, memorization, exhaustive schedules of testing, mechanical drilling in reading and counting, and the punitive indoctrination of Christian catechetics. Widespread adoption of a version of the monitorial teaching system, entirely lacking in proper teacher training and dependent upon the corralling of large numbers of children of disparate ages in huge classrooms, seemed to signal a complete severance of any lingering attachment to the Owenite ideals in the corridors of educational decision-making in London and Edinburgh. Even as the surge in journal literature in the 1850s and 1860s began to signal the first stirrings of a distinctively British 'tradition' of educational science, including the quest for a historic pedigree for the preferred styles of learning and teaching operating in the new schools, Owen's presence was once again largely invisible. He is either little more than a footnote, or entirely omitted, in important surveys of the educational landscape such as R. H. Quick's *Essays on Educational Reformers* (1868), J. Gill's *Systems of Education* (1876), and J. Leitch's *Practical Educationists* (1876). In Scotland, the immensely important volume by Henry Craik, *The State in its Relation to Education* of 1884, subsequently regarded by many as a milestone in the rise of Scottish education and in the creation of a ground plan for the centralized educational bureaucracy of the twentieth-century welfare state, also makes no mention whatsoever of Owen or his work (Silver 1983, pp. 60–81).

The example of infant education in Britain once again provides illuminating evidence of the fate of Owen's reputation in the high Victorian era. We have seen how in his own lifetime Owen became unwittingly entangled in a disagreement with James Buchanan over credit for the origins of nursery schools. There was a further twist to this story of lasting significance to the unexpected erasure of Owen's legacy in the annals of British pre-5 education. In recording in his autobiography his estrangement from Buchanan over the issue of infant education, Owen discusses the redirection of some of his early years patronage to another pioneer in the field, Samuel Wilderspin (Owen 1993e, 4.207–208). Following in the wake of Buchanan, Wilderspin had set up the second proper infant school in London, in Spitalfields, in 1821, subsequently acknowledging in his influential 1823 publication, *On the Importance of Educating the Infant Children of the Poor*, his indebtedness to Owen and the impact on his methodology of visits paid to the school by Owen in the first months of its activities. Wilderspin soon became something of an educational celebrity in the capital, attracting visitors to his establishment and receiving invites to give advice to important government bodies on the education of the poor. *Infant Children* achieved some considerable renown as a guide to the schooling of the very young and was soon running into several editions. As his fame increased, however, Wilderspin altered his original, admiring references to Owen in the text, subtly reducing his significance as an infant educator and playing down his contribution to the operation of the Spitalfields nursery. The reasons for this deliberate rejection of Owen as a precursor, by a figure destined to assume national recognition as progenitor of infant education in Britain, are complex. Harold Silver has pointed to Wilderspin's prudent sense of Owen's increasing isolation from the educational establishment, amidst the growing political distaste for his eccentric schemes for the remaking of mankind (Silver 1965, pp. 140–141). Appearing in 1835 before the Select Committee on Education in the House of Commons, Wilderspin defended a model of infant learning significantly removed from the Owenite values of spontaneity and discovery, choosing instead to highlight the potential contribution of effective, regimented pre-5 teaching to later attainments in literacy and numeracy. It is unfair on the basis of this evidence to label Wilderspin a simple reactionary, ingratiating himself with new national educational paymasters. A Swedenborgian, Wilderspin faced his own battles with authoritarians and Church evangelicals, firmly resisting their determination to ensure that infant education became neither compulsory nor secular. His struggles to sustain infant education as a genuinely popular national movement, and to maintain an international dialogue between British nursery teaching and the parallel initiatives of the continentals, undoubtedly required compromise and sacrifice. It may have been that in his defense of his movement, Wilderspin realized that Owen was simply too subversive a forerunner to invoke too openly. Owen's experiments might well have succeeded within the relatively sequestered surroundings of the Falls of Clyde, but subject to the glaring political and ecclesiastical scrutiny of the metropolis they needed to adapt if they were to survive at all (McCann and Young 1982, pp. 41–47, 167–183).

Wilderspin's readiness to temporize with increasingly powerful state authorities was an implied reproach to the stubborn idealism of the Owenites, whose increasing exile from mainstream educational developments risked reducing them in the middle of the nineteenth century to the status of a sect. It is true that within the various

Owenite associations, centered upon the growth of initiatives such as the Cooperative Society, early trade unionism and the Chartism of the 1840s, Owen's educational principles continued to be revered. They remained, moreover a vital element of the educational programs of these organizations as they manifested themselves in activities such as evening classes and the extra-mural courses of trades colleges and specialist institutes. Few of these initiatives came close, however, to replicating the achievements of New Lanark in its heyday or to implementing the principles articulated in *A New View of Society*, or any of Owen's subsequent works. The beginning and end of Owen's educational thought had been schooling and although his concept of schooling had opened out on to compelling notions of recreation and lifelong learning, the crown of his achievement as an educator had been the teaching of children. As long as Owenism remained peripheral to national debates about the education of the young, it had failed the vision of its founder, settling for the support of special interest groups and in-house devotees almost certainly condemned to toil forever at the edges of national educational policy-making. This was another version of the utopianism that Hazlitt had detected in Owen's writings and that he had seen as the 'one idea' that would ultimately consign Owen to philosophical and educational oblivion. Unwilling to make concessions, Owenism assumed the character of a remnant, untainted by compromise but increasingly forgotten by large sections of the general public. It was in part this essentially anti-democratic elitism that drew the criticism of Marx and Engels, when in the third of Marx's 1845 'Theses on Feuerbach' (amended by Engels in 1888 to include the reference to Owen) they noted that:

> The materialist doctrine that men are the products of their circumstances and upbringing [...] forgets that it is men who change circumstances and that the educator must himself be educated. Hence this doctrine is bound to divide society into two parts, one of which is superior to society (in Robert Owen for example).
>
> (Marx and Engels, 1976, p. 7)

Marx and Engels' implied criticism of the Owenite view of the educator pinpoints one of the paradoxes of the 'materialist' or necessitarian worldview that, on the basis of its own logic, there exists no standpoint beyond the closed causal chain of character formation from which meaningful intervention in the processes of education can ever be effected. The determinism of the materialist view insists that anything that is raised above society as a potential source of social change possesses no real existence outside of the social. If the unjust structures of the social are then seen as the domain to be transformed, the materialist educator, suggest Marx and Engels, is forced back on a sense of privileged insight or privileged status (hence Owen's many entreaties to external aristocratic sponsors, perhaps) which will serve, in fact, only to detach him further from the social realities he wishes to alter. This superior position to society is what Armstrong and Tennenhouse describe as the plight of the 'liberal intellectual': 'one foot in the sanctuary of reproduction, the other in an unspecified relation to it' (1992, p. 88). It is also part of the 'utopianism' that Marx and Engels peremptorily dismissed in Owen's socialism (Donnachie and Mooney 2007, pp. 289–290). Years before, in the far more skeptical view of education articulated in *Political Justice*, Godwin had posed the same uncompromising question in terms his disciple Owen must have found sobering: 'Where must the preceptor himself have been educated, who shall thus elevate his pupil above all the errors of mankind?' (1993: 17).

The solution proposed by Marx and Engels to the paradox is to see education as at least potentially a 'revolutionary practice' in dialectical relation to the unjust circumstances it seeks to redress. The discernible revival in Owenism as a critical perspective on the rise of mass education in Britain in the closing decades of the nineteenth century, while painstakingly eschewing a fully revolutionary politics, nevertheless very firmly associated the living legacy of Owenite education with the growing socialist critique of the failure of largely laissez-faire strategies to produce a national integrated system of popular education capable of rivaling the attainments of the other industrial countries. Fabian intellectuals such as H. S. Foxwell and Beatrice Webb tried hard in the 1890s to bring out the fundamental pragmatism of the Owenite approach to schooling, pointing to the historic evidence of New Lanark as a site where an alternative to the laissez-faire industrial model had been both conceptualized and implemented. They tended on the whole to focus once again on Owen's achievements in infant education, contrasting them with the abject failure of Victorian governments to follow through on the provision of nursery schools for the parents and children of the industrial proletariat. Their preference, also, was to use the memory of Owen as a means of reproaching the inadequacies of their contemporaries rather than as a genuine inspiration to those seeking practical alternatives to the teaching regimes of the time through which they were living. This was in some ways a lost opportunity, because in the wake of the major education reform acts of the 1870s and the accompanying expansion in state oversight of schools, there was much renewed debate about the forms of schooling an increasingly democratic and participatory society such as the United Kingdom should endorse. The Fabian Joseph Clayton was led to complain in 1908 that despite the increased citation of Owen in the critiques of government education policy, he was 'still but a shadow of a name, even in circles where Pestalozzi is honored; and the work Owen wrought for education at New Lanark, unsurpassed in the years that have followed, is still to be apprised at its true value' (Clayton 1908, p. 13). It is possible that an undue concentration on infant education, even among his most ardent supporters, skewed the reputation of Owen in a nation destined not to develop a systematic understanding of the place of pre-5 learning within its educational provision until almost a century later.

The Fabian rehabilitation of Owen did briefly succeed in projecting his relevance beyond the confines of infant education in the period after the First World War, when a wave of post-war legislation in England and in Scotland heralded a major reorganization of primary and secondary schooling across the United Kingdom. A. E. Dobbs' outstanding study of *Education and Social Movements, 1700–1850*, published in 1919, sought at last to assimilate the internal, Owenite and Cooperative hagiographies of Owen and his reforms to a broader narrative of modern British educational history, for the first time highlighting the important element of *conflict* between Owenism and the dominant, instrumentalist educational philosophies of the early nineteenth century. Accepting that the theme of infant education somehow crystallized Owen's divergence from the established modes of learning and teaching in early industrial society, Dobbs went further, arguing that:

The new Lanark experiment has a twofold interest. It drew attention to the problems of the infant school, and it represents the first important attempt made in this country to base a practical scheme of education on an original study of the child [...] The fact that the problem is still one of primary importance, although its urgency was recognised and treatment successfully applied in isolated cases from an early period, affords an example of the slow movement of new ideas and a warning against generalisations based on favourable instances. Nevertheless these experiments have probably done more than anything else to raise the question of educational aims and methods.

(Dobbs 1919, pp. 167–168)

As well as pointing out that Owen's alternative approach to education posed a serious (and unmet) challenge to the still authorized styles of mass education in his own time, Dobbs is one of the first twentieth-century commentators to place Owen's humanistic understanding of the 'original study of the child' at the centre of the overall appreciation of his work. Dobbs sets aside any detailed engagement with the abstract complexities of character formation and networks of village communities in favor of close attention to the Owenite vision of the needs and aptitudes of the child learner as the ethical and emotional heart of education. This was an element that the Owenites, of course, had always recognized, but it had often been submerged in their concern with broader social and political questions. In foregrounding it again as one of the distinguishing features of Owen's thought and practice, Dobbs subtly altered the general perception of Owen as an educationalist and helped enlist his legacy in the service of a new kind of educational reform agenda. Amplified in the writings of other sympathizers such as J. W. Adamson and Frank Smith, this interpretation of Owen as one of the first 'child-centered' educators won for Owenism in the inter-war period an attentive audience of politicians, policy-makers, and practitioners stretching well beyond the familiar boundaries of Fabian socialists and kindergarten activists. As a result, the highly influential Hadow Reports on *The Primary School* (1931) and *Infant and Nursery Schools* (1933) both made extensive historical references to Owen, very much in the spirit of Dobbs' observations. Much more importantly, while the term 'child-centered' does not figure directly in either of the Hadow volumes, they each quite deliberately build on carefully documented Owenite foundations – undoubtedly reinforced by the many submissions to the Hadow Committee from trade unions and cooperative guilds – to advocate a remarkably far-sighted conception of the needs and propensities of the 'whole child' as the kernel of the educational experience. 'The curriculum is to be thought of,' notes the 1931 Report, 'in terms of activity and experience rather than knowledge to be acquired and facts to be stored [...]':

> We desire to see the child as an active agent in his early schooling, making his approach to the activities necessary for an understanding of the body of human civilisation and for an active participation in its process, through his own experiences and his own activities, and relating his growing knowledge at all points to the world in which he lives.
>
> (Hadow 1931, Ch. 12, Section v)

This was the sort of language for the recovery of which Dobbs had fought: a revival of the willingness to 'question [...] educational aims and methods' on a scale not seen since the ferment of the revolutionary era. In finally bringing the heritage of Owenite thought back with such vigor into the centers of political decision-making in Britain, the Hadow Reports forged a new and potentially vibrant association between Owen's most radical ideas and the rising phenomenon of progressive education.

Progressive education

It is tempting to assume that the prominence accorded Owen and his educational thought in watershed documents such as the Hadow Reports somehow marks the advent of a just recognition of the man and his contribution to British education. It is certainly true that some of the key ideas and personalities associated with the Hadow Committee went on to exercise a considerable influence over the creation of the most important pieces of British educational legislation in the twentieth century: the 1944 and (in Scotland) 1947 Education Acts, which mapped out the future of compulsory education in the United Kingdom as one of the major pillars of the new welfare state emerging from the convulsions of the Second World War. It would be rash to conclude, however, that the line of liberal educational philosophy that runs from Hadow to the post-war Acts somehow seamlessly and definitively incorporates Owen and Owenism into the genealogy of popular, democratic education in the United Kingdom (Swinerton 1996). Whatever the achievements of mass education in Britain from the 1940s onwards (and they were conspicuous), it is misleading to imply that vital elements of learning and teaching, assessment, pedagogy, curriculum, or teacher-pupil relationships in any meaningful sense carried the imprint of Owen and his reforms. The one possible exception to this might have been nursery education, the repeated rallying-point of the Owenite educators through the decades. But even here the link to Owen was tenuous. Aside from the fact that nursery schools in Britain for generations singularly failed to reach the sectors of the working population for which the Owenites believed them ideally suited, never becoming a proper part of the compulsory local authority system, in their methods and culture they reflected the influence of the Froebelians much more than that of Owen (Reid 2006). Of course there were resemblances between Owen and Froebel's views of pre-5 education and many of the values of the sector would have been perfectly congenial to the Owenites, but evidence of direct imitation is much harder to find and few theorists or practitioners invoked Owen's memory in anything other than the most tokenistic fashion. Any broad overview of the educational life of post-war Britain, between 1945 and 1965, would have found it very difficult to argue persuasively for Owen's importance to contemporary practice in any sector, suggesting that Hadow in fact may well have represented the final, fitful flaring at the end of a tradition of educational optimism, rather than a new beginning on a completely alternative, Owenite roadmap.

It is with the coming to Britain of what became known to its supporters and opponents as 'progressive education' that a stronger case can be made for the alignment of prevailing educational values with principles that Owen might have recognized and endorsed. In a landmark 1938 account of progressivism in education, the American academic Emma Farrell identified seven principles of progressive education and argued strongly for their origins in the work of the New Harmony schools in the periods during and immediately after Owen's leadership. The seven principles as Farrell saw them were:

1 The freedom of children, male and female, to pursue their natural development.
2 Interest as the motivation for learning.
3 The teacher as guide not taskmaster.
4 The scientific study of child development (psychology).
5 Attention to the physical development of the child.
6 Home-school cooperation.
7 Schools and not governments leading educational developments.
(Farrell 1938)

This was a bold step on the part of Farrell, because by 1938 progressive education was indelibly associated with high modernity and seen by its leading exponents as in all key respects a phase in educational history surpassing in every area the primitive romanticism of an Owen, a Maclure, or even a Pestalozzi. Yet Farrell argued passionately that almost all of the hallmarks of the progressivism of her time had been anticipated in New Harmony both by Owen in his capacity as community leader and by Joseph Neef, the inspirational Pestalozzian schoolteacher whom Owen and Maclure had hired to manage learning and teaching in the New Harmony schools. Glossing over the internecine strife that had finally overtaken the New Harmony experiment, Farrell drew attention to the popular journalistic and community-based activism by which Owen had striven to win the hearts and minds of parents and public to support and finance the educational innovations at New Harmony. Farrell clearly felt that there was a lesson to be learned in reconnecting with this prehistory of progressivism, because the North American progressive education of her era (roughly contemporaneous with the Hadow Reports in England) remained – with the notable exception of the infant education sector – a coterie interest of professional educational scientists, psychologists, and teacher trainers, still viewed with great suspicion by the maintained schools and by many politicians. Farrell pointed to the essentially democratic, republican pedigree of the Owenite experiments in Indiana and their emphasis on the equal weighting of the seven principles. This last point was particularly relevant, because the rise of progressivism in the United States, and its export abroad as American cultural authority followed American military and economic power, saw the founding principles of the movement shift and mutate, with greater merit being placed upon the disciplines of developmental psychology and the practices of democratic citizenship. Included in this, in the United States, was a concerted attack on the influence of the Froebelians over kindergarten education, which had been all but expelled by 1920 (Cavallo 1976). In her placing of Owen within the genealogy of twentieth-century progressivism, Farrell pointed instructively to Owen's recognition that popular education could not be separated from the broader life and interests of society, and his understanding that the community had to be fully behind any roster of educational reforms if they were to be in a robust sense 'progressive.'

This was a lesson brought home in the United Kingdom in the period beginning with the educational changes of the 1960s. It is almost as if Owen's conviction that education had to develop in concert with other socially enlightened ideals received its most assured vindication in the sudden re-emergence of progressive educational principles that accompanied the gender and youth revolutions of the late 1950s and early 1960s in Britain. The growing influence of American progressive educational thought in the new colleges and universities responsible for the preparation of schoolteachers, assisted by the recruitment into primary and secondary teaching of large numbers of young men and women from a much wider class base than had been the norm for centuries, created an environment much more receptive to alternative, more radical views of learning and teaching, curriculum and pedagogy (Reese 2001). A younger generation increasingly committed to a socially transformative understanding of education as a means of overcoming class, gender, and racial barriers turned back to the optimism of the Hadow Reports and the suppressed histories with which they had tried to reconnect modern educational thought. As a consequence, across the educational jurisdictions of the British Isles, the decade from the mid 1960s until the mid 1970s is littered with major commissions, policy documents, and curricular reform initiatives once again in many respects close to the spirit of Owenism. Typical of these was the famous report *Primary Education in Scotland* of 1965, commonly known as the Primary Memorandum, of particular relevance since it appeared at a time when the 'Scottishness' of Owen and the events at New Lanark was becoming once more an area of heated historical interest as the two-hundredth anniversary of his birth drew near.

Progressive education is defined in the Primary Memorandum in terms of:

> The most fundamental changes [...] which have arisen from the growing acceptance by teachers of the principles underlying an education based on the needs and interests of the child and the nature of the world in which he is growing up. Through a wide range of experiences the pupil is given opportunities to participate actively in his own learning. As a result, his approach to what is to be learned is livelier and his final understanding deeper.
>
> (SED 1965, p. vii)

These sentiments echo clearly Owen's repeated arguments in favor of an approach to the teaching of the young which begins from an understanding of the child as a whole person. Owen's preference for justifying this in terms of the empiricist view of character formation has been set aside in the Memorandum, but the central principle of the child's own active participation in the acquisition of knowledge and understanding for flourishing in the world is highly resonant with the New Lanark classroom practices that Owen described and defended so lavishly in the face of his more cynical, instrumentalist critics. In the 1960s, political, economic, and cultural conditions allowed for the expression of progressivism as policy in exactly the language typified by the Primary Memorandum in Scotland and the Plowden Report in England and Wales. Politically speaking, successive governments in the 1960s and 1970s either actively promoted, or acquiesced in, the heightened professionalization of education and the creation of a new elite cadre of educational experts trained in the social and human sciences. Within educational psychology – the by now dominant discipline in teacher education – Piaget's developmental psychology held sway. In sociology, the subjectivist strand in social theory, drawing upon Schutz and Berger, and Luckmann, commanded the wide appeal of a teaching force increasingly identified with left-wing political agitation. Phenomenology and symbolic interactionism provided the theoretical basis of a social constructivist view of the curriculum. A loosely Marxian theory of society proposed ways in which the institutions of education could be harnessed to the redistribution of wealth and civic power. These factors combined, in effect, to create a fertile cultural and economic context for progressivism, incentivizing its adoption as a policy because of the pervasive social market belief that it would serve as a necessary condition for the egalitarianism that would inevitably perfect the third, technological phase of the Industrial Revolution.

It is perfectly valid to see these optimistic beliefs as in key senses a fulfillment of the Owenite vision of education as the engine of the new moral world. The technical rationality underpinning them might quite convincingly be viewed as a further extension of the Religion of Reason Owen was certain would replace the tired, useless dogmas of the past and herald the future perfection of man and society. The faith in both the natural and human sciences as the catalysts of far-reaching social change, as well as the almost millenarian attachment to the coming age of universal equality, also reverberate with the rhetoric of Owenite hope. It remains nevertheless problematic to see Owen and his educational thought as directly ancestral to the fashion for progressivism in the middle decades of the twentieth century. Such a view involves establishing plausible continuities in educational thought and practice across vast distances of time and drastically incommensurate social conditions. It was a favorite pastime of the pop and hippy generations of the progressivist period in question to appropriate intellectual forebears from among the luminaries of the Romantic era, such as William Blake and Samuel Taylor Coleridge, and there is some evidence, as we shall see in the final chapter, that Owen figures on this wish list of honorary forebears. But this was rarely more than a parlor game, obscuring profound cultural and epistemic differences, and no substitute for the careful scholarly appraisal of Owen's actual relationship to the social and educational changes of the modern age. A restrained, provisional judgment offered in 1971 by a member of Her Majesty's Inspectorate in Scotland, Margery Browning, just as the tide of progressivism had reached its high watermark in Britain, probably captures an abiding truth about Owen's stature as an educator: that he is best seen in longer historical perspective less as a model preserved and imitated down the generations by beleaguered visionaries and more as a vital, necessary element of the climate of opinion in any healthy, democratic understanding of the purposes of education (Browning 1971).

Extrapolating from this measured assessment to the social and cultural tensions of the present day, it is possible to see a thriving element of Owen's living legacy residing in his insistence that the center of moral gravity in mass education must be shifted from the producer-consumer nexus – with its attenuated, marketized construction of the human person and its atomizing effect on individuals and communities – to a secure locus in the sphere of shared public purpose and civic responsibility. Of course, Browning and others, such as David Hamilton, who offered a fresh assessment of Owen's legacy in 1980 when the reaction against progressivism had set in deeply in Britain and the United States, pointed to one very awkward reality confronting anyone committed to any enduring view of Owen's incontrovertible relevance to enlightened education: the stark fact that his most important monument, the village of New Lanark, had by the onset of the progressive era fallen into a state of almost total dereliction, its links to Owen almost forgotten and its ruin threatening to carry the memory of Owen's work into historical oblivion (Hamilton 1983). Examining the extraordinary feat by which the dissolution of New Lanark was prevented and then unexpectedly reversed by a band of latter-day Owenites throws an infinitely brighter light on his significance for education and society today than would have been conceivable even 25 years ago.

Chapter 6

Education, World Heritage, and Social Change: New Lanark as an Educational Experience

New Lanark lost and recovered

We have seen that throughout the period of Owen's international public career, the functioning presence of New Lanark remained central to his propaganda campaign on behalf of the new system. Owen himself knew that the strongest arguments in favor of his approach to education came from the evidence of New Lanark itself, in the form of its huge commercial success, its attractive environment, and the favorable opinion it won from the vast majority of visitors who came to the site and saw the school in action. The steady dissemination of the New Lanark philosophy to other areas of educational growth in Britain and abroad, most conspicuously infant education, furnished further proof of the success of his methods, reinforcing Owen's conviction that New Lanark could serve as the prototype for an entirely new model of progressive education. The financial and other links that Owen and his family retained with the village and its schools following the dissolution of the final partnership strengthened Owen's claims to be speaking from experience, even while the main audience for his ideas shifted from government ministries to networks of private philanthropy and cooperative organizations.

As the Owen-Dale family connection to the village began to loosen, New Lanark was ironically one of the first industrial locations to be inspected as a result of the factory legislation of which Owen had been one of the chief instigators. The inspection of 1833 was mainly concerned with the welfare conditions of employees, but it heaped abundant praise on the work of the school, including its academic standards and its pastoral care of some 450 children (Donnachie and Hewitt 1993, p. 147). This period between 1833 and 1860 perhaps represented the pinnacle of the school's achievements and saw it continue to operate for some considerable time in accordance with Owen's original goals. The continuity was perhaps understandable, given that ownership of the business had passed to the sons of Owen's esteemed partner, the Quaker John Walker. The two generations of the Walker family managed the village until 1881, a period covering some far-reaching changes in the structure of Scottish education (Donnachie and Hewitt 1993, pp. 141–165). Visitors to the village continued to report very approvingly on the life of the school, including two further formal inspections in 1851 and 1860 which described the conduct of learning and teaching very much in line with the methods codified by Owen and Buchanan when the school had been first created. Perhaps the only ominous observation made in these reports, formal and informal, was the note of a steady fall in the school roll, reflective of the wider decline of the village as a cotton manufacturing center in the face of increasingly stiff competition from Lancashire and abroad. In 1867, the school was visited as part of the comprehensive Argyll Commission investigation into the condition of education in Scotland, which was to pave the way for the 1872 Scottish Education Act, the largest restructuring of education in Scotland since the Reformation. As well as recording pupil numbers that were about half of the figure seen in Owen's time, the Argyll commissioners were in general ill-disposed towards 'alternative' or independent educational institutions, which were strongly associated with an age of piecemeal amateurism and charity that was giving way, by the last third of the nineteenth century, to much greater centralization and state control of mass education (Anderson 1983; McDermid 2006). It therefore came as no surprise that in the wake of the new education legislation, and with the village of New Lanark in a phase of more precipitate economic decline, the school was handed over to the new Parish School Board at Bankhead. The Parish Board closed the New Lanark school premises in 1878.

Wider changes were also overtaking the village in the same period. By the time New Lanark was finally sold by the Walkers in 1881, the material fabric of the village had begun to decay, exacerbated by some botched efforts at modernization and outbreaks of fire. The new owner, Henry Birkmyre of the Gourock Ropework Company (GRC), appears to have been a well-meaning but under-achieving business-man. He brought electrification to the village by 1898, but appears to have found it difficult to relate to the experience of workers on the factory floor. Birkmyre's sons entered into the ethos of the village much more thoughtfully than their father and tried hard from 1900 onwards to recapture some of the principles that had made the settlement a unique and profitable industrial venture for over a century. Their efforts included some renewal of the housing stock, the introduction of a proper sewage system, and concerted attempts to restore some of the social provision familiar from Owen's time. In 1911, they appointed as factory manager John Nicol, a figure who by accident or design stood in the lineage of paternalistic overseers of the village that stretched back to Owen and Dale. The villagers soon revered Nicol as their champion. He played a lead role in assisting them through the social and economic traumas of the first few decades of the twentieth century, deliberately invoking the heritage of Owen and cooperation in his dealings with his employees. Nicol's upstanding approach was perhaps more than fortuitous. As we have seen, this was an era of renewed interest in Owen, which saw many of the leading lights of the international labor and trade union movement attracted to New Lanark as an important monument to an indigenous philosophy of enlightened industrial manufacturing. It seems clear that the Birkmyres saw marketing potential in this as well as genuine inspiration for their own philanthropy (Donnachie and Hewitt 1993, pp. 175–182).

However sincere their ambitions to return New Lanark to some of its founding values, under the Birkmyres serious diversification of production did become necessary. Consequently, in addition to continuing the production of raw cotton, the weavers employed by GRC were required to produce goods as diverse as deckchair covers, military canvas, tenting material, rope, and fishing nets. These new products required new skills and new personnel and a final, if much smaller scale, wave of migrants came to the village from Ireland and other parts of Scotland from the late 1890s onwards. The revived atmosphere of Owenite cooperation under the junior Birkmyres appears to have mitigated some of the religious and ethnic tensions that afflicted comparable movements of workers in other parts of Central Scotland and integration at New Lanark appears to have been achieved with relative ease. There is evidence of a recovery of the spirit of mutuality in the community and among the workers, enduring at least until the advent of piece work and other divisive consequences of the economic slump between the two world wars. This was largely attributable to the closeness of a community continuing to live and work in a kind of microcosm, a self-contained world where managers and mill hands under Nicol's benign aegis worked and socialized together. Against the backdrop of sometimes wildly fluctuating economic cycles, New Lanark also benefited from expanding infrastructure developments along the Clyde Valley, including the arrival of a hydroelectric scheme, telecommunications, and a markedly improved road and rail network connecting it with Glasgow and Edinburgh. Internally, the GRC invested heavily in plant and machinery before and after the Second World War, with the intention of positioning the complex to take advantage of the coming of synthetics and the opening of mass markets for their products in the Commonwealth and, later, the European Customs Union. A symbolic moment came in 1953, with the ceremonial unveiling at the village of a plaque to commemorate Owen and to mark the continuing importance of the ethos of cooperation to the life of the village.

Behind the public displays of civic pride and continuity with the past, however, the executives of the GRC were aware of serious structural economic problems hidden by the brief superficial post-war buoyancy of the textile trade. Alongside the ongoing technical modernization of the factory, the owners confronted the challenge of an essentially eighteenth-century municipal environment that increasingly fell short of the exacting welfare and housing regulations of the 1950s and 1960s. The underlying problem, of course, was that the concept of a 'manufacturing community,' combining industrial production and social care within an arrangement of private commercial ownership, looked increasingly anachronistic, as well as – from the proprietors' view – financially unsustainable as the institutions of the welfare state matured. In recognition of this, the GRC in 1963 entered into a partnership with the newly-formed New

Lanark Association to begin renovation of the housing stock. Greater involvement of the local authority alongside central government conservation agencies eased, but by no means solved, the funding problems of upgrading the village and by 1967 the Association was bridling at the huge costs it faced in securing the long-term future of the site and its inhabitants. Unknown to the Association, the GRC had also embarked upon a major confidential review of its investments and in September 1967 all of the company's employees were called to a meeting in the Institute where it was summarily announced that the mills were to be closed by the end of the year. The peremptory actions of the GRC, despite their irrefutable commercial logic, threw the partnership into disarray. They left the Association and its public sector backers with responsibility for a village whose dwindling population now had little real reason to remain in New Lanark, alongside an increasingly derelict complex of abandoned cotton mills. The crisis deepened in 1970 when the GRC sold the mill buildings to Metal Extractions Limited (MEL), an industrial recycling and salvage company. MEL's activities on the site immediately compounded the problems faced by residents and conservers alike, because its industrial processes discharged large quantities of scrap metal and chemical effluent hazardous to human health and destructive of the fabric of the village. The mills as a result soon began to deteriorate and the roof of the neglected Old School collapsed. The effect of such rapid disintegration was to reduce the population of the village from 300 in 1968 to around 80 by 1972, effectively bringing the Association's restoration work to an abrupt halt. For a time, the future of New Lanark hung in the balance, raising the specter of its complete demolition as the only reasonable solution to a seemingly insoluble financial and environmental impasse.

In 1971, prompted by the Scottish Civic Trust, whose members were keenly aware of the crucial heritage and history of the village, Lanark Town Council convened an emergency meeting to respond to the deep crisis faced by New Lanark. A working group was formed to consider a range of options and the net result was that the New Lanark Conservation Trust was formed under the chairmanship of Harry Smith, then provost of the Royal Burgh of Lanark. Led by Smith, the long campaign for the complete restoration and revitalization of New

Lanark began. In 1973 New Lanark was designated as an Outstanding Conservation Area and the local planning department set in motion the process of listing the village buildings in the highest possible conservation category. In 1974, quite remarkably, *all* remaining village buildings in New Lanark were listed Category A and the Conservation Trust was constituted as an independent charity dedicated to the revival of the site as an authentic historical center. The Trust appointed Jim Arnold as its first manager and it is widely recognized in Scotland and beyond that Arnold's appointment was a crucial factor in determining the fate of the village. It is indeed hardly credible that, had it not been for the creation of the New Lanark Conservation Trust and the appointment of Arnold, the whole of New Lanark village and mills would almost certainly have been cleared by bulldozers and razed to the ground. Jim Arnold would eventually be awarded an MBE in 1989 in recognition of his leadership of the project to rescue the village and return it to the international attention it had once enjoyed.

In 1979 the Trust served a Repairs Notice on MEL and in 1983 a Compulsory Purchase Order placed by George Younger, Secretary of State for Scotland, secured recovery of the industrial plant from the scrap-metal firm. This was the first time such legislation had been used in Scotland to preserve a historic building. The costs were grant-aided by the National Heritage Memorial Fund, which underwrote the purchase and subsequently transferred ownership of the buildings to the Trust. Other crucial stakeholders in this vital period of survival and renaissance were the Scottish Development Agency and its successors, the Lanarkshire Development Agency and Scottish Enterprise Lanarkshire, which funded major environmental improvements including the clearing of scrap and aluminum slag from the industrial compound. During the 1980s, 20 house units in the village were sold to owner-occupiers for private restoration and two more tenancies were refurbished by the Housing Association. A major grant of £400,000 from the European Regional Development Fund in 1986 demonstrated that the site had achieved international status and in the same year New Lanark was finally nominated for UNESCO's World Heritage List. Three years later, in 1989, New Lanark Trading was established as the commercial arm of the Trust, putting in place the final institutional building blocks of a sustainable partnership of private investment and public finance to guarantee the long-term future of the site (Donnachie and Hewitt 1993, pp. 197–204).

In tandem with the work on the village, renovation and refurbishment was also carried out on the industrial and community buildings. Between 1977 and 1983 restoration work was completed on Owen's school to repair the collapsed roof and damage to the floors. Between 1986 and 1990 the Institute for the Formation of Character was meticulously returned to its former state. From 1994 to 1995 major restoration work was carried out to rebuild Mill One to its original height and – to coincide in appropriately Owenite fashion with the coming millennium – in 1999 and 2000 there was restoration and development of the school as an Interpretive and Educational Centre. This phase of the Trust's work marked an important turning point, some of the symbolic and educational implications of which will be explored later in this chapter. In line with the Trust's carefully planned and managed program of repair and restoration, there was simultaneous development of visitor facilities, which had been seen from the outset as vital to the long-term financial health of the Trust's whole operation. Picnic and play areas, car parking facilities, and direction signs to New Lanark on major motorways were completed during the 1980s. The New Lanark Visitor Centre opened, supported by cafeteria and exhibition areas in the former Institute for the Formation of Character, the Engine House and Mill Three. In 1993 the New Lanark Village Store reopened as part of the Visitor Centre, the restored water-wheel was installed at Mill Four wheel pit, while work began on the Petrie steam engine, returned to its original location in the Engine House. In 1994 the Millworkers' House in New Buildings opened as part of the Visitor Centre while Wee Row was refurbished as a 62-bed Scottish Youth Hostel Association youth hostel. In 1998 the New Lanark Mill Hotel and Waterhouses self-catering cottages opened and, from 1998 onwards, the Lanarkshire Development Agency and European Regional Development Fund became major sources of capital outlay for a further round of renovation.

Underpinning and supporting the rolling program of restoration and development in New Lanark were the strategically managed commercial investments made in the site from the 1980s onwards.

From 1985 to 1990 commercial tenancies were developed in Mill Three (Level 6), the Dyeworks, and David Dale's House and restoration work on the Mechanics' Workshop allowed the development of further commercial space for rent. By 1995, the number of businesses operating in the village had risen to 20. In the same year, there were two further commercial launches, one of national and the other of international significance. First, the completion of restoration work on the Mill Lade and Turbine House, and the reinstatement of hydro-electric power generation using a 1930s turbine and generator, meant that the electricity generated at the site was able to be sold to the National Grid, thus creating income for the Trust in a manner of which the Owenites would certainly have approved. Secondly, an award by the Overseas Development Agency of an international consultancy contract was given jointly to New Lanark Conservation Trust and Wanlockhead Leadmining Museum to develop business and development planning for Wieliczka Salt Mine, near Krakow in Poland. The number and variety of major awards that New Lanark received in the period after 1967 was indicative of the rising international profile and respect that the site had attained, not just in Scotland and the UK but across the globe. In 1976 the New Lanark community was brought to the attention of thousands of school students throughout Europe when Lanark Grammar schoolteacher, John Goldie, worked with sixth-year pupils to produce a video broadcast by the Olympus Satellite Project to schools in Europe. In addition, thanks to the enthusiasm and vision of the then education officer at New Lanark, Lorna Davidson (currently at time of writing, deputy managing director of the New Lanark Conservation Trust), adventurous teaching materials and resources were exchanged between New Lanark and New Harmony so that pupils and students were enabled to gain greater knowledge of their own community and its history as well as being encouraged to compare different lifestyles and cultures on either side of the Atlantic. Further recognition and evidence of esteem came in the form of accolades, national and international, for both tourism and conservation, including the Europa Nostra Medal of Honour (1987), the Heritage Education Trust Sandford Award for Educational Services (1999), and the Scottish Tourism Oscar for the best visitor center of the decade (2005). The zenith of these achievements was without doubt the inscription of New Lanark as a UNESCO World Heritage Site on 14 December 2001.

The rescue of New Lanark from the brink of extinction to its millennial entry on the World Heritage List rehearsed many of the themes of the village's chequered history, including its unique claims on educational attention. While promotion of the educational dimensions of the site's story remained prominent throughout its sustained period of recovery, they continued to be very firmly embedded in the broader social, architectural, and philanthropic narratives of its past, including its locus within industrial archaeology and its role in the foundation of the Cooperative Movement. This multiple profiling of New Lanark was also perfectly consistent with its history, because neither Owen nor his disciples had ever conceived of the educational innovations as anything other than a reflection of the values and attitudes of a new type of manufacturing community founded upon an enlightened anthropology. Similarly, it had always been part of the Owenite presentation of New Lanark to combine the ongoing internal remodeling of education in the village with a much more public showcasing of its innovations and achievements to the wider world. In this sense, the recent rehabilitation of the village and its inscription as a World Heritage Site is remarkably consistent with the dreams of its founders, particularly with Owen's aspiration that New Lanark be seen as both a proof of his theories and a catalyst for a much grander social and educational transformation. Criterion VI of the World Heritage bidding procedure highlighted what UNESCO termed an association with 'living traditions, with ideas or with beliefs, with artistic or literary works of outstanding universal significance.' The New Lanark submission's successful response to this criterion drew attention to the tangible legacy of Owen's breakthroughs as a writer and activist in 'progressive education, factory reform, humane working practices, international co-operation and garden cities' (Historic Scotland 2000, pp. 38–39). The 'living tradition' prized by UNESCO comes from a reimagining of the original educational mission of New Lanark as an obligation no longer discharged by a working school, by teachers, by buildings, or by a pedagogy – all of which have been overtaken by the march of time – but by the New

Lanark experience *as a totality* assuming its rightful station in a vital lineage of progressive educational thought with much insight still to offer to the contemporary world.

New Lanark and Utopia

Included in Historic Scotland's extended proposals for recognition of New Lanark as a World Heritage location was a bold description of what its sponsors called 'New Lanark as a Utopian Village' (Historic Scotland 2000, pp. 27–29). Clearly influenced by the scholarship of Thomas Markus and others, the authors gestured to the renewal of interest in utopian communities among European religious radicals of the later Reformation (especially the Moravians), by whom, as we have seen, Owen was in important ways influenced. This citation of what the document terms 'a practical model to Utopians' challenges directly the powerful skepticism evinced by William Hazlitt, whose recognition of the utopian strain in Owen's thought had served as a basis for derision rather than commendation. In returning to the undeniably utopian element in Owen's thought, the case for World Heritage status sought deliberately to highlight the utopian character of New Lanark as a resource to future generations rather than merely a forensic curiosity of a bygone age.

Owen's first heirs and disciples, especially in the Cooperative Movement, helped classify his sometimes protean utopian ideas into an educationally empowering lexicon, the vocabulary of which is instantly recognizable to modern progressivists. They achieved this principally through social action, in the creation and development of a range of schools movements and 'alternative' educational communities that eventually included initiatives in learning and teaching covering the complete spectrum from early infancy to adulthood. Terms such as 'imagination,' 'cooperation,' 'energy,' 'activity,' 'emulation,' 'play,' 'curiosity,' and 'liveliness' came to form the doctrinal core of this system of belief and practice, evolving a theoretical coherence and self-confidence firmly at odds with the dominant functionalist models of education against which Owen had fought. William Thompson defined the distinguishing characteristic of the New Lanark experience to be 'sympathy' between adults and children, inaugurating a countervailing *therapeutic* conception of pedagogical relationships in the classroom that anticipated much twentieth-century thinking in guidance, counseling, and the pastoral care of young people (Harrison 1969, pp. 220–222). It is, as we have suggested, possible to see in the Owenite reassertion of millenarian ideals an extension of the 'Romantic' critique of Enlightenment political economy, in which the consolidation of Owenite educational thought (and its increasingly secure positioning in wider socialist hermeneutics) helped lay the foundations of an alternative vision of activist utopian inspiration and polemic (Kumar 1990). Such a view places Owenism, warily perhaps, in a far more problematic relationship to the empiricist elements of the Enlightenment of which it is often alleged to be a predictable outgrowth. It emphasizes, instead, affiliations between Owen's utopianism and certain strains of counter-Enlightenment transcendentalism, through which the subversive, sometimes esoteric, inner light and evangelical longings of the late Renaissance found fresh articulation and social purchase, and the advent of which may well be taken to mark a faultline in the unfolding – and eventual decay – of the Enlightenment (Allan 1993, pp. 231–241). This interpretation helps explain the determination of Wilderspin, for example, to preserve older religious impulses alongside Owen's secularism in the understanding of the development of young children within the patterns of progressive infant education. Wilderspin argued, to Owen's eventual chagrin, that the effective provision of nursery education built on enlightened principles would raise a generation superior to any before it in 'religious and intellectual requirements,' which would in turn produce 'a glorious change in the moral world' and even the creation of 'a paradise.' The intention, he underlined, was 'to make *good* men rather than *learned* men – men of *wisdom* rather than men of *knowledge*' (McCann and Young 1982, p. 155). This is Owenite rhetoric in some senses marshaled to oppose Owenite materialism. Much it reprised in important respects the extravagant designs of the primitive Reformers, which the Enlightenment had striven in the name of critical rationality to consign to the dark age of religious enthusiasm.

If there is indeed a genealogy that links Owenite educational utopianism to the liberal-radical strands in modern educational thought, then its heritage has been obscured almost as completely as its ancestry. It is not a straightforward family resemblance, because beyond the initial flurry of followers and satellites there are undoubted lacunae in the lines of descent that make direct imitations of New Lanark, or any other Owenite site, almost impossible to discern or to arrange unambiguously into a meaningful historical tradition. The rise throughout the British Isles of a distinctive, centralized educational culture in the second half of the nineteenth century, from its earliest stages imposed on the social practices of mass education a set of values obeisant to the interests of the commercial-industrial complex, the regional and cultural hierarchies of imperialism, and the concerns of the social elites whose perpetuation relied on the unquestioned maintenance of both. The rapid advance of a state-sponsored, professionalized bureaucracy created to police the ideological purity of education in Britain, at precisely the time that its international reputation began to soar, resulted in an instrumental scientism inimical to the open, dialogic procedures of Owenite-style methods, which swiftly fell into disuse in most places where they had been adopted (Humes 1983). In his 1880 essay 'Signs of the Times,' Thomas Carlyle, with his immersion in the very different traditions of German idealism, was quick to identity the governing metaphor of this new outcome-obsessed intellectual regime regulating the nation's schools through its instruments of attainment and accountability – the machine:

> Were we required to characterise this age of ours by any single epithet, we should be tempted to call it [...] the Mechanical Age. It is the Age of Machinery, in every outward and inward sense of that word [...] Not the external and physical alone is now managed by machinery, but the internal and spiritual also [...] Thus we have machines for Education: Lancastrian machines; Hamiltonian machines; monitors, maps and emblems. Instruction, that mysterious communing of Wisdom with Ignorance, is no longer an indefinable tentative process, requiring a study of individual aptitudes, and a perpetual variation of means and methods, to attain the same end; but a secure, universal, straightforward

business, to be conducted in the gross, by proper mechanism, with such intellect as comes to hand.

(Carlyle 1899b, 27.59)

From a perspective close to Owen's suspicion of 'mere animal machines' stifling human freedom, Carlyle unmasks the tangible sense of alienation that informs the experience of 'individual Mammonism and Government by *Laissez-faire*' (1999c, 10.186) in the modern systems of mass education. 'This is indeed a time when right Education is, as nearly as may be, impossible,' remarks his fictional savant Teufelsdrochk in his novel *Sartor Resartis* (1899a, 1.97).

For these reasons, the modern afterlife of the Owenite utopian impulse in British educational thought has been confined to a subterranean current of individualized, eccentric, and isolated radical commentary, breaking out only occasionally into a fully self-contained working alternative to the status quo. If this 'dissenting tradition' of British education possesses a unifying feature – and one which connects it to the radical movements of which Owen may be considered one of the founders – it lies in its adherence to the deliberative application of ethical, spatialized utopianism as a critical practice for the interrogation and defamiliarization of the prevailing values of the governing cultural and educational order (Halpin 2007b). As the polymath town planner and Scottish social reformer, Patrick Geddes, recognized, utopian visions of education require to be 'thickened,' to be made culturally convincing and meaningful, by exhibiting their consistency with a comprehensive understanding of the good society. This was a view also maintained by Owen. For Geddes, the roots of such an understanding were to be found in a complex ecology of self and community, heightened awareness of which would 'place brains in the conditions most favourable to their development and activity,' and enable 'the problem of psychological economics to pass over into that of education' (Geddes 1884, p. 978). Idealized forms of educational experience could exist only in a material continuum with the other social, economic, civic, and domestic dimensions of the total *environment* (a word, ironically, as we have seen, unknown to Owen and in fact coined by Carlyle), enveloping and nurturing the individual and lending purpose to existence (Sorensen

1995). Geddes' sense of the *spatial* imperative in learning and teaching, the importance of 'local habitation' and a *belonging to place*, stems from his ambitious (and largely unfulfilled) aspirations as a utopian planner of modern urban communities in a lineage of which Owen is a key if controversial figurehead. Exposure to the scale of educational failure in the urban squalor of the late nineteenth century UK cities prompted Geddes to search out an underlying malaise or 'mental arrest' in the intellectual assumptions of the age. The most egregious error, in Geddes' view, was the Enlightenment obsession with 'formalization,' a rationalistic fixation on division, sequencing, product and output – typified by testing – which sought to 'enclose' the boundless possibilities of the educated life in the prudential calculus of unaided reason:

> The would-be educationalist [...] (coldly and dully, hence stupidly), [tries] to impress those high products [...] upon his pupils' everyday feelings [...] Education is turned to instruction, and this tested by memory-examination, so with the result of all these – as COPY, as CRAM, as JAW.
>
> (Boardman 1978, p. 455)

Only by recovering an organic, embodied sense of interdependence, in which schooling would be seen to arise naturally out of the interactions and exchanges of a questing, self-renewing polity – and in which knowledge would be integrated with work, celebration, and self-development – could education genuinely hope to encompass the thoroughgoing restoration of humanity needed to avert the coming catastrophe of hyperindividualism and unsustainability. Geddes called this desired state, this longed-for place, 'Eutopia' and his language amplifies many of the most urgent claims of Owen and his followers, cleverly disinterring from the ancient etymology of *u-topia*, 'no-place,' the *eu-topia*, 'good place,' which is, as Owenites knew, forever inscribed in the history of the word (Meller 1990, pp. 311–312).

The utopian (or 'eutopian') critique of modern instrumentalist and performative interpretations of the purposes of education seems always to find its greatest resonance in areas where the system's internal contradictions become most manifest. This may be, as Raymond

Williams famously suggested, one of the purposes of 'heuristic utopias' – 'to strengthen and confirm existing feelings and relationships which are not at home in the existing order and cannot be lived through in it' (Williams 1983, p. 13). Such was the view that visibly informed the utopian educational initiatives of R. F. Mackenzie at Summerhill Academy in Aberdeen in the 1960s and 1970s. Influenced by his reading of Owen, Combe and Froebel, his experience of the Second World War, and his admiration for the Summerhill experiments in 'de-schooling' of A. S. Neill in England, Mackenzie set out to offer a radical alternative to the orthodoxies of the education around him, redesigning the patterns of participation, decision-making, authority, and academic assessment, while criticizing the complacency of an educational culture that claimed to maximize access but in fact structurally excluded the majority of children from success. Mackenzie's strategy drew heavily on the moral temper of the dissenting tradition of the Owenites, dilating on many of their key critical themes: the self-perpetuation of an establishment ideologically disguised as consensus; the insidious barbarism of the logic of control, discipline, and compliance in the systems of schooling; the reification of notions of curriculum serving only to circumscribe knowledge, wisdom and experience, and confirming most pupils only in their exile and failure. Mackenzie offered instead:

> a search for excellence, a love of doing things well, a self-forgetting absorption to putting every scrap of ability one possesses into a picture, a poem or a song [...] we want to give [children] an education which will help them endure and survive the Industrial Revolution which is disrupting their lives and to choose wisely when they take their place in tomorrow's world.
>
> (Mackenzie 1967, p. 189)

This historicization of the Industrial Revolution resonates again with the sense that seems to have grown in Owen as his career advanced that effective education would not simply compensate for the brutalities of the capitalist mode of production, but would release the human mind to think through entirely different modes of organizing work and distributing its fruits in a post-capitalist society.

Mackenzie's recognition of the complicity of existing education with unjust structures of control and confinement represents an abiding reproach to the 'knowledge economy' conception of education gaining ground in the period of his headship, and which was destined finally to overwhelm his and most other efforts at resisting its encroachments. Mackenzie's thought breaches the insularity of a system unwilling properly to acknowledge its collusion in wider patterns of historical change, wedded to a mythic account of its own ancestry, and too often blind to its worst defects as a supposed vehicle of social inclusion. The tenor of his commentary on the prophetic witness of Summerhill Academy to a wholly contrasting conception of the enfranchised educated polity and the empowered subject unavoidably invokes Owenite motifs of utopian and millenarian idealism:

> We'd gone back to first and last things and asked, in a crisis in the history not only of Scotland but of Western civilisation, how do we bring up Scottish children to live fully and happily in an integrated society of which they all feel themselves members?
>
> (Mackenzie 1976, p. 30)

Mackenzie's sense of crisis reasserts the subversive force of the utopian impulse in its continuing confrontation with ideologies that naturalize their own compromised conditions of existence and dominance. The modalities of utopian thought and experiment involve, as Mackenzie's opening words suggest, the invocation of an archaic language of accountability, but only to move beyond the potentially outdated rhetoric suggested by notions of millennium and apocalypse to a new kind of secular eschatology of which Owen is arguably one of the first architects – a citation of judgment where the shifting ratios of utopia and Enlightenment, held in permanent dialectical tension one with the other, enable each generation to test and historicize the limits of any totalizing order in which education is said to have achieved its final, fittest or inevitable form.

Hazlitt had critiqued Owen's utopianism for its implicitly hubristic and authoritarian tendencies. Later skeptics were more likely to point disparagingly to its escapism, its implausible disconnection from the lived realities in which social institutions such as schools must continuously compromise their ideals for social transformation in the face of the insurmountable truths of political power or the unalterable venality of the human condition. Owen would have protested against both of these latter-day objections, declaring them a part of the fatalistic moral economy he believed progressive education would help overthrow. His position, however, would at no time have been that of a deluded fantasist, heedless of the realities in which men and women live. On the contrary, Owen's utopianism, and his concerted efforts to realize it in the daily life of New Lanark, was hard-won, founded on a gritty appraisal of the often grim, *dystopic* circumstances in which the bulk of mankind was in early industrial culture compelled to toil, while at the same time fully alert to the sheer enterprise needed from anyone trying to wrest improvement from the recalcitrant materials of nature and society. Ironically, 'dystopia', an eighteenth-century neologism formulated in direct opposition to 'utopia,' and therefore meaning something like 'worst place,' was given one of its earliest public expressions by the anti-Owenite John Stuart Mill in a House of Commons attack on the social policies of the Disraeli government: 'It is, perhaps, too complimentary to call [the government] Utopians,' he announced, 'they ought rather to be called dys-topians, or cacotopians. What is commonly called Utopian is something too good to be practicable, but what they appear to favour is too bad to be practicable' (*Hansard* 1868, 1517.1) Owen would have protested not only at the supposed impracticability of a utopian vision of society, but also at Mill's careless suggestion that dystopias are equally impossible to invent. Dystopic visions of industrial society were not, for Owen, nightmare imaginings of a remote future condition, but part of the present fabric of daily life for millions of working-class people.

In these regards, Owen's utopianism and its legacy for modernity anticipates the revival of interest in educational utopias seen in recent postmodern theory. Owen's practice combines the vision of *utopia as territory* with utopia *as temporality*: utopia can inspire, for Owen, the reform of social and cultural space in the here and now; it can also point forward to an ongoing pursuit of perfection into the future, in which rational education will assist both in the removal of evils and in the progressive embrace of the good. It is therefore no mere illusion or consolation, but an assertion of human agency wrested from the intractability of the present and motivated by practical hope for the building of something better (Halpin 2002, pp. 31–45). This version of 'human freedom', argues Marianna Papastephanou (2008. P. 94):

> as constant creative reaction to empirical reality precludes a totalizing and non-revisable determination of utopian contents [...] Along with it, the finitude of human existence, the limits of knowledge and existential scope, preclude the finality of the perfect time and the finalism of the perfect space. Utopia emerges only as a possibility, felt through disconnected instances of the good embedded in everyday life and in various social contexts.

It is perhaps this pragmatic principle of 'utopian embeddedness' that the material recovery of New Lanark, more than any other aspect of the Owenite legacy, succeeds in communicating to posterity: the dangerous, subversive, alternative memory of an educational past that can also go on sustaining itself as an inspiration for the remaking of education into the indeterminate future.

New Lanark as heritage

If New Lanark is itself an educational experience, then in what does that experience consist today? In keeping with their subtle reading of the aspiration of the founders of the village, refracted through almost a century and a half of Owenism, the officers of the Trust have succeeded in projecting the educational relevance of the village along the three distinct but related axes of past, present, and future. As a result, New Lanark has become a magnet location for parties of students and teachers – ranging from primary school pupils to university graduates – interested in both the history of education and in the continuing salience of the values of the site for current debates on the relationship of education to work, citizenship, and international social justice. Focusing briefly on some of the prime locations that figure in the itinerary of a typical fieldwork visit to New Lanark further reinforces the sense in which the principles of Owenism are inseparable from their material realization in place and time. It also facilitates reflection upon the bearing of these principles on some of the challenging social questions with which education is interwoven globally at the outset of the twenty-first century.

The most imposing and iconic building in New Lanark remains what it was in Owen's era: the Institute for the Formation of Character. The Institute has evolved into the main entry-point to the modern Visitor Centre, thereby necessarily losing any obvious or direct association with the purposes for which it was built. This change of function reflects important transitions that have taken place in the understanding of the relationship of education to character formation. In standard liberal-democratic educational ethics, the notion that human beings can be exhaustively understood as the products of their circumstances and nothing else has run up against concepts of autonomy, rationality, and individual human rights first articulated by John Stuart Mill – partly, as we have seen, in reaction to Owenite determinism. This assertion of rights and individual freedom undoubtedly prompts appreciable modern-day skepticism towards totalizing schemes such as Owen's, bent upon the inscription of character exclusively though the operation of environmental factors. Indeed, programs rooted in a moral psychology of this kind would routinely be associated today with authoritarian regimes and held in deep suspicion because of this. It seems nevertheless obvious that progressive education has by no means set aside entirely the belief that the attitudes and values of the individual form as the result of the social and cultural influences to which he is exposed from early life onwards.

Contemporary initiatives in social inclusion, full-service schooling and, most conspicuously, education for citizenship, continue to demonstrate the liberal conviction that education can be harnessed systematically to the active formation of specific values and dispositions in individuals and groups for the purposes of social change (Arthur 2005; Davies 2005). The imposing presence of the Institute for the Formation of Character signifies more assuredly than any other feature of the New Lanark site Owen's unswerving belief that effective education was integral to the creation of flourishing citizens. Amidst the economic and cultural fragmentation that seems to accompany the processes of globalization, the reawakening of interest across the educational systems of many democratic societies in notions of civic participation and active citizenship can stand as a vindication of Owen's insight, even if the approach to citizenship education would today assume forms that Owen would not recognize. The major difference would be a fundamentally political one: the operation of the Institute in Owen's time and after, for all its far-sighted recognition of the wholeness of the human person as learner, worker, and citizen, remained essentially paternalistic and paternalism represents a value with which modern liberal education would be at root incompatible. We have suggested throughout this book that in order to understand Owen's paternalism it is necessary to engage with his conflicted views of fatherhood, family, and power. These were issues endemic to the shifting social and cultural valences of the Industrial Revolution, which, Owen instinctively realized, had precipitated a crisis in the social and cultural reproduction of the family unit, in both its domestic and extended forms (Nielsen 1994). A beneficiary of extended family networks in his own early life, Owen recognized from his Manchester years onwards that industrialization was vitiating the family as a source of social and symbolic capital. While he was often fiercely critical of the introspection and stagnation of the traditional family, he made repeated efforts throughout his commercial career to intervene in this process of erosion, seeking ways in which working-class family life could be preserved in the face of economic upheaval and the resultant clash of intergenerational values. Veneration of Owen as a 'social father' and condemnations of his paternalism can be interpreted as contrasting responses to the same phenomenon: that the more Owen strove to reinvent the institutions of traditional domestic piety in the face of the volatility of industrialization, the more he found himself becoming, in effect, a substitute father; an unaccountable benefactor looking after the welfare of his workers and residents from out of his own largesse and philanthropy. The Institute for the Formation of Character stands as a monument to these tensions in Owen's thought and practice. A building dedicated to the empowerment of individuals can in certain lights be seen as the supreme demonstration of paternalistic power and indulgence; a center anticipating some of the most progressive developments in popular citizenship can also at the same time symbolize the subordination of the poorest classes to the autocracy of one arbitrary plutocrat. The Institute serves as a reminder that the modern concept of citizenship has a mixed pedigree and that some of its covert associations with social regulation may continue to test its relationship to liberal democratic education and the goals of genuine participation (James 2008).

None of these wider reservations diminishes the unique status Owen accorded education within the Institute. Even if the premises functioned within a system of paternalistic governance, they quite transparently promoted styles of learning and personal growth conducive to the exercise of faculties likely to prove in the long run fatal for paternalism. It seems clear that in his open-ended embrace of education, Owen fully realized this, accepting his own status as a transitional figure between two different understandings of society. In offering at the Institute opportunities for workers to continue their learning in fully socialized contexts, Owen furnished the embryonic movements in adult and continuing education in early industrial society with a vital source of ideas. Once again, it is possible to argue that subsequent developments in, for example, the formation of the Mechanics Institutes for adult education, and the trade unions, moved rapidly in directions that would isolate New Lanark as a rural exception to the large-scale industrial models evolving in the major cities. Nevertheless, an important part of Owen's living relevance is his readiness to open up debate about the relationship of adult education to vocational training, lifelong learning, and personal recreation. These questions have become more urgent than ever in a post-industrial age where the self is routinely regarded as the last resource to be exploited, and where workers in the infomatics economy are promised only a lifetime of competitive retraining and self-reinvention (Coffield 1999; Crowther 2004). Owen believed that a rationally organized industrial system would mean progressively less labor and more leisure, provided the problems of access and accountability were resolved. For this reason, although the Owenite scheme maintained a close association between education and work, and acknowledged the need to provide a skilled workforce for a mechanized and highly competitive economy, the Institute came quickly to represent an enriched conception of vocational learning to which the recreation of the self was integral.

Determining the appropriate balance between the elements of training, recreation, leisure, and self-fulfillment in post-compulsory education has since become central to the cultural politics of adult education. Even where its contemporary champions advocate an emancipatory and politicized understanding of lifelong learning, they often do so in a moral language that Owen and Owenism helped to craft (Rogers 2006).

The fieldwork visit to the Robert Owen school at New Lanark is an encounter with a series of paradoxes parallel to those raised by the Institute and which need to be thought through with equal vigilance in the assessment of Owen's legacy and contemporary relevance. Children, especially, when visiting the school are enabled to take part in entertaining mock lessons imitating aspects of the Owen-Buchanan methodology, which they can then contrast with their knowledge of some of the more punitive approaches common at the beginning of the nineteenth century. Visiting children are also given access to sample reproductions of the resource materials employed in the school in Owen's time. The enlightened character of learning and teaching as they were practiced at New Lanark is immediately obvious to all visitors, as is the school's paramount ethic of care. In some ways there is much less ambivalence about this dimension of Owen's contribution to the creation of popular education, with the school museum succeeding in conveying to onlookers Owen's exceptionalism as a patron of education for the working poor. Owen's efforts to elevate positive classroom relationships, between teacher and pupils and between children themselves, were without doubt astonishingly far-sighted and a major source of the respect that his innovations commanded in radical circles. If they were subsequently eclipsed for many decades by the revival of monitorialism and the 'industrialization' of state-controlled schooling in the later nineteenth century, their eventual resurgence in the discourses of progressive education certainly owes much symbolically to the precedents set by Owen and his collaborators.

The classroom pedagogy favored by Owen was initially indebted to established rationalist practice of the kind pioneered by Joseph Lancaster, but Owen's dislike of memorization and rote learning for their own sake censured these seemingly enlightened methods and offered a convincing alternative that later generations of teachers were to embrace. Owen's most important contention as a creator of classrooms was that successful learning depended upon the prior happiness of the learner and that such happiness was the fruit of virtuous relationships and the kind treatment of children by adults. Owen was not the first to propose this, but he was quite probably the first to attempt to implement it and to raise it to the level of an international public campaign, the propaganda for which centered on the living proof of his teachers' practice. We can see with progressivist hindsight that the main pedagogical breakthrough achieved by Owen was to take the principles of self-motivation and rational participation previously the preserve of educated elites and to extend them to a sector of the population hitherto excluded from education. 'It was quite new,' Owen noted in his autobiography 'to train the children of the working class to think and act rationally' (Owen 1993e, 4.288). Against the drilling in *habit* preferred by the Lancastrians for large-scale learning and teaching, Owen advocated an embrace of knowledge based upon rationalist values of consent and *agency*, to be incentivized naturally through the creation of a classroom environment open to discovery and the shared construction of meaning by all present within it. Once again, this philosophy was to a great extent marginalized in the educational reforms of the Victorian period, but the record of it remained and its preservation continued in part in some of the alternative schools established by the Cooperative Movement and related organizations. The recovery of its relevance for mainstream schooling by progressive practitioners in the twentieth century, reinforced by the developmental psychology of Piaget and the child-centeredness of John Dewey, reminds us of the role it continues to play in challenging every diminished or instrumental account of the purposes of schools (Lowe 2007, pp. 159–173).

Principles of pupil motivation, exploration, and discovery have become absolutely central to the practice of teaching in liberal democratic societies in the modern period. The interest in cooperative learning in many of today's classrooms, where pupils collaborate in the allocation of roles for the completion of tasks, in hypothesis-formation and in joint problem-solving, has roots deep in the values promoted by Owen. Similarly, the general outward-facing attitude of contemporary schools, aware of their locus in the community and stimulated by the educational possibilities of the external environment, echoes Owen's profound concern with the relationship between the inner realm of the school and the needs of the external world to which the school belonged. For Owen, the primal expression of this value was the direct pedagogical engagement with the outdoors as a unique source of physical growth and experiential learning for the young. The fieldtrips led by Buchanan and Young were often seen as eccentric by their contemporaries – and certainly they seemed at the time highly dependent upon the picturesque natural landscape in which New Lanark was fortuitously set. But they were also clearly vital in the cultivation of the emotions of pleasure and surprise that Owen held to be integral to successful education. Hence the popularity they have subsequently gone on to enjoy with initiatives ranging from the Outdoor Education Movement to the Norwegian *Friluftsliv* (or 'free air') campaign, which has elevated the open-air exploration of landscape and nature by schoolchildren to a distinctive educational ethic for the twenty-first century (Gelter 2000).

The New Lanark Trust has recently reinforced this strong association of education with the outdoors by the opening of a 9,000 square-foot roof garden and viewing platform on top of the restored Mill 2, designed by landscape architect Douglas Coltart. The ambience of the roof garden takes up many contemporary themes not only in the practices of outdoor education, but also in the values of education for sustainability and ecological awareness. While these are peculiarly modern preoccupations, to which the social studies and citizenship curricula of many democratic nations are now urgently required to respond, the garden is organized so as to illustrate their historic consistency with Owen's core values. Chief among these – as several quotations from his writings inscribed around the garden demonstrate – was Owen's belief that immersion in therapeutic natural surroundings could help nurture sympathetic, gregarious personalities among any population of adults and children. It could heal some of the damage inflicted by industrial living and assist in attuning human beings to the needs of others, firmly rooting the community in a responsible sense of organic continuity with nature. In the development of the roof garden, the contemporary New Lanark captures skillfully the synthesis of the 'Enlightenment Owen' and the 'Romantic Owen' and proves deftly the abiding relevance of each. The importance of place to an educational ecology makes the powerful Owenite point for contemporary educators that no amount of formal instruction in the ethics of sustainability can match the felt experience of inhabiting a location where the human and natural interact in a morally creative synergy of self and environment. This amounts, ultimately, to one of Owen's most lasting and tangible legacies: the placing of education at the heart of a thoroughgoing communitarian ethic.

Of almost as much importance for Owen as the outdoors was the school playground – an intermediate zone between the formalities of the classroom and the open-ended discoveries of the fieldtrip. The key to understanding the playground lay, for Owen, in the recognition that the free play of children in the spaces adjoining the school contained the potential to bring together the unselfconscious embodied joy of childhood with the impulse towards mutual understanding that would arise necessarily in the unstructured social interactions of even the youngest pupils. The spontaneity of the playground would prove the hypothesis that human beings possessed a natural propensity for cooperation, for the compelling scientific reason that cooperation in play, games, and physical activities maximized the happiness of all, individually and collectively. Owen's suggested regulation of the playground at New Lanark was, as a result of these idealist assumptions, light, involving some limited adult supervision alongside the informal care of younger children by older ones. In the playground, Owen believed:

> the child will be placed in a situation of safety, where, with its future school-fellows and companions, it will acquire the best habits and principles [...] The area is also to be a place of meeting for the children from five to ten years of age, previous to and after school hours [...] and a shade will be formed, under which in stormy weather the children may retire for shelter.
>
> (Owen 1993f, 1.58)

It is also true that Owen saw that one purpose of the playground was 'to serve as a drill-ground' where boys would receive rudimentary training in military-style exercise. This intended use of the playground was later a source of some discomfiture for Owenites, many of whom gravitated into pacifist politics as the nineteenth century wore on. It is important to recognize, however, that Owen's original remarks on the drilling of boys were intended as a criticism of the standing armies that had dominated the political landscape of the Napoleonic period and which had often been used for internal repression in Britain during and after the wars with France. Playground drilling was, for Owen, a sign of the school's contribution to citizenship, and a reminder that in the renewed society he hoped to see emerge out of the Village Schemes, any resort to military force would be subject to the general will and the consensus of the community. While this supplementary use of the playground highlights the necessary limitations on any effort to conscript Owen to a progressivist educational politics quite alien to his time and situation, it also demonstrates the need for a subtle reading of his educational programs as they took shape in New Lanark. Viewed as a whole, the New Lanark school represents a values system that cannot be localized to any of its discrete elements, but which communicates in its rounded entirety an understanding of childhood, of learning, and of egalitarian well-being highly prophetic of the best practices of later progressive education. In the light of this, part of the legacy of the building for the modern age resides in its continuing assertion of these values in an era when they have come under concerted attack from performative measures of school effectiveness, attainment, and knowledge production. An important educational purpose of an expedition to New Lanark can be seen as the effort to engage each fresh generation of young people in the conversation about the nature and purposes of schooling as the capitalist society that Owen helped both to create and critique appears to be entering another phase of its evolution, and once again draws the institution of the school into its complex, conflicted designs (Ryan 2008).

In an analogous spirit of free enquiry, joining the wisdom of the past with the best practices of the present and the dynamic imagining of the future, the New Lanark Trust has recently introduced to the village what is termed an 'interactive gallery.' Unlike the Institute or the school, the gallery does not tie itself to the traditions of any specific building within the complex. Nor does it simply commemorate or re-enact the practices of the past. Instead, it is a modern interactive playroom, the purpose of which is to celebrate the contemporary relevance of Owen's 'progressive ideas of infant education' by showcasing their affinity with instances of some of the most advanced methods currently available for the education of the very young. In what is one of the boldest gestures on the site, visitors are taken not backwards, to the recreation of the Owenite methods of the nineteenth century, but outwards and forwards to examples of leading-edge pre-5 and kindergarten facilities most strongly associated with the world's foremost nursery education centers, such as Reggio Emilia in northern Italy. The gallery offers a multisensory experience of color, sound, and light, enabling visitors to move around a sequence of self-contained rooms dedicated to the stimulus of the young child's mind through visual and aural displays, interactive surfaces, and the open, playful investigation of space. The overall impact is appropriately futuristic, tied firmly to current understandings of the development of infant minds and allied to the most vigorous assertions of the uniqueness of the pre-5 curriculum. It represents a radical attempt to associate Owen and New Lanark with all that is currently most prized in infant education internationally, almost in riposte to the erasure of his influence in the standard histories of infant schooling which began with Buchanan and Wilderspin and which continued with the rise of Froebelian nursery education in Britain and North America (Whit-bread 1972, pp. 17–28).

It is certainly the case that Owen's role in the founding of nursery education has never been properly acknowledged, mainly because his ground-breaking methods were initially altered beyond recognition by some of his own followers and then assimilated to a national system of infant education in many respects remote from his original values. The re-emergence of a progressive pre-5 educational ethic in the later nineteenth century in the English-speaking world then turned to Froebel and Pestalozzi for inspiration, largely sidestepping Owen's example. Even the famous Reggio Emilia philosophy, to which the interactive gallery pays inevitable homage, has its own independent ancestry in the thinking of Loris Malaguzzi and before him Rousseau (Rinaldi 2006, pp. 53–61). The main purpose of the gallery perhaps then needs to be seen as genealogical rather than historical. Although no unbroken historical continuity can reasonably be established between the New Lanark infant school and the burgeoning of progressive pre-5 education in the nineteenth and twentieth centuries, the creation and operation of the gallery restates the significance of Owen's original breakthrough and confirms its affinity with much that is most highly esteemed in the sector today, especially its counter-cultural celebration of non-instrumental play as the defining characteristic of early childhood. Moreover, in an era where infant education has been increasingly ensnared in the performative logic of the wider education system, compelling nursery educators to confirm the efficacy of their work with reference to its verifiable contribution to the 'competence' of young children and their 'readiness' for elementary school, the interactive gallery draws attention to the endurance of an alternative model and highlights its indigenous pedigree. It is an intervention of the first importance in consolidating Owen's reputation as a founder of infant education to whom the late industrial world can turn today as it reflects upon its duties to the lives and imaginations of its youngest members.

Reimagining Owen: New Lanark and educational tourism

It is perhaps significant, from the twin perspectives of memory and prophecy, that the culmination of the tourism experience of New Lanark is an encounter with two spirits – the first a ghost of the Owenite past, the second a spirit of a possible Owenite future. It seems fitting, somehow, that the Owen who embraced at the end of his life the 'rational' religion of spiritualism should have his achievements and his ideas spectrally represented at his most important site by two disembodied products of holographic technology, gesturing to the past and to the future in ways which unexpectedly illuminate the educational preoccupations of the present. Of course, 'Annie Macleod,' the mill girl who takes New Lanark visitors back to an imagined recreation of the village in the 1820s, and 'Harmony,' the young female time-traveler from the year 2200 returned to the present day to tell us of the bright utopian future that lies ahead, are figures of entertainment as well as education, perhaps vulnerable to the theme-park criticisms that are often made of commercial heritage sites seeking novel ways of maintaining their competitive standing as visitor attractions. If Annie and Harmony do possess this touristic aura, then it is a satisfyingly apposite one, reminding visitors that New Lanark was a tourist destination long before it was manufacturing community, and that even as a philanthropic cotton-producing village it was a prominent international destination on the itinerary of progressively-minded travelers almost from its inception by Dale and Owen, its two most successful propagandists. Annie and Harmony may be fittingly ghostly guides to a New Lanark that never was and a New Lanark that never will be, but they perform an educational task even in discharging those ambiguous, estranging roles, serving to remind us that, throughout its existence, image and representation have been vital to the identity of New Lanark and seem likely to remain pivotal to its ongoing symbolism of an educational ideal, and its negotiation of the difficult questions that continue to be raised by that ideal. Speaking specifically of the spectral effects of film, Jacques Derrida tells us that all ghosts are 'memories of a past that was never present' (McMullen 1983). Our encounter with the ghosts of Annie and Harmony teaches us that that there may be no 'real' New Lanark to be retrieved from the layers of the past after all, or to be appropriated by the vociferous, competing educational philosophies of the present. Instead, we are offered an experience of the site which simultaneously distances and brings close, makes recognizable and renders foreign – opening up a virtual space within which we can recognize the uncanny familiarity of New Lanark while beginning the subtle task of narrating our own evaluations of it (Bendix 2002; Conroy 2009).

The 'Annie Macleod Experience' is an audio-visual journey into New Lanark's past led by the spirit of a 10-year-old girl who narrates her memories of living in the New Lanark of the 1820s. The sequence elicits from its audience sympathetic human interest in precisely the kind of iconic working-class child that Owen himself emotively invoked to win public support for his schemes. Annie combines the projection of a vulnerable and somewhat harassed young mill worker with remarkably painstaking recreation of the realities of family life, schooling, and employment in the New Lanark of the period of

Owen's stewardship. The characterization may be two-dimensional, but care is taken to present Owen as a demanding as well as a philanthropic employer and the recognition accorded Owen's educational innovations sits adjacent to quite unsparing portrayal of even his relatively enlightened factory regime. The harshness of working-class labor is well drawn and the stress of daily life is effectively conveyed. The 'journey' – as it is appropriately termed – succeeds in making its viewers aware of the distance that separates Owen's New Lanark from the social realities of a modern welfare democracy and ultimately defamiliarizes some of the standard 'visitor center' formulae that accompany the promotion at heritage sites of heroic figures from the national past. Seen in context, the attraction certainly enhances appreciation of Owen's radical social and educational reforms in the village, defending their originality and emphasizing implicitly their contemporary relevance. It does this, however, by capturing some of the tedious and laborious routines of early industrial life, encouraging visitors to ask wider questions about wealth, poverty, work, and power in relation to the system of production that it depicts – and, by implication, in relation to the economic system in which they themselves operate. This effect might reasonably be judged as authentically Owenite in its desire to provoke reflection upon the history of New Lanark and its complex relationship to the present. The exhibition skillfully avoids the cult of personality, according due recognition to Owen's achievements while situating them within a historical reality in which ordinary people were rarely the free agents Owen imagined they one day might become.

The companion to Annie Macleod is Harmony, an audio-visual addition made to New Lanark to commemorate the millennium. The concept of the millennium came to haunt Owen as he grew older, epitomizing his desire to secularize the language of Christian eschatology and harness it to a rational yet revolutionary understanding of future social transformation. This rhetoric grew ever more feverish in Owen's later writings and it undoubtedly played its part in driving him into the ranks of the spiritualists. Nevertheless, millenarian discourse was also a source of powerful political critique in Owen's thought and it served in addition to communicate to his followers his absolute commitment to social progress and, increasingly, to science and technology (Harrison 1969, pp. 136–139). The Millennium Experience at New Lanark, to which the appropriately-named Harmony is the ethereal guide, sits somewhere between tribute and pastiche, ironically rehearsing an optimistic Owenite vision of the utopian future while cleverly distancing it through the visual trappings of science fiction. Harmony looks 200 years into the third millennium, to the age of technologically-enhanced leisure and recreation envisaged in some of Owen's later educational writings; to the age of world government and universal peace; to the realm of justice, equality, longevity, and plenty which Owen felt must certainly follow upon the rational application of the untold resources of human talent and cooperation to the obstacles facing mankind. For all its slightly recherché feel, the Millennium Experience brings the tourist experience of New Lanark to a fitting climax, by reminding visitors of the importance of the utopian impulse driving the New Lanark project from its origins, through its rebirth and on into the range of possible futures that might lie before it. It would be easy to dismiss much of this as gimmickry – and Owen in his time was not above such showmanship in his propaganda campaigns on behalf of the new system – but Harmony is the twin of Annie in the clever symbolic economy of the modern New Lanark. Like Annie she raises more questions than she answers, revealing more of the present than the future or the past and drawing a distinction that Pau Obrador Pons suggests is vital to the delicate moral mechanisms of educational tourism – that between 'visiting' and 'dwelling' (Pons 2003). It is not possible to dwell in Harmony's New Lanark or the future society it presupposes any more than it is feasible to dwell in Annie Macleod's industrial village of the 1820s. But the larger educational invitation of New Lanark today for the many thousands who make their way to it from all over the globe is not to dwell, but to visit, and in visiting and revisiting the refreshingly multiple versions of the place and its stories to refuse any closure, drawing upon its inspiration first to imagine, and then perhaps to fashion, a world better than the present one.

References

Abrams, M. H. (1971) *Natural Supernaturalism: Tradition and Revolution in Romantic Literature*, New York: Norton & Company.

Allan, D. (1993) *Virtue, Learning and the Scottish Enlightenment*, Edinburgh: Edinburgh University Press.

Anderson, R. D. (1983) 'Education and the State in Nineteenth-Century Scotland,' *The Economic History Review*, New Series, 36.4: 518–534.

Anderson, R. D. (1995) *Education and the Scottish People*, 1750–1918, Oxford: OUP.

Armstrong, N. and Tennenhouse, L. (1992) *The Imaginary Puritan: Literature, Intellectual Labor, and the Origins of Personal Life*, Berkeley, CA: University of California Press.

Arthur, J. (2005) 'The Re-emergence of Character Education in British Education Policy,' *British Journal of Educational Studies*, 53.3: 239–254.

Bendix, R. (2002) 'Capitalizing on memories past, present, and future: observations on the intertwining of tourism and narration,' *Anthropological Theory*, 2.4: 469–487.

Bernard, P. R. (1988) 'Irreconcilable Opinions: The Social and Educational Theories of Robert Owen and William Maclure,' *Journal of the Early Republic*, 8.1: 21–44.

Bestor, A. (1948) *Education and Reform at New Harmony: Correspondence of William Maclure and Marie Duclos Fretageot, 1820–1833*, Clifton, NY: Augustus M. Kelley.

Bloch, M. N. and Choi, S. (1990) 'Conceptions of Play in the History of Early Childhood Education,' *Child and Youth Care Quarterly*, 19.1, 31–48.

Boardman, P. (1978) *The Worlds of Patrick Geddes*, London: Routledge & Kegan Paul.

British Parliamentary Papers (1968) *Volume 1: Report from the Select Committee on Education of the Lower Orders in the Metropolis with Minutes of Evidence and Appendix, 1816*, Shannon: Irish University Press.

Brnardi, T. S. (2009) 'Exchange and Commerce: Intercultural Communication in the Age of Enlightenment,' *European Review of History*, 16.1: 79–99.

Browning, M. (1971) 'Owen as an Educator,' in J. Butt (ed.) *Robert Owen, Prince of Cotton Spinners*, Newton Abbot: David & Charles.

Butt, J. (1971) 'Robert Owen as a Businessman,' in J. Butt (ed.) *Robert Owen, Prince of Cotton Spinners*, Newton Abbot: David & Charles.

Carlson, H. L. (1992) 'Care and Education of Young Children of Pauper and Working Classes: New Lanark, Scotland, 1790–1825,' *Paedagogica Historica*, 28.1: 8–34.

Carlyle, T. (1899a) *Sartor Resartus*, in H. D. Traill (ed.) *The Works of Thomas Carlyle, Vol 1: Sartor Resartus*, London: Chapman & Hall.

Carlyle, T. (1899b) 'Signs of the Times,' in H. D. Traill (ed.) *The Works of Thomas Carlyle, Vol 27: Critical and Miscellaneous Essays, Vol 2*, London: Chapman & Hall.

Carlyle, T. (1899c) *Past and Present*, in H. D. Traill (ed.) *The Works of Thomas Carlyle, Vol 10: Past and Present*, London: Chapman & Hall.

Cavallo, D. (1976) 'From Perfection to Habit: Moral Training in the American Kindergarten, 1860–1920,' *History of Education Quarterly*, 16.2: 147–161.

Chase, M. (2007) *Chartism: A New History*, Manchester: Manchester University Press.

Claeys, G. (1989) *Citizens and Saints: Politics and Anti-Politics in Early British Socialism*, Cambridge: CUP.

Claeys, G. (2005a) 'The Revival of Robert Owen: Crafting a Victorian Reputation', in C. Tsuzuki, *et al.* (eds) *The Emergence of Global Citizenship: Utopian Ideas, Co-operative Movements and the Third Sector*, New Delhi: Robert Owen Association of Japan.

Clarke, K. (1985) 'Public and Private Children: Infant Education in the 1820s and 1830s', in C. Steedman *et al.* (eds) *Language, Gender and Childhood*, London: Routledge & Kegan Paul.

Clayton, J. (1908) *Robert Owen: Pioneer of Social Reforms*, London: Fifield.

Cobbett, W. (1817) *Political Register*, 2 August 1817.

Coffield, F. (1999) 'Breaking the Consensus: Lifelong Learning as Social Control,' *British Education Research Journal*, 25.4: 479.

Combe, A. (1823) Prefatory Letter to Robert Owen, in R. Owen, *Metaphorical Sketches of the Old and New Systems*, Edinburgh: Reid.

Conroy (2009) 'The Enstranged Self: Recovering Some Grounds for Pluralism in Education,' *Journal of Moral Education*, 38.2: 145–164.

Crowther, J. (2004) '"In and Against" Lifelong Learning: Flexibility and the Corrosion of Character,' *International Journal of Lifelong Education*, 23.2: 125–136.

Cruickshank, M. (1966) 'David Stow, Scottish Pioneer of Teacher Training in Britain,' *British Journal of Educational Studies*, 14.2: 205–215.

Daunton, M. J. (1995) *Progress and Poverty: An Economic and Social History of Britain, 1700–1850*. Oxford: OUP.

Davies, I. *et al.* (2005) 'Citizenship Education and Character Education: Similarities and Contrasts,' *British Journal of Educational Studies*, 53.3: 341–358.

de Vries, J. (2008) *The Industrious Revolution: Consumer Behaviour and the Household Economy, 1650 to the Present*, Cambridge: CUP.

Dean, R. (1995) 'Owenism and the Malthusian Population Question, 1815–1835,' *History of Political Economy*, 27.3: 579–597.

Dobbs, A. E. (1919) *Education and Social Movements, 1700–1850*, London: Longmans, Green & Co.

Doheny, J. (1991) 'Bureaucracy and the Education of the Poor in Nineteenth Century Britain,' *British Journal of Educational Studies*, 39.3: 325–339

Donnachie, I. (2005a) *Robert Owen: Social Visionary*, Edinburgh: John Donald.

Donnachie, I. (2005b) 'Historic Tourism to New Lanark and the Falls of Clyde 1795–1830. The Evidence of Contemporary Visiting Books and Related Sources,' *Journal of Tourism and Cultural Change*, 2.3: 145–163.

Donnachie, I. and Hewitt, G. (1993) *Historic New Lanark*, Edinburgh: Edinburgh University Press.

Donnachie, I. and Mooney, G. (2007) 'From Owenite Socialism to

Blairite Social-ism: Utopia and Dystopia in Robert Owen and New Labour,' *Critique*, 35.2: 275–291.

Eagleton, T. (1978) *Criticism and Ideology: A Study in Marxist Literary Theory*, London: Verso.

Eastwood, D. (1989) 'Robert Southey and the Intellectual Origins of Romantic Conservatism,' *English Historical Review*, 411: 308–331.

Edinburgh Review (1825) No. 82, January.

Erickson, E. and McPeck, E. K. (1964) *British Sessional Papers*, New York: Readex Microprint.

Evans, E. J. (2001) *The Forging of the Modern State: Early Industrial Britain, 1783–1870*, 3rd edn, Harlow: Pearson Education.

Farrell, E. L. (1938) 'The New Harmony Experiment, an Origin of Progressive Education,' *Peabody Journal of Education*, 15.6: 357–361.

Fitton, R. S. and Wadsworth, A. P. (1958) *The Strutts and the Arkwrights*, Manchester: Manchester University Press.

Gallagher, C. (2009) 'The Romantics and the Political Economists,' in J. Chandler (ed.) *The Cambridge History of English Romantic Literature*, Cambridge: CUP.

Gardner, P. (2007) 'Literacy, Language and Education,' in C. Williams (ed.), *A Companion to Nineteenth-Century Britain*, Oxford: Blackwell.

Geddes, P. (1884) 'An Analysis of the Principles of Economics,' *Proceedings of the Royal Society of Edinburgh*, 12: 943–980.

Gelter, H. (2000) '*Friluftsliv*: The Scandinavian Philosophy of Outdoor Life,' *Canadian Journal of Environmental Education*, 5: 77–90.

Godwin, W. (1993) *An Enquiry Concerning Political Justice* (1st edn, 1793), in *Political and Philosophical Writings*, Vol, 3, ed. M. Philp, London: Pickering.

Goldstone, A. (2008) '"Freedom in a Determined World": John Stuart Mill's Philosophical Engagement with Robert Owen, and its effect on His Politics,' unpublished paper, Australian Political Studies Association Conference, Hilton Hotel, Brisbane, Australia, 6–9 July.

Gomel, E. (2007) '"Spirits in the Material World": Spiritualism and Identity in the *Fin de Siecle*,' *Victorian Literature and Culture*, 35.1: 189–213.

Grenier, K. H. (2005) *Tourism and identity in Scotland, 1770–1914*, Farnham: Ashgate.

Griscom, J. (1824) *A Year in Europe*, New York: Collins & Hannay.

Hadow, H. (1931) *Report of the Consultative Committee on the Primary School*, London: HMSO.

Halpin, D. (2002) *Hope and Education: The Role of the Utopian Imagination*, London: Routledge.

Halpin, D. (2007a) *Romanticism and Education: Love, Heroism and Imagination in Pedagogy*, London: Continuum.

Halpin, D. (2007b) 'Utopian Spaces of "Robust Hope": The architecture and nature of progressive learning environments,' *Asia-Pacific Journal of Teacher Education*, 35.3: 243–255.

Hamilton, D. (1983) 'Robert Owen and Education: A Reassessment,' in W. M. Humes and H. M. Paterson (eds) *Scottish Culture and Scottish Education, 1800–1980*, Edinburgh: John Donald Publishers.

Hansard (1868) 12 March , p. 1517, col. 1.

Harris (2005) *Of Liberty and Necessity: The Free Will Debate in Eighteenth-century British Philosophy*. Oxford: OUP.

Harrison, J. F. C. (1969) *Robert Owen and the Owenites in Britain and America*, London: Routledge & Kegan Paul.

Hartley, D. (1749) *Observations on Man*, London: Johnson.

Hazlitt, W. (1998a) 'A New View of Society' (1816), in *Selected Writings Vol 4: Political Essays*, ed. D. Wu, London: Pickering, pp. 92–97.

Hazlitt, W. (1998b) 'On People with One Idea' (1822), in *Selected Writings Vol 6: Table Talk*, ed. D. Wu, London: Pickering, pp. 51–60.

Helvétius, C. A. (1759) *De L'Esprit, Or Essays on the Mind*, 1st French Edition 1758, trans. anon, London: Dodsley & Co.

Helvétius, C. A. (1777) *A Treatise on Man, His Intellectual Faculties and His Education*, trans. W. Hooper, London: Law & Robinson.

Hilton, B. (2006) *A Mad, Bad & Dangerous People? England 1783–1846*, Oxford: The Clarendon Press.

Hilton, M. (2007) *Women and the Shaping of the Nation's Young: Education and Public Doctrine in Britain 1750–1850*, Aldershot: Ashgate.

Historic Scotland (2000) *Nomination of New Lanark for Inclusion in the World Heritage List*, Edinburgh: Historic Scotland.

Hone, W. (1817) 'Let us alone, Mr Owen', *Reformist Register*, 23 and 30 August 1817.

Houston, R. A. (1982) 'The Literacy Myth? Illiteracy in Scotland, 1630–1760,' *Past and Present*, 96: 98–99.

Houston, R. A. (1985) *Scottish Literacy and Scottish Identity: Illiteracy and Society in Scotland and Northern England 1600–1800*, Cambridge: CUP.

Humes, W. M. (1983) 'Science, Religion and Education: A Study of Cultural Interaction', in W. M. Humes and H. M. Paterson (eds) *Scottish Culture and Scottish Education, 1800-1980*, Edinburgh: John Donald Publishers, pp. 115–137.

James, A. (2008) 'Care and Control in the Construction of Children's Citizenship,' in J. Williams and A. Invernizzi (eds) *Children and Citizenship*, London: Sage, pp. 85–97.

Jameson, F. (1981) *The Political Unconscious: Narrative as a Socially Symbolic Act*. Ithaca, NY: Cornell University Press.

Janiak, A. (2008) *Newton As Philosopher*, Cambridge: CUP.

Jennings, H. C. (1928) *The Political Theory of State-supported Elementary Education* in England, 1750–1833, Lancaster: The Lancaster Press.

Johnson, O. C. (ed.) (1970) *Robert Owen in the United States*, New York: Humanities Press.

Kail, P. J. E. (2007) *Projection and Realism in Hume's Philosophy*, Oxford: OUP.

Kennedy, D. (2006) *The Well of Being: Childhood, Subjectivity and Education*, New York: SUNY Press.

Kumar, K. (1990) 'Utopian Thought and Communal Practice: Robert Owen and the Owenite Communities,' *Theory and Society*, 19.1: 1–35.

Laird, S. (2008) *Mary Wollstonecraft*, London: Continuum.

Lloyd-Jones, R. and Lewis, M. J. (1988) *Manchester and the Age of the Factory: The Business Structure of Cottonopolis in the Industrial Revolution*, Bekenham: Croom Helm.

Lowe, R. (2007) *The Death of Progressive Education: How Teachers Lost Control of the Classroom*, London: Routledge.

MacLeod, E. V. (2007) 'British Attitudes to the French Revolution,' *The Historical Journal*, 50: 689–709.

MacKenzie, R. F. (1967) *The Sins of the Children*, Glasgow: Collins.

MacKenzie, R. F. (1976) *The Unbowed Head*, Edinburgh: Edinburgh University Press.

Markus, T. A. (1993) *Buildings and Power: Freedom and Control in the Origin of Modern Building Types*, London: Routledge.

Marshall, P. (1984) *William Godwin*, New Haven, CT: Yale University Press.

Martin, M. C. (2009) 'Marketing Religious Identity: Female Educators, Methodist Culture and Eighteenth Century Childhood,' in M. Hilton and J. Shefrin (eds) *Educating the Child in Enlightenment Britain: Beliefs, Cultures, Practices*, Farnham: Ashgate, pp. 57–77.

Marx, K. and Engels, F. (1976) 'Theses on Feuerbach,' in M. Cornforth, *et al.* (eds) *Collected Works, Volume 5*, London: Lawrence & Wishart.

Mason, J. C. S. (2001) *The Moravian Church and the Missionary Awakening in England, 1760–1800*, Woodbridge: The Boydell Press.

McCann, P. and Young, F. A. (1982) *Samuel Wilderspin and the Infant School Movement*, Beckenham: Croom Helm.

McDermid, J. (2006) 'Gender, National Identity and the Royal (Argyll) Commission of Inquiry into Scottish Education (1864–1867),' *Journal of Educational Administration and History*, 38.3: 249–262.

McGillivray (2005) 'Fitter, Happier, More Productive: Governing Working Bodies Through Wellness,' *Culture and Organization*, 11.2: 125–138.

McLaren, D. J. (1999) *David Dale of New Lanark*, Glasgow: Caring Books.

McMullen, K. (1983) *Ghost Dance*, Looseyard for Channel 4.

McNab, H. G. (1819) *The New Views of Mr Owen of Lanark Impartially Examined*, London: Morton.

Meller, H. (1990) *Patrick Geddes: Social Evolutionist and City Planner*, New York: Routledge.

Mill, J. S. (1974) *A System of Logic Ratiocinative and Inductive (Books IV-VI and Appendices)*, ed. J. M. Robson, London: Routledge & Kegan Paul.

Mill, J. S. (1981) *Autobiography*, in *The Collected Works of John Stuart Mill, Vol I: Autobiography and Literary Essays*, ed. J. M. Robson and J. Stillinger, London: Routledge & Kegan Paul.

Mirayes, J. R. V. (2005) 'The Prejudices of Education: Educational Aspects of the Scottish Enlightenment,' *Atlantis*, 27.2: 101–118.

Morgan, K. (2004) *The Birth of Industrial Britain: Social Change, 1750–1850*, London: Pearson Education.

Moseley, A. (2007) *John Locke*, London: Continuum.

Musgrove, F. (1962) 'Two Educational Controversies in Eighteenth Century England: Nature and Nurture; Private and Public Education,' *Paedagogica Historica: International Journal of the History of Education*, 2.1: 81–94.

New Harmony Gazette (1825) 29 October 1825.

New Harmony Gazette (1826) 23 August 1826.

Nielsen, N. J, (1994) 'Lifelong Care and Control: Paternalism in Nineteenth Century Factory Communities,' *Ethnologia Scandinavica*, 24: 70–89.

Owen, J. D. (1968) 'The Principles of Natural Education', in J. F. C. Harrison (ed.), *Utopianism and Education: Robert Owen and the Owenites*, New York: Teachers College Press, pp. 176–189.

Owen, R. (1832) *Address to All Classes in the State from the Governor, Director and Committee of the Association*, 14 January 1832, London.

Owen, R. (ed.) (1838) *The New Moral World*, 4.197, 4 August.

Owen R. (1852) *Robert Owen's Journal*, Vol. III, No. 2, (7 February 1852), London: James Watson.

Owen, R. (1857) *The Life of Robert Owen, Written by Himself* (1971 reprint with an introduction by John Butt), London: Charles Knight & Co. Ltd.

Owen, R. (1991a) 'The Natural and Rational Classification of Society' (1837), in G. Claeys (ed.) *A New View of Society and Other Writings*, London: Penguin, pp. 344–358.

Owen, R. (1991b) *The Revolution in the Mind and Practice of the Human Race* (1849), in G. Claeys (ed.) *A New View of Society and Other Writings*, London: Penguin, pp. 365–377.

Owen, R. (1993a) *A Statement Regarding the New Lanark Establishment* (1812), in *Selected Works Vol 1: Early Writings*, ed. G. Claeys, London: Pickering, pp. 11–23.

Owen, R. (1993b) *A Report to the County of Lanark* (1821), in *Selected Works Vol. 1: Early Writings*, ed. G. Claeys, London: Pickering, pp. 287–333.

Owen, R. (1993c) 'Address to the Infant Schools Societies, and to Patrons of Infant Schools,' in *Selected Works Vol. 2: The Development of Socialism*, ed. G. Claeys, London: Pickering, pp. 155–158.

Owen, R. (1993d) *The Book of the New Moral World* (1842–1844), in *Selected Works Vol. 3: The Book of the New Moral World*, ed. G. Claeys, London: Pickering.

Owen, R. (1993e) *The Life of Robert Owen*, in *Selected Works Vol. 4: The Life of Robert Owen*, ed. G. Claeys, London: Pickering.

Owen, R. (1993f) *A New View of Society*, in *Selected Works Vol. 1: Early Writings*, ed. G. Claeys, London: Pickering, pp. 23–101.

Owen, R. (1993g) *A Development of the Principles and Plans on which to Establish Self Supporting Home Colonies*, in *Selected Works Vol. 2: The Development of Socialism*, ed. G. Claeys, London: Pickering, pp. 337–408.

Owen, R. (1993h) *The Address of Robert Owen...Denouncing the Old System of the World, and Announcing the Commencement of the New*, in *Selected Works Vol. 2: The Development of Socialism*, ed. G. Claeys, London: Pickering, pp. 224–232.

Owen, R. D. (1824) *An Outline of the System of Education at New Lanark*, Glasgow: Wardlaw & Cunninghame.

Owen, R. D. (1874) *Threading My Way: Twenty-seven Years of Autobiography*, New York: Scribners.

Papastephanou, M. (2008) 'Dystopian Reality, Utopian Thought and Educational Practice,' *Studies in the Philosophy of Education*, 27: 89–102.

Paterson, L. (2000) 'Traditions of Scottish Education,' in H. Holmes (ed.) *Scottish Life and History. A Compendium of Scottish Ethnology, Vol. 11: Education*, East Lothian: Tuckwell Press, pp. 20–28.

Pinker, S. (2002) *The Blank Slate: The Modern Denial of Human Nature*, New York: Penguin Books.

Pitzer, D. E. (1989) 'The Original Boatload of Knowledge Down the Ohio River: William Maclure's and Robert Owen's Transfer of Science and Education to the Midwest, 1825–1826,' *Ohio Journal of Science*, 89.5: 128–142.

Place, F. (1813) *Place Papers*, London: British Library, Add. 27, 791, f. 268.

Podmore, C. (1998) *The Moravian Church in England, 1728–1760*, Oxford: OUP.

Podmore, F. (1906) *Robert Owen: A Biography*, London: George Allen & Unwin.

Pole, T. (1823) *Observations Relative to Infant Schools*, Bristol: Goyder.

Pons, P. O. (2003) 'Being-on-Holiday: Tourist Dwelling, Bodies and Place,' *Tourist Studies*, 3: 47–66.

Powell, G. (2008) 'Robert Owen and "The Greatest Discovery Ever Made By Man",' Unpublished conference paper for '*Robert Owen and His Legacy*,' Gregynog Hall, Newtown, Powys, Wales, 14 August.

Quataert, J. H. (1988) 'A New View of Industrialization: "Proto-industry" or the Role of Small-Scale, Labor-Intensive Manufacture in the Capitalist Environment,' *International Labor and Working-Class History*, 33: 3–32.

Reid, J. (2006) 'Free Play with Froebel: Use and Abuse of Progressive Pedagogy in London's Infant Schools, 1870–c.1904,' *Paedagogica Historica*, 42.3: 299–323.

Reese, W. J. (2001) 'The Origins of Progressive Education,' *History of Education Quarterly*, 41.1: 1–24.

Richardson, A. (1994) *Literature, Education and Romanticism: Reading as Social Practice, 1780–1832*, Cambridge: CUP.

Richardson, A. (1999) 'Romanticism and the End of Childhood,' in J. H. McGavran (ed.), *Literature and the Child: Romantic Continuations, Postmodern Contestations*, Iowa: University of Iowa Press, pp. 23–44.

Rinaldi C. (2006) *In Dialogue with Reggio Emilia: Listening, Researching and Learning*, London: Routledge.

Roberts, A. F. B (1972) 'A New View of the Infant School Movement,' *British Journal of Educational Studies*, 20.2: 154–164.

Rogers, A. (2006) 'Escaping the Slums or Changing the Slums? Lifelong Learning and Social Transformation,' *International Journal of Lifelong Education*, 25.2: 125–137.

Royle, E. (1998) *Robert Owen and the Commencement of the Millennium: A Study of the Harmony Community*, Manchester: Manchester University Press.

Rusk, R. R. (1933) *A History of Infant Education*, London: University of London Press.

Ryan, K. (2008) 'On Power, Habitus, and (In)civility: Foucault meets Elias Bauman in the Playground,' *Journal of Power*, 1.3: 251–274.

Scotland, J. (1969) *The History of Scottish Education, Vol. 1: From the Beginning to 1872*, London: University of London Press.

SED (Scottish Education Department) (1965) *Primary Education in Scotland*, Edinburgh: HMSO.

Silber, K. (1960) *Pestalozzi: The Man and His Work*, London: Longman.

Silver, H. (1965) *The Concept of Popular Education*, London: MacGibbon & Kee.

Silver, H. (1977) 'Aspects of Neglect: The Strange Case of Victorian Popular Education,' *Oxford Review of Education*, 3.1: 57–69.

Silver, H. (1983) *Education as History: Interpreting Nineteenth- and Twentieth-Century Education*, London: Methuen.

Smith, M. A. (2007) 'Religion,' in C. Williams (ed.) *A Companion to Nineteenth-Century Britain*, Oxford: Blackwell, pp. 337–353.

Smout, T. C. (1979) *A History of the Scottish People, 1560–1830*, Glasgow: Fontana.

Sorensen, D. (1995) 'Postmodernism and the Disappearance of "Environment": A Carlylean Perspective,' *Carlyle Studies Annual*, 1995: 101–22.

Southey, R. (1929) *Journal of a Tour in Scotland in 1819*, ed. C. H. Herford, London: Murray.

St Clair, W. (1990) *The Godwins and the Shelleys: The Biography of a Family*, London: Faber & Faber.

Steedman, C. (1995) *Strange Dislocations: Childhood and the Idea of Human Interiority, 1780–1830*, Cambridge, MA: Harvard University Press.

Stobart, J. (2008) 'Manchester and its Region: Networks and Boundaries in the Eighteenth Century,' *Manchester Region History Review*, 19: 66–80.

Stocking, M. K. (ed.) (1995) 'Fanny Imlay to Mary Godwin, 29/7–1/8/1816,' *The Clairmont Correspondence, Vol. 1, 1808–1834*, Baltimore, MD: Johns Hopkins University Press, pp. 54–56.

Swinerton, B. (1996) 'The 1931 *Report of the Consultative Committee* on the Primary School: Tensions and Contradictions,' *History of Education*, 25.1: 73–90.

The Cooperator (1829) No. 20, 1 December.

The Crisis (1834) Vol. 3, No. 20, 4 January.

The Economist (1821) Vol 1, No. 8. 17 March 1821.

Thompson, W. (1830) *Practical Directions for the … Establishment of Communities*, London: Strange & Wilson.

Turner, D. A. (1970) 'The State and the Infant School System,' *British Journal of Educational Studies*, 18.2: 151–165.

Von Arx, J. P. (1985) *Progress and Pessimism: Religion, Politics, and History in Late Nineteenth Century Britain*, Cambridge, MA: Harvard University Press.

Waller, J. C. (2001) 'Ideas of Heredity, Reproduction and Eugenics in Britain, 1800–1875,' *Studies in History and Philosophy of Science Part C: Studies in History and Philosophy of Biological and Biomedical Sciences*, 32.3: 457–489.

Whitbread, N. (1972) *The Evolution of the Nursery-infant School: A History of Infant and Nursery Education in Britain, 1800–1970*, London: Routledge.

White, D. E. (2006) *Early Romanticism and Religious Dissent*, Cambridge: CUP.

Williams, G. *et al.* (2007) *The Welsh Church from Reformation to Disestablishment, 1603–1920*, Cardiff: University of Wales Press.

Williams, R. (1983) *Towards 2000*, London: Chatto & Windus.

Wilson, J. F. (2008) 'Social Capital, Trust and the Industrial Revolution,' *The Economic History Review*, 61.4: 1009–1011.

Withrington, D. J. (2000) 'Church and State in Scottish Education before 1872,' in H. Holmes (ed.) *Scottish Life and History. A Compendium of Scottish Ethnology, Vol. 11: Education*, East Lothian: Tuckwell Press, pp. 47–65.

Wollstonecraft, M. (2008) *A Vindication of the Rights of Men; A Vindication of the Rights of Woman*, ed. J. Todd, Oxford: OUP.

Wood, N. (1992) 'Tabula Rasa, Social Environmentalism, and the "English Paradigm,"' *Journal of the History of Ideas*, 53.4: 647–668.

Woodley, S. (2009) '"Oh Miserable and Most Ruinous Measure": The Debate between Private and Public Education in Britain, 1760–1800,' in M. Hilton and J. Shefrin (eds) *Educating the Child in*

Enlightenment Britain: Beliefs, Cultures, Practices, Farnham: Ashgate, pp. 21–41.

Wordsworth, D. (1941) 'Journal of My Second Tour in Scotland (1822),' in E. De Selincourt (ed.) *Journals of Dorothy Wordsworth, Vol. 2*, London: Macmillan, pp. 337–399.

Yeo, E. (1971) 'Robert Owen and Radical Culture,' in S. Pollard and J. Salt (eds) *Robert Owen: Prophet of the Poor*, Lewisburg, PA: Bucknell University Press, pp. 84–115.

Index